The Future of Higher Education

The Future of Higher Education

Rhetoric, Reality, and the Risks of the Market

Frank Newman

Lara Couturier

Jamie Scurry

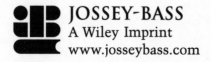

JOSSEY-BASS
A Wiley Imprint
www.josseybass.com

33.00

Published by Jossey-Bass
A Wiley Imprint
989 Market Street, San Francisco, CA 94103-1741   www.josseybass.com

Jossey-Bass books and products are available through most bookstores. To contact Jossey-Bass directly
call our Customer Care Department within the U.S. at (800) 956-7739, outside the U.S. at (317) 572-
3986 or fax (317) 572-4002.

Jossey-Bass also publishes its books in a variety of electronic formats. Some content that appears in
print may not be available in electronic books.

Library of Congress Cataloging-in-Publication Data

Newman, Frank, 1927-
  The future of higher education : rhetoric, reality, and the risks of the market / by Frank Newman,
Lara Couturier, and Jamie Scurry.— 1st ed.
    p. cm.
  Includes bibliographical references and index.
  ISBN 0-7879-6972-9 (alk. paper)
  1. Education, Higher—Aims and objectives—United States. 2. Education, Higher—Economic
aspects—United States. 3. Educational change—United States. I. Couturier, Lara. II. Scurry, Jamie.
III. Title.
  LA227.4.N494 2004
  378.73—dc22
                            2004006400

Printed in the United States of America
FIRST EDITION
HB Printing 10 9 8 7 6 5 4 3 2 1

**The Jossey-Bass Higher and
Adult Education Series**

Contents

Preface

Over the past four years, the Futures Project staff has focused on the impact of a set of powerful forces that are transforming the American system of higher education. These include an intensifying competition among traditional institutions; rapid expansion of the new for-profit and virtual institutions; technology and its influence on the way learning takes place; globalization of colleges and universities; and the shift toward restructuring higher education as a market rather than a regulated public sector. What has motivated our efforts to understand these forces is the concern that American higher education, feeling successful and satisfied with itself, will fail to understand the speed and significance of the changes under way and drift into new and unexamined structures that undercut higher education's traditional purposes.

The Futures Project staff has already published a great many articles, each of which focused on one of the forces for change that is taking place. We have, as well, presented the evidence of change and our concerns about the potential impact of a range of meetings here and abroad. Fortunately, a small but growing number of higher education scholars have begun calling attention to one or another of the dangers ahead, helping to raise the level of concern about the need to plan rather than drift.

In creating this book, we felt it was essential to go further than what has been published so far. We wanted to:

- Make readily available an analysis of the impact of the most important forces of change. We have gone beyond the first anecdotes to include as much data as are available about the extent, rate, and impact of change so far as well as the cumulative impact of these forces taken together.

- Suggest policies that are necessary to shape an intelligent and workable higher education market. We have not focused on how to avoid a higher education market—it is already here. The issue is whether it will be thoughtfully structured or unintentionally damaging.
- Propose strategies that individual institutions as well as higher education as a whole should consider as they face this changing environment.
- Call for a renewed focus on the public purposes of higher education that are endangered by the changes under way.

Our goals in this are several. First, we want this book to serve as a wake-up call to the leaders of our colleges and universities. They must provide informed, skillful, and aggressive leadership that brings constructive change to their institutions. They must, as well, be engaged collaborators in the effort to create a new market-oriented structure for the system of higher education.

A second goal is to provide policy makers—governors, legislators, commissioners, board members at the state level, as well as congressmen and the administration at the federal level—with policy solutions that have emerged worldwide to restructure higher education. There is a danger that, in the absence of visible progress toward a more responsive and accountable system, they will act on whatever ideas are available without careful analysis. There is a danger as well that in their frustration they will act without drawing in the higher education leadership as partners.

A third goal is to convince both of these groups—the academic and the political leaders—as well as the engaged civic leaders, including business and community leaders, that American society has an enormous stake in preserving, clarifying, and enhancing the public purposes of higher education. We have found these to be eroding steadily. Americans now need to see that higher education is not just a private good. When a low-income student graduates from college; when a researcher solves a vexing mystery; or when a campus undertakes an open, thoughtful discussion of a complicated issue troubling society, it is not just the graduate, the researcher, and the audience that benefit; it is society as a whole.

Finally, we hope to provide a useful guide to the current issues for students of higher education. We are in the midst of a transformation on a scale we have not seen in our lifetimes. This is a first attempt at chronicling the change, analyzing the impact, and proposing solutions. Usually such books are written at a later point when the smoke has cleared and the authors can say with greater certainty what has happened. Our purpose is not to record the change but to influence it.

The structure and nature of higher education is important—more important than ever before. It is no time to stand on the sidelines waiting to see how things turn out.

Acknowledgments

It would be impossible for us to thank all of the people who have contributed to this book and helped to make it a reality. We have spent four years calling upon the expertise of friends and colleagues at universities, colleges, associations, and commissions all over the world. Each conversation, article, book, and report has helped us to form our theses and back them up with evidence. There are, however, several people we would be remiss to not thank individually.

Laurinda Custodio deserves our enduring gratitude for her patient acceptance of draft after draft, as she painstakingly made changes, sought out sources, updated references, and organized and reorganized the process. Laurie kept the book-writing process, and the authors, on track and in good humor. We owe thanks to Melissa Nicholaus for her extraordinary commitment in a similar vein.

Our Advisory Board served as our main source of comments and constructive criticisms. We knew we could always count on the highest quality of thought and assistance, and the book was improved immeasurably by their input. In this capacity, we thank Russell Edgerton, Kay McClenney, Kathy Spoehr, Terrence MacTaggart, Blenda Wilson, and Ray Handlan. We also called upon the expertise of several other experts and readers, whose insights were tremendous. For this we thank, especially, David Kirp, Bob Dickeson, Laura Freid, and Ellen Liberman.

Over the years, a number of undergraduate and graduate students have assisted us with our research. They have always brought enthusiasm, passion, and hard work to our team. Our appreciation is extended to Alison Leff, Miranda Chen, Kristi Hutchinson, Karen Dulitz, Joe McGrath, Pauline Lauterbach, Jamie Olson, Milena Ivanova, Andrea Castaneda, Briana Huntsberger, Natasha Lewis, Felix Lo, Anjali Nigalaye, Elisabeth Preis, Rachel Silbermann, Jamie Crook, Kevin Novell, Alex Carp, Eduardo Arellano, and Caroline Frank. A number of students who worked with us during the actual book-writing process deserve special thanks: Priya Cariappa, Thilakshani Dias, Kristin Sinclair, Kathy Bacuyag, and Nyema Mitchell.

Finally, we would like to thank our families. They have been kind, supportive, and patient, and we are grateful.

Frank Newman
Providence, Rhode Island
April 2004

The Authors

Frank Newman, a leader in American education for more than thirty years, was director of the Futures Project: Policy for Higher Education in a Changing World. He also had academic appointments at Brown University, where he was visiting professor of public policy and sociology, and at Columbia University, where he was visiting professor at Teachers College.

He held a Ph.D. in history from Stanford University, a master's of science degree in business from Columbia University, a bachelor of science degree in engineering from Brown University, and a bachelor of arts degree in naval science and economics from Brown University.

In July of 1999, he stepped down as president of the Education Commission of the States (ECS) after fourteen years. ECS is a national nonprofit, nonpartisan organization that helps governors, legislators, and other state education leaders develop and implement policies that improve education. Dr. Newman was the president of the University of Rhode Island from 1974 to 1983; after that he was a presidential fellow at the Carnegie Foundation for the Advancement of Teaching.

He was the author of a number of books on higher education including *Report on Higher Education* (1971), *Higher Education and the American Resurgence* (1985), and *Choosing Quality: Reducing Conflict Between the State and the University* (1987). He passed away in May 2004.

Jamie E. Scurry is a research associate with the Futures Project: Policy for Higher Education in a Changing World. Her work focuses on the quality of student learning, the role of technology in improving pedagogy, issues of equity, and promoting meaningful opportunities for low-income students, students of color, and nontraditional students to gain access to and successfully complete a degree. She has authored several publications on these topics, including: "Online Technology Pushes Pedagogy to the Forefront" (*Chronicle of Higher Education,* July 2001); "In Jeopardy . . . New England's Reputation in Higher Education" (*Connection* Magazine, 2002); "Dealing with *U.S. News* College Rankings" (*Providence Journal,* Sept. 2002); and Access and Attainment Building Block (ERIC, U.S. Department of Education, 2003). Scurry is a master's degree candidate in American civilizations at Brown University. Previously she has worked for Wake Forest University and Stonehill College.

Lara K. Couturier is associate director and director of research for the Futures Project: Policy for Higher Education in a Changing World at Brown University. In addition to her work at the Futures Project, Lara is working on her Ph.D. in history at Brown University, focusing on the intersections of race and policy in U.S. history. She holds a master's degree from the Harvard Graduate School of Education, a bachelor's degree from the University of Richmond, and is an associate of the National Center for Public Policy and Higher Education. She previously conducted research for the Harvard Project on Faculty Appointments and worked as a consultant and global marketing manager for Andersen Consulting. Her other publications include: "Balancing Autonomy and Accountability in Higher Education" in *Double the Numbers: Postsecondary Attainment and Underrepresented Youth* (2004, Harvard Education Press); "Balancing State Control with Society's Needs" (*Chronicle of Higher Education,* June 27, 2003); and "The New Competitive Arena: Market Forces Invade the Academy" (with Frank Newman, *Change,* Sept./Oct. 2001).

The Future of Higher Education

Chapter One

Higher Education in the Grip of Transforming Change

Whether an effective, publicly oriented system can emerge during this period of change is no small issue. The university is one of society's great inventions. Much is at stake.

This is a demanding, exciting, and risky time for colleges and universities. Suddenly, higher education is in the grip of transforming change. Part of this change flows from the demands of political leaders for access for a greater share of the population to meet the needs of the New Economy; part from the growing concern that the skills and attitudes young people bring to their roles as workers and citizens are inadequate; part flows from the growing impact of external forces such as information technology and globalization.

But the main force for change flows from a new level of competition and market-orientation among higher education institutions—a competition for students, faculty, research grants, athletic titles, revenue, rankings, and prestige. Competition promises the opportunity to improve learning, broaden access, or focus attention on efficient use of resources. But if not skillfully structured by thoughtful and strategic interventions of government, the market and growing competition will distort the purposes of higher education and further widen the gap between rhetoric and reality. It is, as a result, a time of both opportunity and risk.[1]

The New Competition

Compared to most other countries, the United States has always had a diverse and competitive system of higher education—part public, part private—and has functioned at least partially as a market. However, the basic nature of the higher education system is changing. Competition among traditional, nonprofit institutions is intensifying. Exacerbating this competition, the number of degree-granting for-profit universities and colleges has grown rapidly. Virtual or online programs have mushroomed over the last decade and now enroll millions of students. Corporate universities and certificate programs offer alternative ways to gain skills and credentials. The impact of technology on teaching and learning challenges every institution's ability to keep up and opens new opportunity for aggressive institutions. To complicate matters further, higher education is in the early stages of becoming a global enterprise, and colleges and universities must choose whether to go beyond their national boundaries or not.

These trends are amplified by a growing willingness on the part of political leaders to use market forces as a means of structuring higher education in order to increase the impact of the competition. Their hope is to improve access, affordability, and the quality of learning. The result is an evolution of the higher education sector toward operating far more as a market, with universities and colleges competing to supply the service of education, as opposed to the concept of higher education as a public sector structured principally by government regulation. As an example, in the old world, government would tend to depend on regulations to control costs. In the new world, government instead tends to hope that growing competition will slow the rapidly rising costs of higher education.

The students arriving at the admissions office door are also changing. They are more diverse (in age, race, ethnicity, socioeconomic status, understanding of technology, and nationality). This diversity of backgrounds brings to higher education a variety of demands that institutions have never faced before, from racial sensitivity to night classes to child care. A new consumerism is especially evident at selective institutions, where we see a well-documented demand for more amenities, better services, and

competitive financial aid packages. Students today are more willing to search the Internet to find programs with the quality and
convenience they need and are more aware of the alternative
programs and institutions available to them to help meet their
goals. In short, the pressures for institutional change mount as
many students become more demanding, sophisticated, and diverse
consumers of higher education.

The competition of the past several decades was largely benign.
Today it is more powerful, the consequences more serious. As a
result of the changes under way, a new higher education landscape
has emerged. Universities and colleges that were accustomed to an
established place in their segment of higher education and in their
geographic area now find that the competition crosses both these
boundaries. At first it was easy to argue that these changes were
"interesting but don't affect our campus," but today it is clear that
every campus will be affected. In the United States, the impact of
competition has been masked in part by the overall growth in the
number of students applying for admission and by growth in various sources of funding. Now, with the downturn in the economy,
funding sources are under pressure. As the competition escalates
and the new providers multiply, a growing number of applicants
will not be enough to save institutions lacking strong leadership
and focus.

The Risks of a Market

One danger of the shift toward competition and market forces is
that it is almost certain, unless addressed by specific policies, to
exacerbate another trend already evident: a growing gap between
the public purposes that need to be served by colleges and universities and the reality of how higher education is functioning. From
the establishment of the first college in America in 1636, there has
been an understanding that higher education, though it clearly provided private benefits, also served important community needs.
Over the three-plus centuries since then, the public purposes have
been formalized in the charters of institutions and in the laws of the
federal and state governments. They have been steadily expanded
from preparation of young men for leadership in the community
to preparation of a broad share of the population for participation

in the workforce and civic life; from polishing the elite to providing widespread social mobility; from generating scholarship aimed at supporting certain beliefs to supporting unfettered, evidence-based debate about social issues as well as wide-ranging and trustworthy research essential to modern society.

Higher education has been accorded a special place in society, separate from and above the marketplace throng. Today, however, the growing influence of the market in higher education means that the search for truth is rivaled by a search for revenues. As the gap between higher education's rhetoric about its public purposes and the reality of its current performance grows, the special place of higher education—a place supported by the public because of the benefits it receives in return—is imperiled.

There is not automatically or necessarily a "market" for public purposes. Markets have brought important improvements to many sectors of society around the world; even so, they often bring in their wake unexpected and undesired effects, such as the problems that developed in the airline industry with deregulation, or the chaos that developed with the shift to a market for California electric power, or the frustrations that have emerged in the attempt to create for-profit schools.

The Need for Thoughtful Policy

The first critical question, then, is whether new state policies can create a market structure for the complex and expanding array of institutions that will serve the public purpose. Policy makers, particularly governors and legislators, face the need to formulate new policies that address these new circumstances. The demand for institutional accountability by political leaders has become a major issue. They recognize that higher education is ever more central to their goals of economic development and civic renewal, while at the same time more frustrating to deal with and more set in its ways. The result has been a growing interest in and experimentation with market forces as a means of structuring higher education. If the current regulatory approach cannot encourage institutional responsiveness to public needs, perhaps the market can—or so the theory goes.

But using market forces to achieve public purposes is not a simple task for policy makers. Establishing a successful market is not as easy as decentralizing the sector. All markets need some regulation (the role of the Securities and Exchange Commission in regulating the financial markets is an example); most require some subsidized activity (support of the airline industry by the subsidy of air traffic control is such a case). A critical task for legislators is to determine where and how the government should intervene to make the market work effectively, without acceding to short-term pressures to overregulate. The Futures Project: Policy for Higher Education in a Changing World has been studying the impact of the market on higher education for the past four years (the authors are director and research staff of the Futures Project, a higher education think tank based at Brown University). As a result of our analysis, we believe the state has a strong interest in two issues: defining institutional missions and creating effective means of accountability. We also believe it should deregulate operational issues to a great extent.

These are not just American concerns. In country after country across the globe, in Denmark and China, in Austria and Australia, the demands of governments are changing—moving toward new approaches to higher education governance that encourage a greater level of competition, that permit more institutional autonomy but also call for greater responsiveness and accountability in return.

The Challenges of Policy Making

The task for legislators is difficult. Even for those in favor of the concept of the market, the temptation to regulate is deep-seated, and the chance to undermine institutional autonomy is ever-present. Concrete rule making is often easier to explain and take credit for than the abstract concept of a balanced "market." The devotion of political parties to competing ideologies often makes the debate difficult.

Another difficulty is the risk of creating a winner-take-all competition that leads to the failure of useful institutions. Many economists looking at higher education as a market will make the case that we should expect that those institutions slow to respond will—and should—fail and that other, more nimble institutions will take their place. Certainly, with four thousand colleges and universities, the loss of one, or ten, or a hundred is not fatal. At the

Futures Project, we believe that the public will be better served by a level of competition that fosters a determined attempt at institutional reform rather than by a Darwinian thinning of the ranks. There is much to preserve and much to gain from enhancing what we have developed.

Higher Education's Public Purposes

Colleges and universities were intended to be institutions that safeguard fundamental societal needs, most notably the search for truth. This often leads to efforts undertaken within the academy that make some parts of society uncomfortable (such as the recent investigation of the role of the slave trade in building the fortunes of prominent New England families, including several involved in founding the very universities that now foster the academic freedom that makes such research possible).

Some academics go so far as to argue that the search for truth is the only societal purpose the university should serve. This seems an extraordinarily narrow definition of higher education's role in a society that is as dependent on "knowledge" as is today's. In a world of market forces, technology, globalization, and the enormous capacity of new knowledge to enhance the public well-being, higher education institutions must be held, in Stanley Katz's phrase (2002, pp. 430–431), to "a higher standard than that to which corporations, and perhaps even governments, are held. . . . The university is in manifold ways the provider of common benefits and the doer of social good." This expands the obligations of colleges and universities to include functions such as creating a skilled and educated workforce, encouraging civic engagement in students, serving as an avenue for social mobility, and establishing links with primary and secondary education.

The Need for Institutional Strategy

The second critical question is whether individual colleges and universities can develop a strategy and the leadership necessary to succeed in and take advantage of this new climate.

To thrive and even survive into the future, each university and college needs a clear strategy that defines the role the institution is determined to play and a concrete plan to implement that strategy. In other words, there must be institutional change that responds to the changing nature of the broader system of higher education. To achieve this requires different and more effective leadership, not just at the top but throughout the institution, leadership with the ability to draw the whole organization into the process of change, assessment, and constant and unremitting improvement. It requires as well a clear commitment to the institution's responsibilities to the public.

In the higher education market that has already begun to emerge, institutional leaders often feel compelled to chase revenues and rankings rather than concentrate on the public purposes of providing a high-quality education to an ever-expanding share of the population. How should each institution respond to these powerful new forces? How can each ensure that it thrives in the new world? How can each ensure that it is meeting the public purposes of society?

The Task Ahead

For the last three years, the Futures Project has been examining the growing competition and increasing role of market forces. What follows is a summary of what we have found and what we propose as a pathway forward. The project goal is first to understand the impact of these forces; then to help fashion appropriate policy initiatives and institutional strategies to respond to these changes; and finally to help create a debate among political leaders, academic leaders, and the public, a debate sustained and intense enough that American higher education moves thoughtfully and purposefully into the new century. Whether an effective, publicly oriented system can emerge during this period of change is no small issue. The university is one of society's great inventions. Much is at stake.

The task for policy makers is equally demanding. Creating an effective, socially responsible market in higher education is not as simple as just eliminating burdensome regulations. Market forces do not necessarily foster the public good; they often exacerbate societal inequities. Those without resources and without access to information are at a great disadvantage.

The United States has learned from a variety of experiences—for-profit health care, the dot com boom and bust, deregulation of electricity—that market forces, left to themselves, do not necessarily serve society well. Observing the introduction of market-oriented education policies in New Zealand confirms the relevance of this risk to education. The appeal of the market as a force for responsiveness is gaining widespread attention, but creating an effective market requires thoughtfully structured strategic interventions by government to ensure that the market is a force supporting, not undermining, the public purposes of higher education.

Colleges and universities now live in a sea of changed expectations. Society needs a greater share of the population educated to a higher level of skill and knowledge for the workforce and for civic involvement. Society needs as well the expertise of universities and colleges applied to an expanding array of societal problems—from training corporate workers to preserving the environment to developing gene therapy. Meanwhile, the tasks facing institutions of higher education become ever more complex as the proliferation of knowledge complicates both education and research.

For each university and college, and for higher education as a whole, the new landscape offers greater opportunity than ever. The chance for well-led institutions to excel and contribute to the broader success of society has never been greater. But it is also a time of much greater risk.

Chapter Two

The New Competition

*For the last several years the system has been shifting
steadily toward greater competition, marked by less market
segmentation, more dependence on market forces, and less
dependence on regulation. Colleges have been using a
variety of strategies to compete, some creative and benign,
others shocking in their intensity.*

Higher education in the United States has always viewed itself as
competitive, particularly when compared to systems elsewhere in
the world, with universities, colleges, and community colleges—
public, private, and for-profit—all seeking students and funding.
In reality, however, the competition has been muted, more benign
than ferocious, more focused on prestige than quality or price. It
has been restrained by tradition and by governmental regulation.
Institutions have largely competed within particular segments—by
type of institution, level of prestige, and geography. States have
operated what are basically higher education cartels of public institutions, where three-quarters of the students in the United States
are enrolled. Each institution is assigned specific roles, with regulations that govern price (that is, tuition), funding, enrollment,
operation, and the scope of programs.[1]

The Emergence of the New Competition

For the last several years, however, the system has been shifting
steadily toward greater competition, marked by less market segmentation, more dependence on market forces, and less dependence
on regulation. The competition among traditional institutions—the

nonprofit public and private universities and colleges—for students and for research dollars, in fund-raising and in sports, and particularly for prestige, has been intensifying. Colleges have been using a variety of strategies to compete, some creative and benign, others shocking in their intensity. Depending on how they are used, each of these strategies and competition as a whole can either serve or undercut public purpose.

Financial Aid as Competitive Weapon

The use of price discounting (in the guise of student aid) to attract students is accelerating. Historically, the role of student aid funds was to allow needy students to afford going to college. Over the last decade, however, both states and institutions have been shifting their aid toward "merit" in the attempt to attract the "better" students—students who will enhance the prestige of the institution, or students who can afford to pay the tuition charges remaining after the discount. The danger, now rapidly becoming reality, is that needy students will be worse off.

For states, a key goal is to keep the best students in the state. According to the report *Who Should We Help? The Negative Social Consequences of Merit Scholarships,* state spending on merit programs increased 18.3 percent annually between 1991 and 2001, whereas spending on need-based scholarships increased only 7.7 percent annually. Furthermore, the share of state aid devoted to merit awards rose from 11 to 24 percent (Heller and Marin, 2002).

In a unique use of merit awards, the state of Utah created the New Century Scholarship to keep talented students in Utah while addressing the overcrowding issues facing the higher education system. High school students who achieve an associate degree or complete sixty credit hours at a state institution by the start of the academic year, in the year they would have graduated from high school, are eligible for the New Century Scholarship. The scholarship "can equal 75 percent of an eligible student's tuition cost for up to two years (60 credit hours) at any of Utah's state operated institutions . . . offering baccalaureate programs" ("New Century Scholarship Program," 2002). Students who fail to maintain a B average for two semesters in a row will loose their scholarship ("New Century Scholarship Program," 2002).

Among private institutions, those that can (and some that can't or shouldn't) are discounting their tuitions by offering scholarships for merit and increasing the eligibility requirements for financial aid. Some families making as much as $150,000 a year are eligible for financial assistance from some colleges (Marcus, 2001). More than 80 percent of students at independent institutions now receive some sort of aid (Lapovsky and Hubbell, 2000). New data show that over recent years the average institutional grant aid at four-year institutions, public and private, for students from families with income over $40,000 has risen faster than for students from families with income under $40,000. Princeton University, for example, recently eliminated all student loans in favor of grants. As one of the richest universities in the country (and world), Princeton can afford this strategic move. But Princeton's action has in turn put pressure on other selective institutions, even those with far smaller endowments, to follow suit or lose out on bright students (Clayton, 2001).[2] In other words, both attention and money are increasingly focused on the so-called better students. Tuition discounting, although easing the problem for wealthier students, is limiting access to grant aid for low-income students, making it harder for them to attend four-year institutions (J. Davis, 2003).

Other colleges with fewer resources have cut their tuition across the board in the hope of increasing application and enrollment rates. For example, Bethany College in West Virginia decreased its tuition from $20,650 to $12,000 for the 2002 freshman class. As a result, the number of applications it received rose from 501 to 658 ("Colleges Lure Students with Lower Tuition," 2002).[3] For a number of institutions, this type of behavior is working, but for others it is creating a financial crisis. Some institutions are finding themselves in a discount war that they cannot afford or sustain. The Lumina Foundation found that not only is tuition discounting not increasing net revenues for some colleges, it is also not producing hoped-for increases in student quality (J. Davis, 2003).

If there were substantial resources—governmental, institutional, and family—available, if student aid for students in need were rising as rapidly as tuition or more rapidly, then the price competition for better students could be seen as a positive. What is emerging is growing financial hardship for less advantaged students and less affluent institutions.

Marketing to Students

The purpose of the admissions office is shifting from selecting a balanced class to maximizing tuition revenue (much like airline passenger revenue management), as is the title of its director—from dean of admissions to director of enrollment management.[4] Early admissions is increasingly used as a key vehicle for enrollment management. It helps colleges to make themselves look better statistically in rankings by increasing the yield (the number of accepted students who choose to enroll).[5] Unfortunately, the strategy tends to reward affluent students from the most exclusive and well-resourced high schools and penalize almost everyone else (Altschuler, 2002). In a new book, entitled *The Early Admissions Game: Joining the Elite,* three economists assert that "applying to an elite college through an early-admissions program can improve students' chances of getting in by as much as 50 percent over their odds during the regular admissions cycle, a difference that is the equivalent of scoring 100 points higher on the SAT." They also found a "disparity of sophistication about the process between students from private and wealthy suburban public schools and those from [other] public schools. . . . As it stands, the strategic nature of early applications has got to be enhancing the advantage of the wealthiest" (as cited in Young, 2003, p. A38; see also Fitzsimmons, 2003).

This emphasis on advertising and recruiting has led individual institutions to try out a variety of competitive strategies.[6] Direct mail campaigns and phone recruiting are on the rise. Gaining the attention of potential students by new means, most importantly by slick Websites, is now critical (Hoover, 2002). In a discouraging display of how far out of bounds the competition can get in the effort to attract the best possible students, the director of admissions at Princeton broke into a Yale Website to find information about students who had applied to Yale (Delbanco, 2002).

The competition for hot prospects in business and law schools has intensified to such an extent that several schools now offer free trips and visits and send out showy and high-tech acceptances. A recruiter for Vanderbilt University Law School went so far as to take a top applicant on a hiking trip. Accepted students can expect to receive phone calls from faculty members, students, and graduates. When Duke's Fuqua School of Business sent out flashy e-mail acceptances that included animations and music, the percentage of accepted students who enrolled at Fuqua increased from 52 percent to 57 percent (Mangan, 2003).

Advertising, once seen as appropriate only for summer school, is now commonplace. A recent "Education Life" section of the *New York Times* had sixty-one university and college ads; ten were for New York University alone—seven of them full-page ads.[7] Advertising has, in a striking change, also become de rigueur for Italian universities, as those bastions of outmoded educational practices struggle to compete in the new European market. Italian universities increased their spending on advertising from $500,000 in 1997 to $5 million in 2001 (Bollag, 2002). Many American universities and colleges have also hired public relations firms to make sure that they receive their share of favorable mention in the media, despite little evidence that it helps (Ross, 2003).[8] Here again, the problem is not that colleges and universities work hard to attract students. They always have, and they should. The problem that has emerged is that, as competition has intensified, the mode of pursuing students, such as early admissions, undercuts the ideals of higher education.

Recruiting by Amenities

Universities and colleges compete as well by offering amenities seemingly far removed from the traditional college experience, such as elaborate fitness centers, luxurious student unions, and other costly adaptations designed to make the life of a student easier and more attractive (Randall, 2002; for a statement on how this competition is affecting the financial health of institutions, see Winter, 2003). Housing with single bedrooms is proliferating to keep up with the "high-priced competition for students who may be just as concerned with residential amenities as they are with the number of volumes in the library" (Rimer, 2003a, p. A1). Here again, the problem is not with the concept of competing for students but with the priorities that have resulted. Fitness centers, as such, are surely not harmful to the nature of higher education, but how are society's needs met by the many decisions made to invest institutional energy and resources in them rather than in addressing consistently poor performance in teaching introductory math courses?

Climbing the Ladder of Prestige

The increasing competition, especially at the top echelon, has, in the words of Cornell economist Robert H. Frank, created a "winner-take-all market" for the student and the institution (Frank, 2001, 2002).[9] In such a market, college rankings such as those produced by *U.S. News & World Report* that consistently list the wealthiest universities as the preeminent institutions in the country play a vital role in shaping the competition. Robert Woodbury, former chancellor of the University of Maine System, has written a scathing indictment of how the rankings encourage perverse behavior in colleges and universities, such as the temptation to use marketing tricks indiscriminately to create "an application deluge" and then reject as many students as possible, because the rankings favor institutions with a high rate of rejection (Woodbury, 2003).

In addition to competing for higher rankings, institutions seek to be "categorized" in ways that connote prestige: as universities, as selective institutions, and as research institutions. Reacting to survey results that showed prospective students see "university" as more prestigious than "college," more than 160 colleges have changed their names to become universities over the past decade alone (Mathews, 2003). The number of research teams applying for federally funded research grants has grown as institutions strive to gain a foothold as research universities. As of the year 2000, more than 261 universities were listed in the Carnegie Classifications as doctoral/research universities (McCormick, 2001).

The percentage of institutions classified as "competitive" or "selective," as opposed to "open door," has increased for both private and public institutions (Hoover, 2002). One way of bolstering the number of applicants, in order to look more selective, is to encourage simplified online application, which encourages the casual applicant and increases the number of applications made by each student. The result is that the institution receives more applications and is therefore able to reject a higher percentage of students.[10]

Another way that institutions are trying to appear more prestigious is to add honors colleges to attract students with high test scores and grade point averages. The National Collegiate Honors Council reports that since 1995, membership rose 50 percent, with more than a thousand institutions running honors programs (Samuels, 2001).

Even institutions that traditionally serve the less economically advantaged students have been caught up in this type of competition.[11] City University of New York, the institution with perhaps the most storied tradition of educating poor but striving students, recently created an honors college at seven of its four-year campuses. In addition, a systemwide scholarship was introduced for the very best students—full tuition, a $7,500 per year stipend, and a laptop computer—all in the service of becoming an "elite institution" (Arenson, 2002).

Newly aggressive community colleges are also busily recruiting top high school graduates. Many now offer full-cost scholarship programs and a more challenging honors curriculum; 168 community colleges now offer honors programs up from 24 fifteen years ago (Walsh, 2003). More community colleges are moving beyond collaborating with four-year institutions, to providing their own baccalaureate degrees at the campus.[12] One can readily understand that community colleges are pleased when they attract students who have the ability to gain admissions to a four-year institution. It is probably also true that having such students on campus helps improve the learning experience, as students learn from each other. Surely, striving to build the prestige of the institution is a rational goal of institutional leadership. The difficulty lies in the narrowness of the goals that have emerged. Absent is any competition based on how much students are learning, or the social mobility afforded to graduates. In the long run, success at garnering prestige will be a hollow victory if it serves only the institution's needs, not the public's.

Chasing New Sources of Revenue

The insatiable thirst for new revenues has led institutions to try a range of moneymaking initiatives, ranging from the mundane to the creative—even the bizarre. Institutional revenues from corporate training (particularly at community colleges) and from patents have been commonplace for years. Fund-raising holds new sway on public campuses. More recently, thousands of traditional colleges and universities have started creating virtual courses, trying to attract students from all over the world. Institutional credit cards—where universities collect a fee based on the consumer purchases their students and alumni make—stand out as an example of crossing the boundary between educational institution and full-service bank.

Programs for older, working students, many of whom are eligible for employer tuition benefits, have exploded in popularity, offering an effective new revenue stream. Older students are increasingly present in higher education. More than half of all postsecondary students are over the age of twenty-one, and the estimates are that this will increase ("Almanac 2002–3," 2002).[13] Sister Joel Read, the president of Alverno College, reports that when they started a weekend college in Milwaukee twenty-four years ago, they were alone. Today, Alverno competes with twenty-seven such programs seeking to serve the area's adult learners.[14]

Success in diversifying revenue sources will be, we believe, essential for institutional stability and capacity to serve the public in the tumultuous times ahead. The danger lies in revenue becoming the end rather than the means, in institutions drifting over the boundary that separates them from commercial enterprises.

The Student as Consumer

In an inevitable response to the behavior of the colleges and universities, prospective college students and their families have more and more taken on the attitude of consumers. Some students and their families—especially the more affluent—are seeking the help of consultants in navigating the admissions process. The Independent Educational Consultants Association (IECA) estimates there are more than two thousand consultants working nationwide, more than double the number a decade ago. It is an industry that is completely unregulated and growing exponentially.[15] Even for the less affluent, the Internet means that students have available far more information than ever before as they examine Websites early in their search. Students now can, and do, search for meaningful information about potential institutions—from class size to undergraduate research opportunities—and it has begun to affect their choice of colleges (see, for example, Hammond, 2002). Today, a student interested in choosing an undergraduate college, enrolling for an MBA, or finding an alternative introductory math course can easily peruse a variety of options on the Internet and choose from a range of virtual, traditional classroom, or mixed courses that match his or her current needs.

Once accepted, it has become gradually more common for students and their families to bargain with a college or university after receiving the financial aid package, employing such tactics as faxing another institution's financial aid package to their top choice, hoping that the latter will be forced to "meet the competitor's price" ("Top Financial Aid Tips," 2003).[16]

Another change from the traditional college experience is the fact that a student enrolled in a university who finds a given course is of poor quality—or even just inconvenient—can easily find a substitute nearby or online; almost half of all students attend more than one institution prior to earning their degree.[17] Commercial sites are now appearing that rate individual courses and professors, making the task far easier and increasing consumerlike behavior of students (Lewin, 2003b). A new online business, called "Pick-a-Prof," allows students in certain schools to view the grade distributions of every course and professor by using state open-records laws to view the statistics of public universities. The University of Maryland's student body is one of fifty-one schools and student bodies that have paid up to $10,000 for this service to be brought to their campus (Lewin, 2003b).

The result is that the behavior of the student as consumer is reinforced. If the student becomes a more informed selector of academic programs, if ratings systems force faculty to confront the perception of their classroom effectiveness, if student desertion of the campus-based statistics course forces the math department to reappraise its approach, then society is surely served. However, two drawbacks to consumer-oriented behavior have already emerged. Professional coaching to improve the student's chances of admission and bargaining over student aid overwhelmingly help wealthy families, while it is those least well off who desperately need this help. More and more, institutions see the student as a customer rather than as a participant in the enterprise or colleague on the voyage of learning. The student increasingly treats the college education as a commodity to be bought. The concept of a liberal education focused on the student's development and preparation for a life of civic engagement and the life of the mind is in danger of slipping away.

What is causing this increased competition that is jumping outside the traditions of higher education? It is not a lack of students; more and more students, from more diverse backgrounds, are applying to college than ever before (Carnevale and Fry, 2000). Nor is it a lack of dollars, for state support, tuition, and fund-raising have all increased substantially over the past two decades. While student numbers and dollars swell, competition and the search for new revenue sources are expanding faster.[18] Gordon Winston has described this new climate as an "arms race" in which institutions engage in a frenetic and never-ending search for better students, better faculty, winning athletic teams, more research, prestige, and—above all—the revenue to make these things possible (Winston, 2001).

The New Providers

The rapidly growing number of new providers of higher education services has become a powerful force pushing higher education toward a market.[19] Counted among the new competitors are some 625 for-profit, degree-granting universities and colleges (Brimah, 1999, 2000). Some of these for-profit institutions have been around for years, a few for a century or more. But recently they have grown rapidly in number and size, moved into offering conventional degrees, and sought accreditation. For-profit institutions now give associate's, bachelor's, master's, law, and Ph.D. degrees. Over the decade of the 1990s, the number of for-profit institutions granting two-year degrees rose 78 percent; those granting four-year degrees rose 266 percent (Kelly, 2001). Just between 2000 and 2001, revenue of the for-profit colleges grew 20 percent (Blumenstyk, 2002). The stocks of publicly traded for-profits have consistently outperformed the Standard and Poor's in past years ("The Chronicle Index," 2003).

There has been as well an explosion of online courses available from virtual institutions, virtual arms of traditional institutions, for-profit universities and colleges, and consortia such as the Colorado Community College Online (run by the twelve Colorado Community Colleges) or the Electronic Campus (run by the Southern Regional Education Board; "Postsecondary Education," 2002).

In 1997–1998, fifty-two thousand courses were offered via distance education, enrolling almost 1.7 million students. One-third of all tertiary education institutions in the United States were providing distance education of some sort, and another 20 percent planned to add distance education to their curriculum (U.S. Department of Education, 1999). The number of programs and their enrollment then began to grow rapidly as institutions focused on online courses rather than correspondence, television, or other modes of distance instructional delivery. By the beginning of 2002, 3,600 academic programs were offered via distance education.[20] One study found that 70 percent of traditional two- and four-year institutions offered online courses in 2000 (as cited in Konrad, 2001). Estimates vary, but total enrollment has probably surpassed three million students.[21] Currently, one of the largest providers is the University of Maryland University College (UMUC). Javier Miyares, vice president for planning and accountability at UMUC, reported a total of 87,423 online enrollments in 2002. Online enrollments now make up 37 percent of all University of Maryland enrollments (Javier Miyares, personal communication, Dec. 2002).

Virtual high schools in Florida and Massachusetts each teach more than 5,000 students. The University of Oklahoma and the University of Nebraska offer online high school diploma programs ("Online High School Program," 2002). Numbers vary, but the Center for Education Reform estimates that there are sixty-seven cyber high schools in the country (Rimer, 2003b). In addition, 15 percent of the high schools in the United States currently offer access to virtual classes, and at least twenty-six states have started virtual high schools (Borja, 2001). As a result, a growing number of high school students now enter college with credits earned online during their junior and senior high school years. These students, versed in online classes in high school, arrive at higher education's door familiar with and open-minded about the online format as an approach for their undergraduate programs.

Not only high schools are socializing students to online learning; so is the military. As of March 2002, 15,834 soldier-students had signed agreements to participate in eArmyU, the Army's online university, growing to an estimated 30,000 today. The Army expects to expand the program to 80,000 students by the end of 2005 (Lorenzo, 2002).

Virtual education does indeed represent a significant new opportunity, though the going is not always smooth (Smith 2000; Lewis and others, 1999). Some universities that entered the domain of for-profit virtual higher education, either to sell courses or electronic course materials, have not succeeded, mostly from insufficient or poor planning. Temple University, New York University, the State University of New York at Buffalo, Cornell University, and the University of California and California State University (jointly) all created now-defunct for-profit online arms (Hafner, 2002). The University of Maryland experimented with a for-profit subsidiary, UMUConline, but closed it in October 2001. (However, as mentioned, UMUC continues to offer a large and growing array of virtual courses.) What has grown steadily is online versions of traditional courses and degrees offered by both for-profit and non-profit institutions.

An emerging body of research makes plain that learning via the Internet can be both effective and satisfying for students, when done well (Newman and Scurry, 2001). Jay Sivin-Kachala and Ellen R. Bialo found that "more than half of the students described as 'seldom' participating in face-to-face class discussions participated online at about the same rate as students described as 'frequent' participants in face-to-face discussions" (Sivin-Kachala and Bialo, 2000, p. 25). A growing number of studies have documented the experience of faculty such as Deanna Raineri, a molecular biologist at the University of Illinois, Urbana-Champaign. After she added virtual labs to her molecular biology courses, her scores on student evaluations shot up, and her students performed better on quizzes covering applied questions ("Online, On Campus," 2001). As students from these programs, or from the growing number of online corporate training programs, become comfortable participating in online learning, it is likely to increase the number of students willing to enroll in one of the growing online graduate programs now available, such as master's in teacher education or MBA courses. There are, of course, poorly run online programs, just as there are poorly run traditional programs; but when done well, virtual learning clearly has the capacity to create effective and satisfying learning.

Beyond the array of traditional higher education institutions jostling for position, there are additional institutions that are not formally part of higher education but serve some of the same functions. This includes the information technology companies running certificate programs (which have already granted more than 2.5 million certificates); corporate universities that train their own employees (which have grown from four hundred a decade ago to more than two thousand); as well as museums, publishers, and even government agencies offering courses.[22]

Not only is there an expanded universe of providers of higher education, but—in the spirit of the student as consumer described earlier in this chapter—the Internet gives students an easy way to access this wider variety of choices. The students who spend four residential years on a single campus will soon be an anomaly among the Internet-savvy students empowered to map out their own educational path. The sum of these challenges is a fundamentally changed climate of competition.

Technology in the Classroom

To date, the growth of virtual education has been the most significant change in education wrought by technology. However, as important as the capacity is to educate at a distance, the impact that digital technology is beginning to have on learning, particularly in the traditional classroom, is, over the long run, of far greater significance. Much of the early use of computers and the Internet in traditional classroom settings has served to do ordinary tasks more efficiently: distributing the course syllabus and readings, providing a communication link between faculty and students and among students, creating the means for more effective student research. New technology is used principally to replicate traditional classroom-based experiences (for example, Microsoft PowerPoint instead of a blackboard; Werbach, 2000). The opportunity ahead lies in the capacity to use information and communication technology to transform learning in ways that capitalize on what we have known for a long time about powerful pedagogy: that students learn more, learn more profoundly, and remember over a far longer period when they are actively engaged in a self-driven learning activity rather than when they are engaged only passively, sitting and listening. Technology can give professors a practical approach to those methods that have been recognized as far more effective than lecturing. Technology can as well make visible and help address the different learning styles of students.

Now emerging are new software approaches that encourage much more exciting forms of learning. Our estimate is that over the next six or eight years, the use of such software will become commonplace, truly transforming how learning takes place in most settings—in traditional classrooms on campus and in virtual courses online. Software, for example, allows students to simulate experiments in all sorts of fields—in chemistry, physics, biology, geology, and more—that are too complicated, expensive, dangerous, time-consuming, or simply impossible to do in a real laboratory experiment. The Fly Lab, for example, is a technology module that can be used in the classroom to allow students to design their own fruit flies by varying their phenotype and then mating them to yield progeny. Analysis of the progeny allows students to understand the rules of inheritance (Bell, 1999; see also Newman and Scurry, 2001). Virtual, Web-based surgical simulators allow medical students (and experienced physicians) to practice surgical techniques without putting patients at risk. Among other procedures already available is simulation software for ventricular catheterizations, pedicle screw insertions, and liver biopsies ("Web-Based Surgical Simulators . . . ," 2002). The "cognitive tutors" in a growing number of disciplines—including that bête noire, statistics—developed at Carnegie Mellon give students easily visualized help twenty-four hours a day, seven days a week.

Many faculty are still wary as to whether the technology is simple and reliable enough to use for more sophisticated learning tasks. Every day, however, software is emerging that is better, faster, cheaper, more reliable, and easier to use and that allows students to take part in more engaging and effective learning. One of the most compelling demonstrations of the capacity of technology to help transform the classroom has been the Pew Grant Program in Course Redesign led by Carol Twigg. It has taken aim at redesigning large introductory courses (often the least effective and most disliked). Rio Salado College, for example, designed new approaches to teaching introductory algebra. The University of Wisconsin-Madison created thirty-seven "Web-based instructional modules" for chemistry. After the student has completed a module, a series of questions are presented to determine whether or not the student sufficiently absorbed the material. Students found the tutorials extremely helpful and were especially appreciative of the option to link directly to a tutorial if they had difficulty with a problem.

Evaluation of the participating institutions has been completed. The team found that when the faculty analyzed carefully how the course was currently structured, applied the most advanced concepts of pedagogy, and used technology effectively, improvements in student learning, retention, and student satisfaction resulted. Perhaps most surprising was that all showed cost savings, ranging from 20 percent to 84 percent (Twigg, 2003b).

As higher education moves forward, every postsecondary institution should recognize that digital technology has already begun to change how students learn in every setting—online courses, elementary and secondary schools, skills training centers, as well as the traditional classrooms. Indeed, as the capacity and use of technology continue to advance, the traditional and the online course will look more alike to the student. Each will use technology to enhance learning. Each will encourage active learning as well as frequent communication with the faculty member and other students. Each will use faculty members as mentors and guides rather than as the primary source of information, thereby altering the student-faculty relationship forever.

Today there is a spectrum of collaboration employed in the creation of a course: from the traditional mode of the entire preparation by a single professor, to a professor with help from one or two other technology professionals, to a small team involving a graphic artist and a technology expert, to the large group method preferred by the institutions such as the University of Phoenix or the British Open University. While the single professor creating his or her own course is still the dominant mode, the more technology is used, the more course preparation moves toward the team approach. The two ends of this spectrum could be compared to the work of individual craftsmen and the specialized labor of modern production.

Our assumption is that, over the next several years, a different scenario will emerge. Even now, few faculty have the capacity or support to create their own software. More technology will be available in a module form, professionally created, that the course instructor uses much like an interactive, far more exciting textbook. As this occurs, the need for campus-based teams to create learning software will diminish, and their efforts will instead be focused on helping faculty find and employ software from professional sources. The use of technology in the classroom will accelerate. More and more learning will involve interactive software. Increasingly, learning, including on campuses, will involve a mixture of both classroom and online instruction. Creating the modules will require faculty as content consultants and specialists (that is, the backup of a sophisticated team) but will probably be done commercially. To date, the impact of technology in higher education is slower than in many fields (such as banking or telecommunications). Still, it has been far more rapid than is typical for higher education.[23]

A National Academy of Sciences panel examining the impact of technology on the university noted that the change is likely to be revolutionary—in the way both teaching and research are conducted—resulting in fundamental changes in how universities are structured. The most profound changes, the panel noted, have come in those organizations engaged in gathering, manipulating, analyzing, and disseminating information. There is no organization that this better describes than the university (National Research Council of the National Academies, 2002).[24] Higher education faces a sea change for which it must prepare.

All of this raises important questions that each college and university should consider. Soon those institutions skilled in the use of technology to improve learning will be seen as more dynamic and effective than their less engaged competitors. The use of technology will become a source of prestige and competitive advantage. Therefore, institutions and faculty that view themselves as excellent at teaching now need to excel at the use of technology if they are to remain leaders.

The Globalization of Higher Education

Recently a new phenomenon has emerged: the globalization of higher education (see, for example, Green, Eckel, and Barblan, 2002; Altbach, 2003). We mean here the emergence of global rather than international institutions. International institutions have foreign students enrolled; their domestic students often spend some time studying abroad. Similarly, faculty come from other countries to study, teach, or do research, and the home institution faculty frequently go abroad. All of these activities have become routine for the best-known universities in the United States and increasingly so for all types of institutions, including American community colleges. It is common in other countries as well. In Canada, for example, 84 percent of universities report that "internationalization" is included in their institutional strategies (Green, Eckel, and Barblan, 2002). The British have stepped up their efforts at attracting more international students, with an increase of almost 20 percent in 2002 compared to 2001, becoming a formidable rival to the United States. The number of American students accepted into undergraduate programs in Britain rose by 17 percent in 2002 (Galbraith, 2003).

Global institutions, on the other hand, conduct operations (educate students, do research, generate revenue) in multiple countries.[25] This may be accomplished by establishing campuses (for instance, Monash University in Malaysia and South Africa), by creating learning centers (the British Open University throughout Europe and in more than thirty non–European Union countries), or forming alliances with local institutions (as with the Singapore-MIT Alliance; "Global Development," 2003).[26] Any virtual (online) program is by its nature global, and a number of global online consortia are popping up as well (such as Cardean University and Universitas 21). Technology makes content delivery increasingly a global enterprise. What is appearing more and more are mixtures—programs that use intense short trips to the home university campus or to nearby learning centers to supplement a base of virtual course work. Several business schools have begun to offer executive education this way (Duke University, for example). Australian universities with strong financial support from their government are using all of these methods, in one way or another, to create a higher education presence across Asia that generates a sizable balance of trade.

American academics tend to believe the globalization of higher education presents only opportunity, not risk. To date, the total enrollment in global academic programs is still small. Far more programs are under discussion than under way. What is important to recognize is that the barriers to global higher education enterprises are falling, and the trend is up. Beyond this, the conditions favoring more intense competition from the universities of other countries are growing.

In an important but generally overlooked development, the World Trade Organization (WTO) is now proposing to regulate higher education as part of the General Agreement on Trade in Services (GATS), as it would any other form of trade—by removing barriers to its traffic.[27] The goal of GATS is gradual liberalization of the trade in services, which is likely to have a broad and troubling impact on the nature of higher education by affecting such issues as subsidization of higher education, quality assurance, financial aid for certain students, and the ability to gear teaching and research to local culture and needs (GATS—Fact and Fiction, 2002). The U.S. delegation has already proposed inclusion of for-profit higher education and all testing materials and services, and it has announced that it expects soon to propose inclusion of all of higher education, despite the fact that there has been almost no debate within the academy about the impact of this on higher education. This form of rapid and potentially harmful globalization is an example of how higher education is drifting into a market-oriented system without adequate debate and planning—here and abroad.

An advance look at how some aspects of globalization may affect the way higher education functions can be seen in the workings of the European Union, the one place where a great deal of planning has taken place. The development of the Common Market led to a strong interest in facilitating the movement of professionals across country borders. This has led in turn to a joint effort to increase the number of students from other Common Market countries at each EU university, with a target of 10 percent of total enrollment. To help reach this target, the European Union created a range of programs that encouraged and subsidized such "study abroad." One of them, the Erasmus Program, uses financial aid and promotes collaboration between universities to encourage mobility of both students and faculty members. Since its establishment, more than one million people have taken advantage of the opportunities it offers, with some twenty-five hundred universities from twenty-nine European countries involved.[28]

In time, it became evident to the Europeans that more than access was involved—that Europe needed to compete for the best students, many of whom head to the United States or Britain. Among other concerns, the Europeans felt they needed to reduce

the confusion over different types of degrees (and the unwillingness of universities to accept each other's degrees) and to improve
the attractiveness of their universities. In 1999, in Bologna, a European Higher Education Area was formed. Among other steps, the
Bologna Accord called for standardization on a three-year bachelor's degree and a two-year master's by 2010. (The Netherlands,
Italy, and Spain have already begun implementing the change.) A
new quality agency, the European Network for Quality Assurance
in Higher Education, has been established to ensure standards.
The Europeans also moved to teach some programs in English,
which is fast becoming the international language of business.
Thirty percent of universities in continental Europe—even some
French universities—now offer programs in English, almost all of
which were established since 1990 (Rocca, 2003). Recruitment,
advertising, and marketing campaigns have been launched.
Frans Zwarts, the rector of the University of Groningen in the
Netherlands, summed up this activity: "Traditionally, European
educational systems focused on accessibility. Now they are realiz-
ing that they have to compete for top talent on a global level"
(Riding, 2003). The EU has also established a substantial fund
(about $20 billion yearly) for the support of European research (a
sum roughly comparable to the U.S. investment in university
research). In meeting after meeting, the Futures Project has heard
the determination of European leaders, political and academic, to
compete with the United States. Unnoticed by most American academics, this country has been surpassed on a number of educational
measures. OECD comparisons rank the United States tenth for high
school graduation, thirteenth for entry rate to a four-year (baccalaureate) education, and tenth for entry to a two-year (associate's)
education (Mortenson, 2003).

Given the right circumstances, societies can gain from the
entry of global higher education institutions into their communities. In cases where the existing institutions are set in their ways
and outmoded in their approach, new institutions are bringing a
breath of fresh air, pushing the older institutions to new action. In
many settings, new institutions are needed to keep up with demand.
The number of tertiary students worldwide doubled in size in just
twenty years, growing from 40.3 million students in 1975 to 80.5
million students in 1995, and the growth is continuing (Task Force

on Higher Education and Society, 2000). Where existing access and funding is limited, new institutions from abroad are expanding opportunity. New institutions may also bring needed diversity to the type of experience available to students. For example, programs taught in English are permitting students broad access to the global workplace and the worldwide network of academia.

At the same time, there are dangers. Cross-border initiatives are subject to the vagaries of political changes, as MIT recently learned when its collaboration with India's information technology ministry, called Media Lab Asia, fell apart after the appointment of a new minister (Rai, 2003). A foreign institution may be insensitive to the local culture and students' needs. Criticism has already arisen that the quality of some overseas programs is less than that at the home campus and that universities from developed countries have not focused on local concerns in developing nations. The use of English raises for some people questions about cultural imperialism and homogenization. Developing countries would surely be ill-served if universities from the outside replaced local universities rather than supplementing them.

There are other profound changes in progress that deserve greater attention. One is the aggressive growth of for-profit global institutions. For example, the parent corporation of the University of Phoenix has begun operations in Brazil, Mexico, India, and the Netherlands and is eyeing several other countries (Jorge Klor de Alva, personal communication, Mar. 2004). Sylvan Learning has been acquiring small private universities (the eighth was just announced) around the world (Blumenstyk, 2003). The goal is to build a worldwide network that shares curricular materials and other resources. If, over the next decade, a global higher education sector led by for-profit institutions emerges, what are the concerns for the public purposes of higher education?

The Implications of the New Competition

There is a deeply held tendency within the academy to respond to these changes by commenting that American higher education has always been competitive and not much has changed. This overlooks three profound shifts.

First, a large number of changes are happening at once, reinforcing the impact of each change. To review some of the trends covered in this chapter:

- Public, private, and for-profit institutions alike are competing to attract students, in ways and with an intensity never seen before, using financial aid, advertising, and campus amenities.
- Traditional universities are more focused on developing new revenues than ever before, including starting for-profit ventures that blur the once sacrosanct dividing line between for-profit and nonprofit.
- There has been huge growth in the number of for-profit universities and colleges, the degrees they give, and the acceptance of their degrees by students and employers.
- Thousands of virtual programs are growing rapidly, altering the way many students attend college and how classes are delivered as new forms emerge.
- Corporate universities and certificate programs are widespread, in some fields becoming the preparation preferred by employers.
- New organizational forms are emerging, such as those at the British Open University or the University of Phoenix, that rely heavily on technology and challenge the hegemony of the traditional faculty and the academic discipline-oriented college or university.
- For the first time, higher education has gone global. Even the degree structure of ancient European universities is changing to make them more competitive.

Second, as more information becomes available—about what courses are available; how much students are learning; how much contact students have with the faculty; whether students are satisfied with a course, a program, or an institution—the workings of the market and the pressures of the competition will accelerate.

Finally, as is made plain in the next chapter, the interest of governments in encouraging the growing competition has begun creation of a huge market of diverse institutions: public, private, for-profit; universities, colleges, technical institutes, corporate universities; online, traditional classroom, hybrid; domestic and foreign. All of these, and more, are competing for a place in the sun, sanctioned and supported by policy makers who hope the market will bring a new form of accountability.

Despite its capacity to resist change, higher education is unlikely to be the same. But will it serve us better or less well? Competition in each of these facets can help—or hurt—higher education build its capacity to serve the public or undercut its commitment and capacity to this end. The future depends on the ability of government to fashion effective policies and on the ability of campus leaders to create institutional strategies that acknowledge public responsibilities.

Chapter Three

The Coming of the Market

There are many forces transforming higher education, but the most powerful and certainly the most striking is the shift of policy makers toward a market-oriented system of higher education and away from a regulated system. The shift toward a market represents a reversal of a long trend—more than five decades—toward state-structured systems.

In our examination of the transformation of higher education, we have focused on five underlying forces: the growing competition among traditional nonprofit universities and colleges; the impact of the new providers of higher education, including for-profit degree-granting institutions, virtual programs and institutions, and corporate universities; the impact of digital technology; the globalization of higher education; and the growing dependence of political leaders on market forces to structure higher education. All of these forces are interactive and tend to reinforce each other, but the most powerful and certainly the most striking is the shift of policy makers toward a market-oriented system of higher education and away from a regulated system. The convergence of all five of these forces is proving to be powerful enough to bring change to what has been a remarkably stable system.

The Shift from Regulation to the Market

The shift toward a market represents a reversal of a long trend—more than five decades—toward state-structured systems. As the number of public universities and colleges exploded in the 1950s and 1960s, governance moved from the single campus (the University of California, as Berkeley was then known) to the multi-campus system (the University of California System, the famous multiversity named, described, and extolled by Clark Kerr) to, in many states, a system of systems (the California Master Plan, which firmly fixed the places of the University of California System, the California State University System, and the California Community College System). Most states developed as well a statewide coordinating or governing board (for example, the California Postsecondary Education Commission, or CPEC). The goal of this superstructure was to bring order and efficiency to the rapidly growing array of state universities and colleges. Responsibilities included defining institutional roles, reducing program overlap, easing the task of the legislature in allocating resources to the individual campuses, and affording a degree of protection for higher education from the politics of the state ("About the Commission," 2003).

Now the tide is turning. The existing superstructure, although effective in orchestrating the expansion in size and scope of the public system of higher education, has been largely ineffective in preventing mission creep and program overlap. It has not been able to address issues of cost and efficiency or the quality of learning, nor has it been able to mobilize higher education in support of the reform of elementary and secondary education. Legislators have grown impatient, and accountability has become a hot-button topic.[1] The National Governors Association has argued, "Now more than ever, the responsiveness of [postsecondary] institutions to the changing needs of students and employers is critical to state economic competitiveness" (National Governors Association, 2001). The governors feel that there is a need "for postsecondary education to improve its productivity and its accountability" (National Governors Association, 2002; see also Feemster, 2003). There is, as a result, a growing interest in shifting from dependence on regulation and oversight to using the market as a means of ensuring public purposes. This move away from broader, systemwide regulation sometimes (though not always) includes specific agreements with the individual institutions about mission and accountability.

Examples of decentralization and deregulation abound:

- In 1994, New Jersey dismantled the Board of Higher Education and eliminated the office of chancellor as well as most of the Department of Higher Education, creating a simpler, more decentralized structure. Institution-level boards gained control over tuition, academic programs, personnel, trustee nominations, and construction. The new system, however, depends on "self-regulation" (McLendon, 2000, p. 17; McLarin, 1994).
- In Colorado, one institution was given a ten-year funding plan and freed from most state regulation in return for an agreed-upon plan for measuring its performance. Two other institutions were removed from their systems and given their own boards. A sweeping bill was introduced in the legislature to replace the state subsidy to the institutions with a program of vouchers that students would carry to the institution.[2]
- In North Dakota, a "flexibility with accountability" bill was signed in 2001 that gives institutions spending flexibility, block grants, and the ability to keep tuition and private donations in exchange for new measures of accountability (Gouras, 2001; State of North Dakota, 2001; Sullivan, 2002; Hanson, 2000).

In some states, a confusing mix of motives has led to a political debate that is based on an accountability-autonomy trade-off, but with the process so politicized that the resulting outcome is not clear. In Florida, controversy erupted over a proposed shift to decentralization. The governor proposed, and the legislature passed, a bill abolishing the Board of Regents and creating a new board that oversees all education for the state. Each university was given its own board, with greater powers. But in 2002, less than a year after the change took place, a former governor of Florida led a successful referendum for a constitutional amendment restoring the board and leaving the trend toward greater institutional autonomy confused (see Kumar, 2002; Schmidt, 2003; Hebel and Schmidt, 2002; Gibson, 2001). New proposals from the universities, which would restore some of the shift toward deregulation, have been under consideration in 2003 and 2004.

In other states, the debate has been limited to questions of accountability, without considering ways of creating new autonomy for the institutions. The Illinois Board of Higher Education has just mandated that all public colleges and universities submit annually a set of "performance indicators." Each discipline will devise its own means of evaluating what students have learned. The plan makes plain that the board and the higher education community are "serious about quality and accountability" ("Plan to Test Student Learning, Enact Performance Measures Top IBHE Agenda," 2003). A more detailed description of state-by-state changes is in Chapter Seven.

Nationally, there is a growing movement toward seeing the state higher education system as an array of institutions all competing for their place in the market, with each public college and university following the specifics of an individually negotiated mission and mode of accountability. With the entry into higher education of a large number of for-profit, degree-granting universities and colleges, added to the presence of hundreds of private nonprofit institutions, the system of higher education in the country is already partly structured as a market. With more than four thousand degree-granting institutions, perhaps only a market can serve the public effectively. Across the world, the same shift is evident in country after country. Even in nations where the higher education system has been far less diverse and much more regulated than in the United States, new modes have emerged designed to create a market and encourage competitive pressures.

The Causes of the Shift

Why is this reversal of public policy occurring now? There are two main causes at work. One is a set of forces that flow naturally from growing competition. As competition intensifies among the traditional public and private nonprofit universities and colleges, augmented by the growing pressure of the new for-profit universities and colleges and the new virtual programs, the leaders of the public institutions press harder for autonomy. Their interest in gaining greater autonomy, already strong, is now buttressed by a new and compelling argument: "We need greater autonomy in order to compete."

The clearest case of how this pressure has played out is the move by the Darden Graduate School of Business Administration at the University of Virginia to phase out its public funding by 2008 so as to free itself to compete more effectively in the lucrative but highly competitive market of elite business schools and executive training. (Darden is actually moving ahead of this schedule, and the UVA School of Law has announced that it will follow suit.) It will essentially become a private institution within a public university.[3]

The pressures of competition have led most institutions as well to an intense search for new revenue streams: higher tuition, the use of "enrollment management" to maximize tuition revenue, virtual programs, fund-raising, corporate contracts, research grants. According to David Kirp, "Market talk is increasingly heard, and it's more than talk—from the periphery, money moves closer to the core; from a means, making money has become an end" (David Kirp, personal communication, Mar. 19, 2003; see also Kirp, 2003). As the push for new revenue escalates, increasing the ratio of private revenues to public revenues, so does the pressure for greater autonomy from public control. More and more, public presidents have taken to arguing that their college or university is now a "state assisted," rather than "state," institution.

The other side of the coin is that governors, legislators, and statewide boards, rather than protecting their institutions from the market and from competition as they have done in the past, now more often welcome the idea of the market as a potentially positive force. The line of reasoning goes that "if five decades of regulation have been unable to develop any workable mode of accountability and responsiveness, perhaps the discipline of the market can." The *American Statesman* in Texas reported, "Many Republican legislators believe that competition should be the key constraint. As with electricity and telephones, they believe education should respond to market forces." The *Statesman* also quoted State Sen. Florence Shapiro as saying, "We must remember that these are public institutions, and they must be competitive" (Kay and Jayson, 2003). In Colorado, State Rep. Keith King, a Republican, has said that it is time to "force market realities on higher education."[4] The same argument is gaining strength in other countries. For example, Margaret Hodge, the United Kingdom's minister of state for higher education, has stated publicly that she favors serious free-market reforms that would allow the market to "play a much stronger role in determining student choice and research investment," possibly resulting in the closure of some institutions (Crane, 2003, p. 6).

The academic community needs to understand that this interest in market forces does not come out of the blue but rather is a further extension of a broader push toward the use of markets for an array of sectors—the "rightward shift." For example, the changes already under way in telecommunications, health care, and the airline industry serve as market-oriented backdrops in the private sector. New market thinking has created imaginative approaches to what traditionally has been addressed by regulation. The federal government, for example, created an alternative approach to environmental regulation: the buying and selling of "pollution credits." Companies that beat uniform emissions standards can accumulate and sell credits to companies that fail to meet standards. The hope is that such an economic incentive will push companies to reduce emissions on their own; as one environmentalist wrote, "We must set up the rules of the game so that companies' own self-interest lies in safeguarding the environment" (Engle and Truax, 1990, p. 12; see also Mandel, 1989; Golden, 1999).

In the public sector, the shift in higher education policy mirrors a similar trend toward creating a market in elementary and secondary education. At the state level, this has produced an evolutionary push in policy from magnet schools to public school choice, to charter schools, to home schooling, and to voucher programs—all modes of organization that challenge the traditional identity of education as a heavily regulated public sector.[5]

Market Forces Go Global

This is a shift seen far beyond the borders of the United States. In country after country, the same shift toward market forces, or one even more pronounced, is occurring. In Egypt, Singapore, China, Poland, Germany, Malaysia, and a host of other countries, governments have, for the first time, encouraged establishment of new, private, often for-profit universities to compete with the traditional state universities. In several Asian countries, notably Japan, South Korea, the Philippines, India, and Indonesia, the majority of students, sometimes as many as 80 percent, are now enrolled in private universities (Lewis, Hendel, and Dundar, 2002; see also Quddus and Rashid, 2000). In Singapore, the government recently announced that it would meet the expected growth in higher education enrollment entirely by expansion of its already substantial private sector, holding the number of state universities at three.[6] In 1996, the Malaysian government changed its educational policy to actively recruit international branch campuses to its shores (Bennell and Terry, 1998). Indonesia is modeling the expansion of its education system after Malaysia's 1996 plan (Banks and McBurnie, 1999). In China, the emergence of *min ban,* or people-run, private institutions reflects the government's belief that a private sector in higher education is needed to ensure access to all students, especially those with modest test scores. Of the one thousand *min ban* institutions, one hundred have so far been accredited by the government. Legislation creating a structure for this sector is pending (Altbach, 2002a). In Poland, the growth rate of private institutions has been equally impressive. Over the past eleven years, the number has risen from zero to almost two hundred, with the largest, the Academy of Humanities and Economics, enrolling twenty thousand students and just recently receiving approval to offer Ph.D. programs (Lewis, Hendel, and Dundar, 2002; Makary Krzysztof Stasiak, personal communication, Jan. 2003).

In many cases—China, Britain, New Zealand, Australia—the move to encourage competition among state institutions represents an extension of a broader shift in government philosophy toward the market. In Great Britain, Chile, and New Zealand as well as the United States, the focus of government on market forces has included an effort to apply them to elementary and secondary education.

The Differing Motivations of Academic and Political Leaders

Although many American leaders from both the political and the academic worlds have embraced market forces, the motivation of the two groups is quite different. The Futures Project's interviews and formal focus groups with leaders from both groups have revealed stark differences (Immerwahr, 2002). Both see American higher education as the best in the world. Governors and legislators, however, see significant problems, ranging from the failure to address steadily rising costs to a lack of assessment of learning. They want some mode of accountability. University and college presidents, on the other hand, do not see the problems noted by the political leaders as serious. They want greater funding and autonomy (see Chapter Five).

Left alone, this disconnect is likely to lead to a growing confrontation. There is however, a clear opportunity for a trade-off: greater autonomy in return for greater accountability. What state leaders need, and what would serve the public most effectively, is state control principally of two factors: mission and a range of workable means of assessing institutional performance. What institutional leaders need is greater autonomy in the operation of the institution to fulfill the agreed-upon mission. Here again, a trend is emerging, both in various states in this country and in a growing number of other countries, to experiment with a new approach: more operating autonomy combined with an agreement with the state that spells out the specific mission of the institution, what the institution should be held accountable for, and how the institution will measure and report its performance.

One of the best examples of a dynamic performance agreement, created after constructive negotiations between government and academic leaders, is the one in place for the Colorado School of Mines. The performance agreement is a clear, four-page document that reflects the mission of the institution. The agreement is not excessively long or bureaucratic, and it includes performance criteria that the faculty and administrators of the School of Mines consider fitting for their institution. The agreement spells out how Mines is responsible for providing mentoring programs, maintaining graduation rates, and measuring learner outcomes through exit surveys and field-specific licensing exams, as well as how it will report progress to the Commission on Higher Education ("Performance Agreement: Colorado School of Mines and CCHE for FY 2002–2007," 2002).

Negotiations over autonomy and accountability are not always smooth, as other factors including politics enter the debate. In a striking example of the conflict over performance and accountability,

Kentucky Gov. Paul Patton and Charles Wethington, then the president of the University of Kentucky, squared off in a bare-knuckled political fight. The governor proposed a reorganization separating the state's community college campuses from university control. The move was designed to free the university to focus on its mission—specifically, on improving its lagging status as a research university. At the same time, the change encouraged full development of the community colleges into badly needed centers of educational opportunity and skill development, a task the university had largely ignored. Despite inclusion of a $50 million addition to the university's budget base, the university leadership was unwilling to agree to what it saw as a loss of turf and a set of local community college campuses that helped it to develop statewide political support. Marshaling compelling evidence of the need for change, the governor was able to carry the day. A report from the National Center for Higher Education Management Systems stated that "Kentucky's progress since the 1997 assessment is nothing short of remarkable" but went on to note that the existing institutions continue to compete with each other voraciously and to find ways to "'end run' the system" for short-term gain, thereby illustrating a need for a state compact with each institution to define its mission as well as the need for cooperation among universities and legislators (Chellgren, 2002; see also "Turf Battles Still Endanger State's Higher Education," 2002; Hawpe, 2003).

The Opportunity in the Current Budget Crisis

In a perverse way, the current budget crisis for state governments in the United States represents an opportunity to create such trade-offs. Essentially all states have a budget gap, many severe. In April 2002, the National Conference of State Legislatures reported that forty-three states had a deficit. By 2003, it was forty-four, and the deficits have only grown since. Unable to provide much funding, governors and legislators are more open to discussions of autonomy. Presidents, already working hard at expanding other revenue streams (particularly from tuition), are more open to new ideas for governance. It is a time when a more realistic, constructive approach can emerge.[7]

Officials at the University of Colorado System, for example, have argued that given a voter-initiated constitutional amendment that has limited state spending since 1992, "they need greater flexibility to attract and retain high-quality faculty, build better academic programs, and use their money more efficiently" (Hebel, 2002, p. A29). They have proposed a trade-off recognizing that the university receives a decreasing proportion of its revenues from the state, in exchange becoming a "state enterprise" with greater control over such issues as purchasing and tuition setting. The state-enterprise status was passed by the legislature but vetoed by the governor in June 2003 ("Owens Ties CU's Purse Strings," 2003; Hebel, 2002). The idea is back on the table in 2004.

Oregon presidents have similarly proposed to their legislature a trade-off, informally called "the Deal." It calls for the state to provide funding equal to 80 percent of the average of a group of comparable state universities elsewhere, rising to 90 percent in five years. The universities would gain control over tuition and a set of "flexibility initiatives" that would allow them greater autonomy in their operations. In return, the universities would agree to increase enrollment from the current 78,000 to 100,000, double sponsored research funding, increase the graduation rate, keep the cost to taxpayers below the national average, and set aside a portion of tuition revenues for financial aid for needy students ("Universities Ask for Freedom to Set Own Tuition Policies," 2003).

In Massachusetts, the governor, Mitt Romney, proposed restructuring the public universities to partly privatize the system. The University of Massachusetts System office would be eliminated, the main campus at Amherst would become largely autonomous, tuition would be sharply increased to make up for budget cuts (in some cases by as much as 28 percent), and the other universities and community colleges would be restructured into regional clusters that would collaborate in areas such as purchasing agreements. This proposal became highly politicized. The former president of the University of Massachusetts system, William Bulger, the former leader of the senate in Massachusetts, accused Romney of "attempting a 'corporate takeover' of public higher education" (Healy, 2003, p. B1; see also Butterfield, 2003; Healy and Russell, 2003; Russell, 2003). Bulger, under fire for other issues, has stepped down, and the move to restructure the university system has been abandoned, but many of the elements are being implemented piecemeal.

All of these proposals involve ideas on how to improve higher education, how to meet the budget crisis, and just plain politics.

In some cases, such as Colorado and Oregon, they also reflect a growing trend for university presidents to represent themselves as "state-located" rather than "state-supported" so that they can maneuver for more freedom from state regulations.

The Concern over the State Share of Funding

As the push for new revenue streams developed over the last decade, it became increasingly common for higher education leaders to cry abandonment by state government. Asserting that state support has been on the decline, academic leaders have suggested that they were left with no alternative but to seek new revenue elsewhere and that their increasingly private status should come with more autonomy from the state.[8] Mark Yudof of the University of Texas has been a leader in making this case publicly. Yudof has asserted: "Unfortunately, the agreement between the states and their flagship universities has deteriorated for 25 years, leaving public research universities in a purgatory of insufficient resources— low tuition and flat appropriations" (Yudof, 2002a, p. 18; see also Yudof, 2002b). The American Association of State Colleges and Universities made the argument that "the total funding 'pie' for states and for institutions has gotten bigger, but higher education's piece of the state funding pie has not concomitantly grown, nor has the state's share of the higher education funding pie" (American Association of State Colleges and Universities, 2001, p. 2). Looking at the data from another perspective, higher education analyst Tom Mortenson has argued that appropriations of state tax funds per $1,000 of personal income have been on the decline since the 1970s ("State Investment Effort in Higher Education, FY1962 to FY2003," 2002).

Though we sympathize with institutional presidents' desire for more autonomy, our analysis of state revenues finds the case to be quite different. State appropriations to higher education actually increased over the last two decades (up until the budget crisis of the last two years), even on an after-inflation and per-student basis (Figure 3.1). In the past decade alone (1993–2003), the amount spent on higher education by state governments has increased on average by 60.2 percent (or about 13 percent on a per-student, after-inflation basis; Grapevine Project, 2003; see also Callan, 2002).[9] What clearly is the case is that, even as state funding was expanding, colleges and universities were aggressively expanding other sources of revenue (tuition, sponsored research, corporate contracting, fund-raising).[10] The result is that the state appropriation now represents a smaller share of the total budget of public institutions—not because it was declining but because other revenue sources were growing faster for the institutions to feed their "insatiable appetites," as Pat Callan, president of the National Center for Public Policy and Higher Education, describes it (Allen, 2002, p. 1).

Figure 3.1. Revenues for Public Institutions per Full-Time-Equivalent Student (in Constant Dollars)

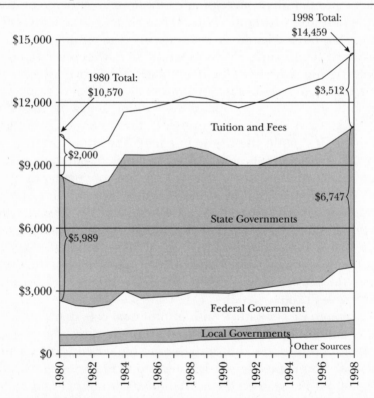

Source: Callan, P. M. *Coping with Recession: Public Policy, Economic Downturns and Higher Education.* San Jose, CA: National Center for Public Policy and Higher Education, 2002, p. 9.

All across the country, and across the world, as governments have been faced with the costly need to expand access to higher education for an ever-broader share of the population and to balance higher education's needs with other pressing social issues such as health care or support of elementary and secondary education, they have been willing, even eager, to see other funding streams finance a larger share of higher education. Given the current downturn in state finances, with real reductions occurring in some states (thirteen, as of March 2003), there is even greater willingness among states to see the other sources (reluctantly but clearly in the case of tuition) shoulder a greater burden.[11] But political leaders still see the urgency of higher education's public purposes and want greater accountability—even in return for a dollar amount that is a smaller share of the institutional budget. They continue to feel that not only does the massive increase in the amount of state funding over the last five decades demand greater accountability, so does the greater significance of higher education in the welfare of the state (Wellman, 2002).

Market Forces and Public Needs

Market forces in these cases offer the promise of improved performance in meeting public needs. After deregulation in the airline and telecommunications sectors, the public reaped the benefits of plummeting costs to the consumer. In higher education, when the GI Bill was introduced after World War II, it created the beginnings of a partial higher education market by putting money in the hands of students, which they carried with them to the institutions. The result was to overcome the resistance of the presidents who had originally opposed the GI Bill but later responded enthusiastically to the availability of these well-funded students. The ensuing expansion of the share of the population that entered higher education changed public perceptions as to who and how many could and should go to college and led to a continuing growth in access and in total enrollment (Bennett, 1996).

Market forces, however, carry risk as well as promise. One need only remember the American experience with health care, which resulted in large segments of the population being denied service.

In the case of health care, almost 44.5 million people have been left without coverage, over 15 percent of the population (U.S. Census Bureau, 2000). Minorities, the poor, and the unemployed are the most likely to be without coverage. As one expert summed it up, "The market is destroying our health care system. . . . We have had a decade or more of policies aimed at making healthcare a business, and they have failed" (Stolberg, 1999, p. A18).[12] One might also cite the current woes of the power industry in those states that have tried deregulation.[13]

Already there are signs that the pressures of the market in higher education are causing an erosion of critical public purposes. The push to enroll the so-called better students and to move up in college rankings has led to pressure on the states, the federal government, and institutions to expand merit aid—designed to attract the better students—at the expense of aid aimed at students with financial need. Universities, eager to secure corporate research dollars, have signed over control of publication rights to the sponsors. A few institutions, already feeling adverse market pressures, are merging and consolidating (Martin and Samels, 2002). Everywhere, one hears cries about the commodification of education (reducing the value of learning to simply "the opportunity to earn more upon graduation") and about the outsourcing of higher education's core purposes of teaching, learning, and service (Kirp, 2002; see also Benson and Harkavy, 2003). Higher education cannot afford to blindly accept the adverse consequences of the market. (See Chapter Six for a more detailed description of market risks.) Now is the time for careful thought about how to structure the market so that it is successful not only in creating institutional accountability but also in ensuring a system of higher education that serves the long-term needs of society.

Preparing for a Successful Market

Given these circumstances—growing competition, more diverse sources of revenue, interest among policy makers in the use of market forces to achieve some measure of institutional accountability—how market forces are structured is the key.[14] Competition won't automatically lead to better colleges and universities. These forces must be strong enough to encourage change. At the same time, they must be channeled or restrained in ways that prevent damage. All effective markets have some degree of regulation or channeling as a result of strategic intervention by government.

The United States has learned the hard way from the recent surge of corporate corruption cases, most notably Enron and Worldcom, that transparency—the availability of relevant and dependable information—is essential for an effective market. A requirement of a workable market in higher education is information about institutional performance. A number of states have proposed requiring their institutions to make public the information necessary to make a market work. In May 2003, the Board of Governors of Florida's public institutions voted to create an "accountability committee." The committee will consider how much (or how little) students at the state's public institutions are learning. The state is intent on holding public institutions accountable in much the same way as it does elementary and secondary schools. However, under this plan assessments would not be tied to graduate requirements; rather, they would be tied to the institution's funding. Steve Uhlfelder, a current member of the board, stated, "I want to know which universities are doing the best jobs." Board members and Gov. Jeb Bush want to "make sure students are learning" (Kumar, 2003, p. 18).

Kentucky, North Carolina, and Wisconsin have required all of their public institutions to participate in the National Survey of Student Engagement (NSSE). All three states have indicated that the results of the NSSE survey may be used "in their performance-indicator systems—and perhaps even in funding" (Kuh, 2003). NSSE results will furnish prospective students and their parents with better information when choosing where to apply for college.

Legislators, governors, and boards need to develop policies that encourage the positive aspects of market forces while simultaneously mitigating their potentially negative effects. At the same time, institutional leaders need to develop strategies that allow their universities or colleges to succeed in this new setting. They need to keep in mind that, as market forces emerged in other sectors of society, the ability of organizations and their leaders to cope with a new level of change was crucial to success and even to organizational survival. (See Chapters Seven, Eight, Nine, and Ten for proposals about policies and Chapter Eleven for proposals about institutional strategies.)

The Need for a Debate

To create a new and more effective structure for higher education, there is another change needed as well: generation of serious discussion, state by state, engaging both political and academic leaders as well as key community leaders as to how to restructure the system of higher education.

A debate is needed so that all parties can examine the alternatives and share data and analysis about the critical questions that are involved in a move toward a higher education market. What is the appropriate role for the state? What must the state support financially so that critical public purposes are met? What are the responsibilities of the institutions? A debate serves another purpose: building understanding and support among the public, which is essential if the new approach is to succeed in the long run. By *debate* here we mean more than just a simple discussion—rather, the complex process of discussion and negotiation by which ideas are transformed into policy.

This means overcoming the traditional reluctance of both policy makers and academic leaders to engage in any substantive discussion with each other about the nature of higher education. In the absence of such debate and of conscious planning, the system of higher education will likely drift into some new market-oriented format without adequate restraints and with an ongoing erosion of its fundamental purposes, a format difficult to change once established. The result is likely to be the loss to society of some of the attributes of higher education that are essential to a free and effective society.

Time is important. Political leaders need to address these issues while the system is still in flux and before it settles into some new mode that will, once again, be hard to change. As societies everywhere have found, a poorly thought through move toward market forces is difficult if not impossible to reverse. The leaders of universities and colleges need to recognize their responsibility to join with political leaders in developing thoughtful policies that safeguard the essential nature of higher education's contributions, now before it is too late. They need to recognize as well that for every institution to succeed in a changed environment, each needs its own strategy that helps it focus on what it does best and how it can improve performance.

Chapter Four

The Growing Gap Between Public Needs and the Reality of Higher Education

The quest for prestige often looks appealing to those who champion individual universities, but the reality is that it is a costly endeavor that often stretches and diverts state budgets.

Within the leadership of American higher education there is, as yet, not much sense of impending change or the recognition of danger in the status quo. This is, Americans believe fervently, the greatest higher education system in the world. For more than fifty years, there has been striking growth in enrollments and funding. Students from other countries, more than five hundred thousand of them, have come to colleges or universities in the United States because they see the quality. So, what is the problem?

The problem is a growing gap between the public needs and the reality of the performance of the institutions of American higher education. We believe the growing gap stems from broad changes that have been transforming American society and American higher education. We believe as well that the growing gap has received too little attention within universities and colleges because of a strong sense of satisfaction with how things are and because of the lack of performance measures that would serve to connect institutional performance to society's changing needs. Higher education has instead depended on the assumption of quality buttressed by a polished and familiar rhetoric describing the benefits of a college education. (See Chapter Five for the view of higher education quality from differing groups.) If the gap is not successfully addressed, it will increasingly impede higher education's ability to serve the public and ultimately threaten its special place in society. If it is addressed and corrected, this can be a period of great promise for American higher education.

The Changing Nature of American Society

Societal changes have generated new expectations of higher education. The last six decades, since the end of the Second World War, have been a period of change and turbulence in American life. As society struggled to understand and master these changes, higher education became ever more central to the process of adapting.

One of the most significant changes has been demographic. Populations within the society that were constrained or discriminated against have pushed themselves forward, insisting on the opportunity for full participation. This included, in turn, African Americans, Hispanics, women, the disabled, Native Americans, Asian Americans, and immigrants. A central concern of each group has been access to higher education. The changing makeup of the population—more from low-income backgrounds, more people of color, a greater share from immigrant families with less involvement with and understanding of a formal system of education—requires a higher education system able to address the needs of a new and more diverse society.

As the nature of the economy changed from industrial to "postindustrial" (or "knowledge-based," or "new"), the demand grew—first for a greater share of the workforce to have a college education and more recently for graduates to gain a more effective college education. (See the description of the demands of the business community for greater skills in Chapter Five.) At the same time, the increasing complexity of society requires ever greater civic skills, including the ability to understand complex issues such as environmental warming or in vitro fertilization. The changing nature of the media and the rapid advance of new modes of communication also require a more sophisticated citizenry able to make sense of an overload in information from an expanding array of sources. The result is a public need for a larger share of the population with ever greater knowledge and skills.

The advance of technology has also led to the need for a more sophisticated population. New technologies add to the demand already noted for workforce and civic skills, but they also add to the need for citizens able to analyze, reason, and make critical judgments. At the beginning of the last century, technology was seen principally as a boon, as the agent of a better life. At the beginning of this century, it is seen as a boon and a danger, as the agent of a more complicated life. Penicillin was a great advance; now society worries about overuse of antibiotics. Atomic energy, genetically modified crops, cloning . . . the list is overwhelming.

Adding to all of these changes is the steady progress of globalization. Many segments of society—business, the media, the arts— are already deeply affected by the change from operating in a local setting to operating across boundaries. This requires not only the ability to understand diverse customers and diverse employees but also the ability to compete with new and unfamiliar competitors. This adds further to the need for citizens capable of more thoughtful analysis and understanding.

Many more profound changes can be added to this list. Even from this limited selection, it is clear that the tasks facing higher education are becoming more complex, more numerous, and more important to society. All of these changes also require the development of a far more effective system of elementary and secondary schooling, a system capable of educating all students rather than focusing on the most able. Higher education, as the educator of teachers and school leaders, the researcher of the workings of education, and a large influence on the structure of elementary and secondary education, has here as well a pivotal role to play in improving the schools.

The Changing Nature of Higher Education and the Competition for Prestige

While American society has been changing in ways that raised the level of demand placed on higher education for both a greater share of the population to gain entrance to higher education as well as for graduates to gain greater knowledge and skills, American higher education has been focusing principally on a different issue. The post–World War II evolution of American higher education led to the emergence of a form of competition not based on improving the skills and knowledge of graduates but rather based primarily on institutional prestige (Brewer, Gates, and Goldman, 2002).

This competition has been exacerbated by the rise, over the last two decades, of an expanding array of college and university rankings by publishers such as *U.S. News & World Report,* the *Princeton Review,* the *Financial Times,* the *Wall Street Journal, Business Week,* and *Kiplinger's* among others—many others (see Thompson, 2003). This flood of "best" lists has led to such distortions as the submission of false or misleading data by institutions, the shift toward early admissions to raise yield rates, and even financial incentives for presidents who can move the institution up in the rankings. The flaw, as is argued year after year, is that the rankings are based on factors that do not measure the actual learning experience. As Lee Bollinger, the president of Columbia University, noted, "Rankings give a false sense of the world and an inauthentic view of what a college education really is . . . and contribute to a steadily rising level of competitiveness and anxiety among young people about getting into the right college" (Thompson, 2003). The drive for prestige has led to important gains—most notably, an enormous advance in the quality of university research that has propelled America forward—but it has also led to distortions that have hampered the ability to meet the needs of society. Among these has been inexorable mission creep as institutions push themselves toward the status of research university, often turning away from their intended mission (Arnone, 2003a).[1]

At the same time that society needed a more diverse array of institutions to meet the needs of a more diverse array of students, including a larger share from the less advantaged groups, institutions were moving toward homogenization and a focus on supposedly better students. Teachers colleges became state colleges, then state universities, then research universities. Liberal arts colleges became "research colleges." More and more institutions focused on attracting incoming classes with high SAT or ACT scores. The United States has been well served by having a large number of research universities (roughly two hundred, a huge number by world standards), but within those institutions and in the thousand other universities the allure of research and scholarship (and the necessity of a scholarly record for promotion and tenure) has distracted attention from the hard work of improving teaching.

In 1940, prior to the development of federal sponsorship of university research, teaching *was* the principal role of the faculty. As federal research grants began to expand in the 1950s and 1960s, and as the financial and prestige value of research to the university became evident, universities began to seek grants—and to court scholars who could obtain them. The number of research universities began to expand from literally a handful to several hundred today, and American research surged to the forefront in every field.

This success brought problems in its wake. Soon faculty at the most elite universities were rewarded not for their teaching but for their research. The argument has been made repeatedly that great research and teaching go hand in hand, but the faculty reward structure that emerged made it almost certain that this would not generally be the case. Success led to reduced teaching "loads." Before long, the value system favoring publication and reduced teaching spread, until today it has washed over institutions that do not even remotely resemble research universities. Graduate programs now socialize their students to the belief that success means becoming a published scholar at a research university, not becoming an effective teacher or, for that matter, a leader outside the academy. All of this did not necessarily cause a decline in the quality of teaching (other than lessening student contact), but it did shift the focus of the faculty from their students to their discipline and reduce willingness to invest the time and hard work necessary to seriously assess learning, improve critical flaws, or take advantage of new research and new technology to improve pedagogy. As the authors of a new study of the relationship of faculty to their institutions put it, "The disconnection between faculty priorities and institutional purpose has been widely documented and highlighted in one national conference after another. The changes institutions of higher education and their faculties are confronting have been enumerated so frequently their recitation has become something of a litany. What is most needed now are concrete, campus-based solutions to the structural problems we are facing and constructive responses to the monumental changes about which we have been more than adequately warned" (McMillin and Berberet, 2002, p. xi).

One result of the competition for prestige has been development of low-quality and unneeded Ph.D. programs at literally hundreds of four-year institutions determined to be seen as research universities—not because of a public need but because of an internal drive for prestige. These programs often persist in spite of a contribution that is marginal at best. Christopher Morphew from the University of Kansas conducted a study of new Ph.D. programs in seven states between 1982 and 1992. Morphew found that the new programs were unlikely to award any degrees during those ten years if they duplicated a program already in place at a public university in the state (Morphew, 1996).

As Page Smith of the University of California–Los Angeles argued, "The routine and pedestrian [research] far outweighs the brilliant and original; . . . routine and pedestrian research is not merely a very expensive nullity but a moral and spiritual drag on the institutions in which it takes place and a serious distortion of the nature of both the intellectual and scholarly life . . . [and] the economic cost is also scandalously high" (quoted in Massy, 2003, p. 10).

The quest for prestige often looks appealing to those who champion individual universities, but the reality is that it is a costly endeavor that often stretches and diverts state budgets. As Alex Warner, chairman of the education committee in North Carolina's House of Representatives, remarked about having even more research universities, "Whether we need them or not, we don't have the money to afford them" (quoted in Arnone, 2003a, p. A18).

Although the gains to society from high-quality university research and scholarship are incalculable, they have been accompanied by a huge expenditure of effort and resources on poorer-quality research and seriously detracting from the central role of teaching by reducing both the time and the creativity faculty devote to teaching, undervaluing those institutions whose principal role is teaching and particularly undervaluing those whose chief role is teaching the least advantaged.

The Barrier of Operating Without Measures of Performance Assessment

The success of American higher education has made academics comfortable with the status quo and less open to the idea that all performance should be carefully assessed with an eye toward improvement. Whether it is a question of maximizing performance or of improving efficiency, whether the issue is classroom learning or use of library resources, assessment is a necessity for improvement. Clearly, the most important issue is to enhance learning.

The lack of institutional response to society's need for more effective teaching is to a significant degree a result of the lack of any rational way of knowing what the results of teaching are now and a lack of interest in developing effective ways of knowing. During focus groups conducted by the Futures Project in 2002, many academic leaders were skeptical about measuring student learning despite the centrality of teaching and learning to their institution's role, despite growing demand from political and business leaders for assessment of learning, and despite the growing number of institutions demonstrating that it can be done. Some leaders even stated that there was no way to measure learning in many of their programs (Immerwahr, 2002, p. 1). One president announced, "I think we spend far too much time talking about outcome assessment and worrying about it" (Immerwahr, 2002, p. 17). Another president remarked, "A lot of the assessment efforts are counterproductive to the objective of learning. . . . I see these accrediting bodies come in and talk about outcomes. . . . I want to tell them they ought to go to a trade school, rather than to an institution like ours" (Immerwahr, 2002, p. 17).

The Barrier of Sluggish Campus Governance

The evolution of academic governance has made responding to the changing nature of society more difficult and more cumbersome. Over the long postwar period, the faculty role in governance brought about a needed evolution of greater faculty involvement in planning and implementing academic programming. In part, this was an overdue correction for autocratic presidents and intrusive boards. In time, however, the process better preserved the status quo than seeking out or even supporting innovative new approaches. Formal procedures for faculty participation became even more formal. Faculty committees multiplied. The time necessary for decisions lengthened. One result is that new forms of teaching, no matter how successful at increasing student engagement and improving student learning, tend to remain isolated silos rather than widely accepted ways of operating.

The Futures Project has identified seven areas in which there is a growing—and, we feel, critical—gap between the public's needs and higher education's current performance.

The Need to Take Responsibility for Learning

Society needs greater skills and knowledge in a larger share of its population. To improve learning, institutions need to start by taking responsibility for how much students are learning. To do this requires a conscious institutional effort to focus on the actual learning taking place rather than on surrogate measures of limited relevance such as the scholarly reputation of the faculty (McClenney, 2003). It also requires institutionwide acceptance of responsibility for student success in learning. Rather than assume that the students who drop out were simply a poor admission decision in the first place, or that students who stop taking math courses (despite demonstrated proficiency in high school) are simply too lazy to do the hard work math requires, faculty must begin to ask hard questions about their own responsibility and begin to apply more widely what is known about assessing and improving learning.

Little use is made of the new knowledge developed over the last twenty years about how to improve learning. Much has been learned, for example, about the many ways students learn, including new knowledge about how the brain functions, how it acquires language skills, what causes learning disorders, and how they can be treated. Much has been learned as well about learning styles. Some students prefer learning by addressing a concrete problem, others by a discussion of abstract principles. For still others, visualizing the problem in some form is essential. Research about service learning, where students undertake community service as part of an academic program, shows an increase in students' interest, retention, and comprehension. New software technology has allowed students to participate in simulation exercises that greatly increase comprehension. Software also allows the tailoring of course work so as to adapt to learning styles.[2]

Many of these advances are now in widespread use in corporate or military training programs. Despite the potential gains these new concepts offer in overall student excitement and learning, little has changed in most classrooms. The result has been a widening gap between the current level of collegiate learning and the advancing need for knowledgeable and skilled graduates.

Nine out of ten college graduates reported that their degree was useful in getting a job but did not provide them with the skills they need to succeed in the workplace (Oblinger and Verville, 1998). Employers as well are concerned about the lack of such skills as critical thinking, ability to write clearly, or ability to work on a team (Business-Higher Education Forum, 2001; U.S. Department of Labor, 1999; Mullen, 1997; Oblinger and Verville, 1998). See Chapter Eight for further details.

There is growing evidence, despite the overall value of a college education, of areas where students do not gain the skills or knowledge they will need. One example is in mathematics and science, where only a small share of students gain real understanding of the basic concepts, the ability to apply the concepts to practical problems, or a long-term interest in the subject. Between 1993 and 2000, there was a 14 percent decline in the "number of US citizens and permanent residents enrolling in graduate programs in the natural sciences and engineering" (Zumeta and Raveling, 2002–2003, p. 37). At the advanced-degree level, the United States has compensated for this failure by importing some of the best students from China, Taiwan, India, and Korea. These countries have now begun aggressive programs to expand and improve graduate training so as to keep their best at home (and to recruit back those who stayed in the United States; Southwick, 2002). Graduate enrollments in math and science from these countries are already falling. There is another flaw in our current approach as noted in a recent analysis, "If there is a trend worth watching now, it's companies deciding that it's just as effective and a lot less expensive to simply let the engineer stay in Bangalore and outsource the work to them" (Peirce and Johnson, 2003, p. 15).

Hopefully, these trends will lead universities to ask some hard questions as to how to improve the interest level and the effectiveness of math and science teaching.

Despite the fact that a growing number of institutions successfully measure learner outcomes, notably Alverno College, Truman State University, the University of Phoenix, and the British Open University, most institutions continue to claim that the effort would be too difficult, too expensive, or even impossible for them to attempt.

Where tests and evaluations do exist, they often show poor performance. In an egregious example, only 56 percent of first-time test takers of the Massachusetts teacher certification passed all three components, and only 10 percent of retakers passed.[3]

In his book *Honoring the Trust,* William Massy points to higher education's "respectable B" performance. Massy argues that B performance will not produce a well-educated workforce ready to compete in the knowledge economy (Massy, 2003).

In a publish-or-perish world, teaching at universities is typically given last priority. Quality is too often described in terms of content rather than results. But good teaching is not delivering a lecture that one's colleagues would admire if it were published as an article. Good teaching is creating a setting in which students learn. It is time to elevate the status of teaching—certainly at least to the level of research. The teaching and learning process needs to be more transparent so that constant improvement can take place and so that students can choose their college and their courses on the basis of the quality of the learning experience.

The Need to Move Beyond Access to Attainment

Access to higher education has become vital to full civic and economic participation in society. American society has always treasured the concept of social mobility founded on pluck and determination. Today, social mobility requires more—a college education. A college diploma has now become a required ticket for entry into the middle class. Between 1973 and 1999, the median family income for a high school graduate decreased by 13.1 percent, while for someone with four years of college it increased by 9.9 percent, and the gap continues to grow (Mortenson, 2002).

The future well-being of this country depends on access being extended ever further to a greater share of the population. However, with the erosion in the value of need-based student aid and a rapid rise in tuition, the ability of low-income students to take advantage of access is dwindling.

Even more important than further improvement in access is a more critical and less noted problem: the extraordinarily low rate of attainment and graduation of the students who do gain access. While the graduation rate for all students should be of concern, the primary focus should be improving completion rates for students from disadvantaged backgrounds. The evidence is stark:

- By age twenty-four, 48 percent of students from high-income families have graduated from college, compared to only 7 percent of low-income students (Kellogg Commission on the Future of State and Land Grant Universities, 2000).
- According to Tom Mortenson, a higher education policy analyst, "a person by age 24 whose family income falls within the top quartile is ten times more likely to have received a bachelor's degree than a person whose family falls in the bottom quartile" (Mortenson, 1995, p. 1). More startling is that in 1979, "before the redistribution of higher education opportunity began, the difference was four times" (Mortenson, 1995, p. 1).
- Twenty-nine percent of African Americans and 31 percent of Hispanics leave college before completing their first year (U.S. Department of Education, 2000).
- The National Commission on the Cost of Higher Education reported that between 1987 and 1996, "the price of attendance minus grants rose 114 percent at public four-year institutions, 81 percent at private four-year institutions, and 159 percent at public two-year institutions" (National Commission on the Cost of Higher Education, 1998, p. 11).
- In 1999–2000, 87 percent of public and private two-year institutions awarded nonneed institutional aid to undergraduates on the basis of academic merit (or bargaining by students and

their families; "Financial Aid Professionals at Work in
1999–2000," 2002).

- The Lumina Foundation has reported that the shift toward
tuition discounting helps wealthier students attend four-year
institutions, while making it more difficult for low-income students (J. Davis, 2003; see also Heller, 2003).

American society is, in short, turning away from its commitment to access and social mobility. Public policy can no longer
afford to stop at questions of access. The goal must now include
academic success or attainment after access for an ever-expanding
share of the population.

The Need to Address Efficiency and Productivity

As stewards of the public trust and investment, state colleges and
universities are obligated to spend public funds in a way that most
effectively responds to public needs. Private universities and colleges are similarly obligated to their donors, to their students, and
to the public that accords them many subsidies and exemption
from taxes. This requires turning an eye to cost and efficiency.
Recent projects have demonstrated that there can be substantial
cost savings through interinstitutional and interdepartmental collaboration in purchasing, library materials, technology infrastructure, and more. Similarly, savings are made possible by expanding
the use of outsourcing beyond the bookstore and food service to
such tasks as maintenance of technology infrastructure. All of these
tasks remain largely unaddressed at most institutions.

More important, higher education institutions simply do not
analyze their cost structure, particularly on the academic side.[4]
They do, of course, know the cost of the Geology Department or
the Admissions Office but not the cost of mounting different
courses, or the efficiency of using faculty time in varying ways, or
whether a redesign would improve the effectiveness and the efficiency of a large introductory course. Both colleges and universities have found some ways to reduce costs. The most notable has
been replacement of regular faculty with adjuncts (now more than
40 percent of all faculty, as well as the majority of the appointments
made in the 1990s), but this has occurred as a slow drift without

any serious study of long-term results in terms of learning.[5] In contrast to traditional nonprofit public and private institutions, many of the newly prominent for-profit universities analyze the cost of every program regularly and do find ways to improve their efficiency and quality.

Institutions traditionally cross-subsidize activities by using funds from popular and relatively low-cost programs (such as education or business) to support costly and low-volume programs (such as classics or engineering) or to support faculty time devoted to scholarship and publication. There has been little analysis of how cross-subsidizing is functioning, whether it helps institutions maximize revenues, and whether it is being used in ways that meet the public's needs, despite the fact that a few institutions, such as the University of Rhode Island, have undertaken studies and proven that it is possible to analyze the amount and nature of cross-subsidy that is taking place.[6]

The long growth of higher education, coupled with the lack of performance data and low interest in analyzing costs, has resulted in institutions focusing on increasing revenue but not on improving efficiency (Clotfelter, 1996; Ehrenberg, 2000).[7] Instead, universities see their cost problem as a function of the labor-intensive nature of education over which they have no control—what William Baumol calls the "cost disease" (Johnston, 1997). This recently became an issue at Harvard when a group of alumni protested the fact that Harvard does not focus on reducing expenses, instead requesting larger and larger total donations from alumni and friends and increasing tuition to cover rising costs. The university itself has admitted it could save more than $100 million per year if all of the schools within Harvard pulled together to solicit bids on goods and services, from printing to plumbing. But the far more important question is how much could be saved by determined analysis of all operations, including academic programs, with an eye to efficiency (Winter and Rimer, 2003).

The lack of performance data and cost analysis makes it almost impossible to either improve the impact of programs or reduce costs—despite some encouraging evidence that this is possible, especially through the use of technology.[8] As discussed in Chapter Two, the Pew Grant Program in Course Redesign, run by Carol Twigg, set out to analyze large, introductory courses in a number of disciplines at thirty institutions with an eye toward reducing costs as well as improving student learning. The project has reported an average of 40 percent cost savings, plus significant improvements in student learning and retention (Twigg, 2003a). This is hardly surprising, given the experience of essentially every other sector of society that repeated improvement can be made if costs and processes are analyzed.[9] It would be surprising indeed if, after careful analysis, costs and performance following years of unexamined growth could not be improved.[10]

The warning signs of the growing problem as a result of unexamined cost of operation are readily apparent:

- In the first half of the twentieth century, college costs rose more slowly than family income. Tuition remained affordable through the 1950s. Tuition began to increase in the 1960s and 1970s and then took off in the early 1980s (Mumper, 2003). Since 1980, the average price of four years of college has increased more than 110 percent *over inflation.*[11]
- The demand for resources that has been driving tuition increases has not been caused by falling state appropriations. Indeed, they have been rising. State appropriations increased by 60.2 percent from FY1993 to FY2003.[12]
- If tuition continues to increase at the current pace, the Council for Aid to Education estimates that by 2015 half of those students who want to pursue higher education will be unable to afford it (Council for Aid to Education, 1997).
- The issue is drawing increasing attention from political authorities.[13] According to the National Governors Association, "A majority of states do not have the revenue to support continued, unchecked growth in higher education expenses, where increases annually exceed the consumer price index" (National Governors Association, 2001b, p. 2).
- At the federal level, the chair of the House Education and Workforce Committee recently told an audience of university presidents and business leaders that the federal government simply could not afford to continue increasing support for higher education at a rate of three (or even four) times inflation, and if the institutions could not find ways to slow the increases in cost, then the federal government would be forced to do so (Boehner, 2003).

The Long-Overdue Need to Support Elementary and Secondary Education

Not only has higher education paid too little attention to its own effectiveness in teaching and learning, it has been only sporadically involved in the great, two-decade effort to reform American elementary and secondary education. As the National Governors Association has argued, "Higher education, to a large extent, has been absent from state efforts to improve the quality of teachers, curriculum, and instruction in the K–12 system" (National Governors Association, 2001b, p. 2). This involves an array of higher education responsibilities: education and continuing support of teachers and school leaders, alignment of the two sectors in terms of curriculum and expectations, and research that supports efforts at improvement. In teacher education, the disenchantment with university-based programs and failure to adjust their programs to address the conditions that teachers now face has led to a growing number of school districts moving toward training their own teachers or principals. New York City is the latest and most prominent case, establishing its own Leadership Academy to train principals and superintendents. Higher education has a clear self-interest in improving school performance.

The Need to Reduce Conflict of Interest

The trustworthiness of university research is a crucial foundation to American success. The lure of corporate sponsorship of research cannot be allowed to supersede the integrity of scholarship. Higher education must turn to full disclosure of all financial interests held by researchers and institutions, and universities must maintain control over publication and review rights.

In 1980, Congress passed the Bayh-Dole Act in response to concerns about declining U.S. productivity and rising levels of foreign competition. The bill formalized the already growing practice of allowing universities to patent the results of their federally funded research, thereby giving universities the opportunity to create an income stream from the fruits of research conducted within the university but sponsored by the federal government. Following the change in legislation, ties between research universities and corporations grew stronger, and the vision of the university as the place that supplies "commercially valuable" initiatives became widespread (Press and Washburn, 2000).

The act proved to be a turning point. There was an 8.1 percent annual growth in industry funding for academically oriented research between 1980 and 1998, with the figure reaching $1.9 billion in 1997. The positive consequences of this investment (as well as the growth of federal funding of research) were reflected in the number of patents produced in universities; the figure increased from about 250 per year before Bayh-Dole to approximately 4,800 in 1998 (Press and Washburn, 2000).

Corporate influence has surged throughout universities, as overall corporate giving grew from $850 million in 1985 to a whopping $4.25 billion in just one decade (Press and Washburn, 2000). Surely, the growth of corporate gifts to universities and colleges is a positive force and a unique American advantage—if no inappropriate strings are attached. In the era of the knowledge economy, corporate support will only increase. State governments, recognizing research and development as vital to energizing their economies, are pressuring universities to develop closer links with industry. In one telling statement, the National Governors Association suggested that "state policymakers should review barriers to commercialization. . . . Common obstacles include . . . criteria for tenure that focus on publication rather than commercialization" (Berglund and Clarke, 2000, p. 15; see also Schmidt, 2002).

The volume of research has grown, but the risk to its integrity has grown as well:[14]

• In a 1996 study of nearly eight hundred scientific papers in biology and medicine, Sheldon Krimsky, a professor at Tufts University, found that in one out of three cases the "chief author of the paper had a financial interest in the company" sponsoring the research (Clayton, 2001b, p. 11).
• In a survey of almost 2,200 biomedical scientists, 410 admitted delaying the publication of their research results by six months or more over a three-year period for reasons such as "protect the financial value of the results, protect the scientists' lead in the race to produce a certain result, [and] delay the publication of undesired results" (Knox, 1997, p. A1).

- A study out of Stanford University found that "98 percent of university studies of new drug therapies funded by the pharmaceutical industry reported that those new therapies were more effective than standard drugs," while only 79 percent of studies without industry funding reported that new therapies were more effective (Clayton, 2001b, p. 11).
- The decision of three universities, Stanford and the University of California campuses in San Francisco and San Diego, to form a consortium with SRI International to move their research concerning new drugs into clinical trials takes these institutions further into the commercial world, with the inherent shift in purpose from objective research toward successful return on investment. Harvard has set up a similar effort (Pollack, 2003).[15]

A particularly shocking example of the influence of private corporations on research is the case of Dr. Nancy Olivieri, a medical researcher at the University of Toronto and the Hospital for Sick Children. Apotex, a Toronto-based pharmaceutical company, sponsored her clinical trials, beginning in 1996, of a hemoglobin treatment. When Olivieri discovered evidence of toxic reactions to the drug, Apotex threatened to take legal action if she published her findings or if she informed the patients in the trials of the risks. They argued that she was breaking the nondisclosure agreement she had signed with their company in 1993. Olivieri chose to publish her findings regardless of the consequences. At the time, the university was anticipating a donation from Apotex of more than $20 million. Neither the university nor the hospital supported Olivieri in her fight for academic freedom; in fact, Olivieri was removed as director of the department of hemoglobinopathy at the hospital (she was later reinstated when the president of the university intervened).[16] Once lost, trust in the integrity of the university will be difficult to recover.

The Need to Serve as Society's Critic

There was a time when the nation's colleges and universities were viewed as a principal source of criticism about social and political trends. Communities turned to these institutions as a place for open debate and objective research. Academic freedom was designed to protect that very function so that academics would be free to teach and speak on controversial topics, and campuses could tolerate—even encourage—debate that helped illuminate critical social issues. But there has been a marked change in the amount and type of debate taking place on campus.

The growing need for private fund-raising has led to questions as to whether college and university presidents and faculty are willing to be outspoken about pressing societal issues or whether they limit what they say so as not to offend potential donors.[17] Jane Wellman and Robert Atwell have observed that given the need to raise external funds, "The last thing any politically astute college president would want to do . . . is to take positions which their employers and other public and private patrons might find offensive" (Atwell and Wellman, 2002, p. 67). Clara Lovett agrees that fundraising has made presidents wary of controversial subjects, but she sees that as only part of the problem. Lovett blames the presidential search process, which "screens out potential intellectual and educational leaders in favor of men and women who look, speak, and act like candidates for political office" (Lovett, 2002b, p. B20).

The salaries of college presidents are also increasing at a steep growth rate, often supplemented by private money and reaching at the top end close to $800,000 for both public and private universities. These high salaries—which look more and more like the salaries of industry CEOs—are criticized for a number of reasons, among them exacerbating the focus on money for impressionable undergraduates and indebting presidents to donors who have contributed to their personal compensation (Bok, 2002; see also Basinger, 2002).

The privilege of serving as an open center of analysis and debate allows higher education to make a critical contribution to the democratic functioning of society. If it is not used regularly, it will wither.

The Need to Rebuild Political Involvement to Sustain Democracy

Higher education's role in society extends beyond building workforce skills to include helping students understand their role as citizens and community members (Association of American Colleges and Universities, 2002; Corrigan, 2002). Former Gov. Angus King of Maine said, "Just as the students of today must be prepared to face the demands of tomorrow's economy, so too they must be equipped to face the demands of tomorrow's democracy" (King, 2002). Studies over the years have shown that college graduates vote and participate in political campaigns at a higher rate than those who attended high school only. However, involvement in the political process for *all* groups, including college graduates, is falling. Cynicism as to whether voting or citizen participation in politics of any sort matters is rising steadily. Voting rates are now so low that the very process of democracy in this country is endangered.[18] Several large cities, most recently Detroit, have ended election of school board members because low turnout (often 10 percent or less) has allowed fringe groups to dominate the process.

The Committee for the Study of the American Electorate found that in 1998 voter turnout for congressional elections plunged to 36 percent, the lowest level since 1942. Just over 200 million Americans were eligible to vote, but only 72,450,901 turned out on Election Day (a decrease of 2.5 million people from 1994). This was despite the fact that the possible removal of a sitting president was at issue in the midterm election (Committee for the Study of the American Electorate, 1999). American voters have been voting with their feet, staying away from the polls in growing numbers. In Brian O'Connell's words, "It is a fundamental precept of American democracy that citizens are the primary officeholders of government, and we are dangerously neglecting the quintessential responsibility" (O'Connell, 2003, p. 163).

Civic responsibility is not limited to domestic affairs either. James M. Lindsay of the Brookings Institution has been tracking increasing public apathy about foreign affairs. Lindsay expressed concern that public apathy has allowed special interests to garner growing control in foreign affairs, even when their actions are not in the best interests of the nation (Lindsay, 2000).

Higher education has the ability—and the responsibility—to influence understanding of the political system and a sense of civic responsibility through its graduates. What could be more important? The National Campus Compact and several other organizations have begun a determined effort to focus universities and colleges on this task. Yet engaging the attention of universities and colleges, and their faculties, to address this subject has not been easy. Joel Westheimer and Joseph Kahne, in reviewing the slow progress, noted: "As long as we remain at the level of rhetoric we can get most educators to agree that teaching how to be a good citizen is important. But when we get specific about what democracy requires and about what kind of school curricula will best promote it, much of that consensus falls away" (Westheimer and Kahne, 2003, p. 2). Within the new and growing sector of higher education (for-profit, degree-granting institutions), the issue is stark. Conversations with the leaders of the best-known for-profit universities and colleges make plain that they do not see civic education as their responsibility—only the development of workforce skills. They see civic education as an important issue but for public institutions.

The Growing Gap Between Rhetoric and Reality

Scanning the higher education landscape from the figurative thirty-thousand feet, an observer of higher education would see a successful system, far stronger than it was even two decades ago, facing continuous change in the society it serves, dependent on a governance system that resists change, and focused on competition with the principal goal of prestige. It is a higher education system that fiercely defends a rhetoric of excellence and public purpose while the reality slips.

Some of the gaps in the system's performance have been present for decades but have become more visible as the demands on higher education escalate. Others are new. The rhetoric describes devotion to student learning, while in reality the student bears principal responsibility for learning and for any failure. The rhetoric describes devotion to teaching, while in reality the overwhelming time, energy, and creativity of the faculty at four-year institutions are devoted to research, publishing, and outside consulting. The rhetoric calls for broader access to higher education, while merit-based financial aid programs are increasing at a greater rate than need-based financial aid, and institutions are focusing more and more on recruiting the best and wealthiest students. The rhetoric calls for service to the community while attention is focused on improving rankings such as those in *U.S. News & World Report*. The rhetoric proclaims the importance of fundamental and trustworthy scholarship that serves society, while in fact impartiality is undercut by growing corporate control of research and faculty conflicts of interest.[19] The list of such fissures between higher education's rhetoric and its performance is long, and it is growing.

All of this has led to a significant gap between the needs of society that should be met by the universities and colleges and the actual performance of these institutions.[20] The growing power of market forces will, in the absence of skilled intervention in the functioning of the market, make a difficult situation worse. Every one of the problems noted here lends itself to practical solution. But solutions require intentional—and carefully thought out—public policies and institutional strategies, which in turn require the willingness of political and academic leaders to work together.

Chapter Five

The Public, Political Leaders, and the Academy View Higher Education

Within the broad and generally favorable perception about higher education are important differences among specific segments of the population—the public, business leaders, public officials, and the academy itself—including some important and outspoken criticisms. The differences between academic and political leaders could well lead to a confrontation if not addressed promptly.

Across American society there is broad agreement about two aspects of American higher education: it is the best in the world, and it is of great importance to society. It is seen as more important than it was a decade ago, more important than it has ever been (Sosin, 2002; Immerwahr, 1998). A significant factor in this perception is the growing realization that a college education has become the indispensable ticket to the middle class, critical in preparing for a career (Immerwahr, 1999a).

General Perceptions

One outcome of the growing awareness of the importance of higher education to a student's life chances is gradual renewal of concern that no motivated student should be denied access. This concept, first enunciated by the Truman Commission in 1947 but opposed at the time by most university leaders, gained support as higher education expanded. For the last decade or so, it has been sidetracked as the assault on affirmative action took center stage. Now, it is once again a subject of attention.

The biggest problem that most Americans see with the idea that no student should be denied access is the widespread perception that preparation of students in elementary and secondary education is inadequate and that, for many, their experience in school has left them inadequately motivated. Student motivation is seen as a more critical issue than adequate funding (Immerwahr, 1999b). What students get out of college is seen as a function of what effort they put in. As yet, there is little broad-based recognition that improvement of K–12 schooling, and therefore adequate preparation, will be a long, slow process and that in the meantime it is essential for higher education to create programs that motivate and help inadequately prepared students succeed at a college education.

Beyond the respect that higher education receives for providing a college degree of great value, there is also widely shared respect for university research, for its quality and value to society. The value to society of medical research is the most recognized aspect, though the role of research in supporting economic development and as a breeding ground for new businesses is growing.

One other aspect that has surprisingly wide support is the view that higher education is the place where the country does its thinking—the place where important issues are debated. The greater the education of the observer, the more this belief is upheld. Even more surprising, and encouraging, is that about half of the population believes that colleges and universities should do more along this line (Sosin, 2002).

Although society generally has this positive sense about higher education, there are some concerns. For one, there is a concern that higher education's practices remain largely unchanged even as society itself is changing rapidly. This is felt most strongly among leaders in society, but it is a growing general perception. There is as well a sense that institutions should be more accountable for the performance of their students. Lower on the list of concerns but still present is the sense that the college experience is not producing engaged citizens (National Center for Postsecondary Improvement, 2002).

One of the main difficulties in evaluating the performance of higher education is that the academic community and the public are both unclear about what society should expect from higher education. Unlike elementary and secondary education, where there has been an extensive, two-decade debate involving educators, political leaders, and the public, there are no clearly defined standards to which higher education institutions can be held or even to which universities and colleges can hold themselves. As a consequence, there is no clear mandate for change and no clear direction as to where institutions are expected to head.

Within this broad and generally favorable public perception about higher education are important differences among specific segments of the population—the public, business leaders, public officials, and the academy itself—including some important and outspoken criticisms. Judging from a series of focus groups with state legislators and college and university presidents run by the Futures Project, the differences between academic and political leaders could well lead to a confrontation if not addressed promptly (Immerwahr, 2002). As Clara Lovett, former president of Northern Arizona University, said: "In the past decade, but especially in my six years as president of Northern Arizona University, I have observed and experienced a growing dissonance—in anthropological terms, a clash of cultures—between the institutions you serve and the public officials you try to influence on our behalf" (Lovett, 2000, p. 8).

The Public

Among the public, there is broad general support for higher education (Sosin, 2002). On most surveys asking for a letter grade, the public gives higher education a solid B; not excellent, not an A, but clearly a widely shared sense of "good" (National Center for Postsecondary Improvement, 2002; Immerwahr, 1999a; Educational Testing Service, 2003).

The public also recognizes the importance of higher education. A college education is perceived as imparting substantial personal benefits, both economic and social, especially among groups that have been historically disadvantaged and are still striving for equal opportunities in society. Forty-seven percent of African

American parents and 65 percent of Hispanic parents see higher education as "absolutely necessary" for a successful life, compared to 33 percent of white parents (Immerwahr and Foleno, 2000). The benefit to the community is also seen in economic, social, and societal terms.

The goals of a college education have been explored in a number of polls, with generally similar results. In one, the leading objective was basic skills (identified by 85 percent of the respondents) followed by career training (72 percent). Surprisingly, the goal of preparing for effective participation in and leadership of society was lower on the list (56 percent; Sosin, 2002).

The public wants more than a diploma. Generally, Americans expect students to gain workplace skills along with knowledge, maturity, organizational skills, communication skills, technological competence, the ability to get along with others, and the capacity to solve problems. Unlike elementary and secondary education, where the public expectation has shifted over the last two decades of the reform movement and now holds schools responsible for ensuring learning, in higher education the responsibility for success still rests with the student. A student who drops out, for example, is more likely to be blamed than the college or university.

The public also values the research that universities perform, most often associating the benefits with medical research. The value of research to economic development is generally recognized, but it is still a vague recognition. Medical research seems more concrete.

So, from the public's viewpoint, higher education matters in terms of its role in educating students and opening the door to the middle class. Research is valued, as is the university's role in helping create jobs. But there are concerns.

The two concerns that are most important to the public are access and affordability: "Can I, or my son or daughter, get in, and can we afford the cost?" Only half of Americans believe that colleges are doing all they can to try to keep the cost down (Immerwahr, 1998). African Americans are even more likely than whites to feel that little or no attention is paid to costs and efficiency (Immerwahr and Foleno, 2000). Reporting on concerns their constituents raise with them, legislators say that they hear frequently about the rise in tuition. They also hear that students don't see much of professors in their freshman or sophomore classes (Mahtesian, 1995).

The concerns the public does hold are not strong or clearly formed. A series of polls and focus groups showed that the public is not necessarily well informed about higher education's performance (Immerwahr, 1999a). In general, the public is satisfied with the performance of higher education; the principal concern is over cost. But even here, the public is aware of the rising expenses, troubled about whether college is affordable, but often misinformed about the actual cost (American Council on Education, 2002a; Winter and Rimer, 2003.). With regard to the purposes of higher education, the public expects students to be educated so that they will do well in life in terms of career. It would be desirable if they were also better citizens, but that is very much a secondary issue (Sosin, 2002). Despite the language of many university and college charters proclaiming the centrality of public purpose (the mission of the University of Michigan, for example, is "to serve the people"), the public is not at all clear what that entails.

Business Leaders

The picture is not as sanguine when one asks business leaders about their perceptions of higher education. Like the public, the business community also believes that the quality of American higher education is good and that it is still the best in the world. However, the real attitude is that it is the "best in the world, *but*. . . ." Business leaders voice substantially greater and more informed criticism than do members of the general public. Perhaps most significant, the criticism expressed by business leaders is growing. The level of concern that business leaders have been expressing is now close to what they have put forward for some time about elementary and secondary education (Immerwahr, 1999a). The concerns are principally about two issues: the skills of graduates and how higher education operates.

Over the last decade, several organizations representing business leaders have issued reports increasingly critical of the skills of graduates. Academic leaders often assume that business leaders will argue for narrow vocational skills. Regularly, however, the call from the business community has been for skills that sound remarkably like what academics describe as a liberal education. A number of reports from business organizations have complained about communication skills (oral and written), interpersonal skills, reading comprehension, and math and scientific literacy (U.S. Department of Labor, 1999; Mullen, 1997; Oblinger and Verville, 1998). The Business-Higher Education Forum has called for cross-functional skills, including leadership, teamwork, problem solving, analytical thinking, global consciousness, and reading and writing (Business-Higher Education Forum, 2001). Another study found that graduates are seen as lacking "creative" and "practical" intelligence (Oblinger and Verville, 1998).

Among manufacturers, most cite a lack of "basic employability skills" and report difficulties in finding qualified candidates (88 percent). Sixty percent say they typically reject half or more of those that apply as unqualified (National Association of Manufacturers, Center for Workforce Success, and Grant Thornton, 1998; National Association of Manufacturers, Andersen, and Center for Workforce Success, 2001). Employers see this as a serious concern because, in current global competition, the only advantage the United States has is in the supply of knowledge workers. They see this advantage as threatened by the working-skills gap. The skills gap is one area where there is a difference with faculty. Whereas faculty are generally pleased with the quality of graduates, only 46 percent of business leaders think graduates know what they need to know (Immerwahr, 1999a).

It should be noted that in focusing on the skills of graduates, the discussion understates one of the major advantages of the American system: its openness to recurrent opportunities to attend higher education. One reason the American workforce has remained the most productive in the world is the widespread—and widely used— opportunity for a worker to attend or return to higher education, certificate programs, or corporate universities over his or her career. American higher education is far ahead in providing this capacity. It may be an inefficient way to produce a high level of skill and knowledge, compared to getting it right the first time when an employee is a school student, but it works.

Businesses are critical not only about the skills and knowledge of graduates but about how colleges and universities operate. Here again, they differ sharply with faculty. For one thing, they feel faculty do not spend enough time or attention on teaching. They feel as well that faculty have an outmoded view of teaching that has failed to keep up with advancing understanding of how to teach effectively. Most feel this weakness would be helped by eliminating tenure (Immerwahr, 1999a).

In general, business leaders also feel that universities and colleges, and their faculty, are hiding from any meaningful measures of accountability. They feel that faculty and administrators don't take responsibility for the efficiency of the institution and refuse to recognize the need to address escalating costs. Nor do they take responsibility for results. What business leaders say is needed most is assessment of learning as a first step (Immerwahr, 1999a).

One other criticism is that higher education has remained removed from strenuous efforts to reform elementary and secondary education. Business leaders have themselves often been at the forefront of school reform and think that higher education should be an engaged partner. They see higher education as aloof (Business-Higher Education Forum, 2001).

University research is well respected by the business community. There is recognition of industry's dependence on research for economic growth. Still, 51 percent of the business respondents to a recent survey felt that academic research does not adequately address what society needs to know (Immerwahr, 1999a).

An issue that should attract the close attention of academic leaders is that business leaders know substantially more about the workings of higher education than the general public does. The result is that they are considerably more critical (Immerwahr, 1999a). Will this be a trend as the public also learns more?

Public Officials

Political leaders are most critical of the job higher education is doing in educating students—and in serving public purposes. They have raised repeatedly—and lately, more bluntly—the need for greater efficiency and control over rising costs, the need for measures of learner outcomes, the need for greater access, more effective alignment with and support of elementary and secondary education, improved teacher education, and above all effective forms of accountability. As Paul Lingenfelter, executive director of the State Higher Education Executive Officers association, observed, "About every three years, SHEEO takes a poll of state leaders to identify pressing issues. 'Effectiveness and accountability' is the only topic to make the top five in every survey for the past dozen years" (P. Lingenfelter, personal communication, Mar. 23, 2003).

It is important to remember that it was political leaders—not educators or the public—that focused the spotlight on elementary and secondary education, starting the massive two-decade effort at school reform that continues unabated. Three groups of public officials have spoken out frequently about the state of higher education: governors, state legislators, and federal officials (principally from the Department of Education but increasingly also from Congress). They are in general agreement, but there are some distinct differences among these groups.

Governors have stressed the importance of higher education, particularly in terms of its importance for the economic development of the state. Most governors argue this point in their state of the state address, making the case that "investment" in higher education is necessary for the state to be competitive, including investment in research and development. They want to see more student aid and better preparation for college at the high school level. But they have been outspoken as well about their concerns— that there must be better coordination with the schools, improved teacher education, coordination among various academic programs, greater attention to workforce needs and lifelong learning, attention to costs and efficiency, assessment of learner outcomes, and accountability (National Governors Association, 2002).[1]

They expect higher education to mirror the changes taking place in the economy—and in state government itself—and become more flexible, adaptable, consumer-friendly, innovative, technologically advanced, performance driven, and accountable. All these concerns reflect the growing centrality of higher education and in turn lead to the greater gubernatorial focus seen, for instance, in establishment of the National Governors Association effort Influencing the Future of Higher Education (National Governors Association, 2002).

Even as these concerns about higher education become stronger, there is also recognition that future demographics will add

further challenges. Many states now expect a major surge in enrollment demand as a result of the baby boom echo and immigration
(typically called Tidal Wave II). Few states have a well-developed
plan for dealing with this onslaught. Originally most states believed
technology could play a key role in expanding access. While it is
clear that technology will indeed help, it will by itself not be enough
to deal with this looming issue.

Legislators agree with the argument of the governors. If anything, legislators are often more outspoken, in part because they
hear more from their constituents about the annoying flaws of
higher education. They are (with some exceptions) cautiously supportive of greater institutional autonomy (Kettl, 2001). Many legislators recognize that states have placed constraints on institutional
ability to retain tuition, negotiate labor contracts, or gain quick
program approval. However, many want any new moves toward
autonomy closely coupled to measures of accountability (Novak,
2001). Some legislators fear that greater autonomy will be used
only to resist change; others view current forms of accountability
as ineffective.

The strong interest in policies addressing accountability is not
new. Julie Davis Bell, the education program director for the
National Conference of State Legislatures, declared several
years ago that "affordability, accountability and teacher education will be the top three issues facing higher education in state
houses across the nation in the next few years" ("NCSL Education
Expert . . . ," 1999, p. 12). A Southern Regional Education Board
survey noted that twelve of the fifteen southern states adopted laws
aimed at improving accountability in the early 1990s. Their concerns, even then, were the inexorable rise in costs, bureaucratic
bloat, faculty being less involved in teaching, the uselessness of
some scholarship, administrative sabbaticals, students staying too
long, and program overlap (Mahtesian, 1995). Tenure is often seen
as a symbol of these ills, though less mentioned in recent years as
political leaders have come to hold a more complex view of higher
education's problems.

Among most legislators, there is stronger criticism of four-year
institutions than of community colleges. They appreciate the willingness of community colleges to respond to public needs, particularly workforce training. They feel four-year institutions resist

change and skillfully and persistently pursue mission creep. They question whether these institutions are willing or able to respond to the changing state needs (Novak, 2001).

Legislators want to see a greater level of responsiveness and a more student-centered approach (community colleges are typically seen as most responsive). They would like higher education to be more aligned with elementary and secondary education, and they are frustrated by higher education's lack of involvement in school reform. They would also like better use of facilities (Ruppert, 2001).

Legislators are also concerned about economic development. They see first-rate research as critical in this regard, as is the need to raise the level of education of the population (Ruppert, 2001). They are eager to keep the best students in state and thus often support merit aid. (They also argue that some support for merit aid is necessary to gain support for the passage of need-based aid; Ruppert, 2001.) They do see, however, the desirability of a greater share of the population attending college. To this end, they feel strongly that higher education must become far more involved in helping elementary and secondary education prepare all students for entry to higher education (Novak, 2001; Ruppert, 2001).

Both governors and legislators are aware that competition in higher education is increasing and aware that it will have implications for their state (though as yet they are not particularly aware that developed countries are determined to compete with American university research, or that some have already surpassed this country in terms of access and graduation rates). They are concerned that unless institutions make internal changes in their governance, they will not be able to compete (Ruppert, 2001). One issue that has begun to reach their attention is that for-profit universities and colleges are likely to "cherry-pick," that is, to compete for students now attending public universities and colleges in high-volume subject areas such as education or business (Immerwahr, 2002). They are aware that this competition could damage public institutions, taking the most profitable programs and leaving them with costly programs that are either low volume or expensive. Some see this as a positive development because it will help address the state's need for access; some see it as positive because it increases the competitive pressures on the public institutions; and some see it as negative and dangerous (Mahtesian, 1995).

Most public leaders see the need for greater institutional flexibility. For example, there is a strong sense that there should be far more collaboration among the institutions—sharing programs, jointly developing new uses of technology, making transfer of course credits easier, and so on. After years of arguing for this (with results that are modest at best), many public officials hope that the market will drive institutions toward cooperation.

Most federal officials—particularly those in the Department of Education who deal with higher education—are beginning to see higher education more as they have seen elementary and secondary education. Historically, the federal role in higher education has been limited and focused on research, student aid, and regulations protecting certain groups (as an example, Title IX for women). The fundamental arena of higher education policy was left for the states. Lately, the administration and Congress have become more activist, proposing measures of accountability for control of costs and student learning. With federal pressure reinforcing growing state activism about assessment, this issue is likely to move front and center (Burd, 2003; Boehner and McKeon, 2003).

Clearly, legislators and governors agree with university and college presidents that the overall quality of American higher education is the best in the world but disagree sharply on where we are now and what steps are needed. They want accountability, too. One official said, "Accountability will eventually determine the dollars that an institution receives" (Ruppert, 2001, p. 35).

The Academy

A series of focus groups with faculty and university and college presidents, conducted by Public Agenda for the Futures Project, showed that academic leaders see the world in strikingly different terms from those of the political actors. They see their institutions as flexible (several used the term "nimble") but hampered by bureaucratic overregulation. They see bureaucracy as taking a great deal of their organization's time and energy. They feel strongly that they need more autonomy (Immerwahr, 2002; see also Gumport, 2000). (See Chapter Seven for more details on institutional autonomy.)

Even more strongly, the presidents feel that their institutions need more money. They are reluctant to recognize, even when pushed, the significant growth in state appropriations over the past two decades, or the even greater growth of total revenue.

Despite the growing chorus of concern expressed by political and business leaders about poor performance by higher education, presidents see few problems that they would classify as serious. They believe firmly that their institutions are teaching what students need to know. The principal cause of low achievement is, in their opinion, the failure of K–12 schools to educate students to the level needed to succeed in college.

As the debate about higher education heats up, the presidents do recognize the growing pressure for accountability. They particularly feel pressure about measuring learner outcomes. Assessment of learning is still controversial, but some (by no means the majority) are beginning to argue for taking the lead on developing multiple forms of student assessment that are thoughtful, and flexible, so as to head off state or federal action. They fear that this would likely result in the forms of assessment now widespread in elementary and secondary education, which they see as simplistic. Community colleges are most open to the idea of assessing learning.

Presidents now also feel the heat of increasing competition, a recognition that has developed only in the last few years. They are concerned that growing competition from for-profit institutions, coupled with their need to raise tuition owing to what they see as declining state funding, makes them vulnerable to cherry picking of their high-volume programs—particularly education, business, and extension programs for older working students. These are the programs whose revenue has been used to cross-subsidize other activities that do not have sufficient income to support themselves.

Until recently, presidents argued that the competition from for-profit institutions was of low quality and focused on older, part-time, and working students—not much of a concern. Today, there is growing recognition of some formidable competitors out there. Many presidents now described the best for-profits as lean and focused, with a higher-quality student body than was previously understood. A frequently expressed point was that for-profits spend no time on scholarship or graduate study (the training ground for faculty) and were therefore parasites dependent on traditional universities.

The presidents of community colleges and regional four-year institutions see their institutions as the only place concerned about access for low-income students. They argue, with solid evidence, that they get the least funding to do the hardest task.

Faculty views often mirror those of the presidents about these issues, but they are generally focused on their own work. They often have little patience with issues of policy, funding, and public debate. Issues such as efficiency are viewed as an annoyance at best and more often as an inappropriate intrusion.

As a whole, faculty are skeptical about learner outcomes and any form of assessment external to faculty members' own grading. They feel strongly that what they are teaching is what the students need to know. They are less concerned about dropout rates, seeing this matter as basically the fault of the student who was granted an opportunity and didn't measure up.

When faculty do pay attention to external criticisms, they fear that policy makers will push for expectations that could damage the institution and the academic process—cutting costs, increasing access, demanding greater "quality," and embracing technology (Immerwahr, 1999a, 2002).

In sum, both presidents and faculty see quality as high, repeatedly referring to this as the "greatest higher education system in the world," pointing to the large number of foreign students here, often asking "Why do you think they all come here?" This is clearly an important argument, though it ignores the other, powerful reasons—political, social, and economic—for which foreign students are attracted to come here to study.

When all of the evidence is assembled, what stands out is the sharp difference in perceptions. Political and business leaders are increasingly outspoken about the need for accountability. Academic leaders and faculty feel growing pressure for accountability but view it with skepticism and apprehension. All of the groups see the intensifying competition. Academic leaders see it as a challenge to be overcome, whereas business and political leaders see this as a force for encouraging improved performance. All sides have a strong interest in finding common ground and a constructive path ahead. This may well emerge from new and serious discussions about the trade-off between accountability and autonomy (to be discussed in Chapter Seven).

Chapter Six

Creating a Thoughtful Market

Even when market sectors are deregulated, some regulation is essential.

In present-day political discussions, there is a tendency to view the creation of markets in terms of the absence of (or removal of) government controls. However, every effective market needs strategic intervention by government in order to function fairly and efficiently. When such intervention is absent or weak, chaos or catastrophe is the usual result. The emergence of a market economy in Russia has been hampered by the lack of an adequate legal framework. In the United States, we have been reminded, by disasters such as Enron, Tyco, or Global Crossing, once again of the critical need for a strong regulatory framework. Their implosion not only hurt their shareholders but had a major impact on the entire financial market.

Even when market sectors are deregulated, some regulation is essential. When airline deregulation occurred, the federal air traffic system and federal airline safety regulations became more important than ever. In the words of Charles Schultze, "The free enterprise system, therefore, carries the label 'made by government'" (Schultze, 1977, p. 30).[1] California learned the hard way about markets during the electricity deregulation debacle. William Hogan, a utility economist at Harvard University, commented that "The magic of the market is no sure thing." He continued:

"Electricity is an example of an industry where introducing competition leads not to less regulation, only different regulation.
[These] markets are made, they don't just happen" (quoted in
Pearlstein, 2001, p. A01). The *Washington Post* concluded: "Opinions
differ on what . . . doomed the California experiment. There is,
however, general agreement now that most of the missteps flowed
from the faulty assumption that consumers could get all the benefits of free markets without assuming their risks" (in Pearlstein,
2001, p. A01).

The Need for Strategic Interventions by Government

A part of the task, then, is for government to structure the market
or channel the forces of competition and institutional self-interest,
not simply do away with regulations. As Joseph Stiglitz, Nobel Prize
winner in economics in 2001, said about the shift toward the market in recent government policy, "Too often . . . the question was
not, What is the *right* regulatory structure? but How do we get rid
of the regulations as fast as possible?" (Stiglitz, 2002, p. 7).

The task for both legislators and academic leaders is not simply
to make the higher education market work but to make it serve the
public purposes that have emerged over time as the system of
higher education has developed, to create both conditions that help
students select wisely and a force that pushes institutions to constant
improvement. In one of the three basic functions of higher education, research, these conditions are present. The federal agencies
that sponsor research have both the information (through peer
review) and the structure (competitive grants) to select the best proposals, and there is powerful pressure on researchers and their universities to perform and improve. The same conditions are not
present in the other two functions, teaching and service (National
Center for Public Policy and Higher Education, 2003).

How, then, can government intervene in the emerging academic marketplace to create the conditions that serve the broad-
based, long-term public good? There are already-established
government interventions, both federal and state, that serve as a
base. They include regulation (such as accreditation requirements for institutions wishing to be eligible for federal student

aid), information (a requirement to publish graduation rates for athletes), or subsidy (financial aid for low-income students). But as the higher education market gains in strength, these need to be supplemented by more imaginative and significant interventions. (See Chapters Seven, Eight, Nine, and Ten for specific policy proposals.)

To make markets work takes deregulation of rules and procedures that are impediments but also strategic intervention by government to ensure the meeting of public purposes. These interventions might typically include prevention of fraud, public subsidy of necessary but unprofitable services, creation of ground rules that ensure appropriate (and prevent inappropriate) competition (such as antitrust regulations), or establishment of minimum standards of quality (such as the requirement to provide seat belts in cars).

The Public Purposes to Be Served

If strategic interventions are to help ensure that market forces in higher education serve the public's needs, it is necessary to be clear about those needs. Here are the public purposes that the Futures Project has distilled from the voluminous literature on this subject (see Chapter Four for further detail on higher education's performance in addressing these public purposes):

- Improve the quality of learning so as to ensure the skills and knowledge that will be required for the workforce.
- Improve the quality of learning so as to reflect the skills, knowledge, and commitment required for active participation in the civic and social life of the community.[2]
- Provide access and academic attainment for a steadily broadening share of the population of all races, ages, ethnicities, and socioeconomic backgrounds, focusing particularly on access and attainment for those currently underserved.
- Serve as an avenue of social mobility for lower-income and minority citizens.
- Serve as the location (virtual or physical) of open debate and discussion of critical, and often controversial, issues of importance to the community, where the emphasis is on

evidence and analysis and the opportunity exists for all sides to participate.

- Support development of high-quality elementary and secondary education through improved education of teachers and school leaders, alignment of curriculum and purpose with the schools, assistance with school reform, and improved research about education.
- Undertake research and scholarship in a manner that is trustworthy and open, in a widening array of fields that serve to advance society.
- Bring the benefit of the knowledge and skills accumulated in colleges and universities to the benefit of the community through outreach and service.[3]

Information as the Driver of the Market

An important government intervention is provision of the information necessary for a market to work fairly and efficiently. A market system needs good information for transparency. How can the consumer make a rational choice in the absence of reliable and relevant information? Hence the effort by governments to demand such information as the percentage of flights leaving on time for each airline, or the calories in packaged foods, or crash-test results for automobiles. In the words of Joseph Stiglitz, "Recent advances in economic theory have shown that whenever information is imperfect and markets incomplete, which is to say always . . . then the invisible hand works imperfectly" (as quoted in Friedman, 2002, p. 50).

The role of the Securities and Exchange Commission in regulating the financial markets as an example of a government agency strategically intervening is the epitome of a free market. Similarly, to ensure that the public has the information it needs to understand and participate in the economy, and that the federal and state governments have the information they need to intervene in the working of the economy where necessary, the federal government publishes extensive economic data that are relevant, timely, and trusted. Multiple measures are often provided for the same issue (for example, employment or money supply) so as to illuminate a complex subject.

For the market to serve effectively in teaching, the buyer (that is, the student) must have sufficient information to determine which program comes closest to meeting his or her interest. For the minority of students who attend selective institutions, there is some helpful information available. The traditional visits to college campuses, college Websites, and a host of guides to picking colleges help students decide among large or small, university or college, West Coast or East Coast, and a multitude of other variables. For working students, and particularly older students, the choices (which historically were limited) have been growing: evening or day, a traditional university or a new for-profit, online or classroom.

The missing questions in all of these cases are, How well and what are students at this institution learning? How many are graduating? In the absence of this essential information, the most potent competition is about prestige. Prestige does serve a number of purposes, though it is not clear that it serves important societal needs. For example, since students learn from each other as well as from faculty, joining a program with a selective student body is an advantage. It is also clear that students and their parents are willing to pay more for the prestige that results from the student attending a well-regarded institution. Surely it is logical and desirable that institutions should strive to be well known and respected. But the lack of information about learning leaves two holes: students cannot choose programs that maximize their life chances, and institutions do not feel pressure to assess and improve learning.

The value of information about graduation rates and learning outcomes is not relevant just to those upper-tier students applying to selective institutions. In fact, the greatest benefit may accrue to low-income students. In addition to learner outcomes, students entering higher education without advantages such as wealth, or parents who are college graduates, stand to benefit from information about academic support programs, financial aid, and other support structures such as child care. The impact of these programs on the academic success of low-income students is significant, resulting in graduation rates that range from an abysmal 6 percent to an impressive 60 percent. An even more important function of such information is that it creates a pressure on the institution to improve. As we discovered in the focus groups that the Futures Project sponsored, many presidents do not feel that pressure (Immerwahr, 2002).

Higher education, far more than is the case for elementary and secondary education, operates without much of the information that would help ensure a thoughtful, effective market. Even when some information is known, such as graduation rates, it is not available in a form that makes it readily accessible and useful (for example, graduation rate by race, age, discipline, incoming credentials, and so forth). The Department of Education is the major source of information about higher education, supplemented by the states and some nonprofit agencies. Even before the advent of the changes now happening, the current federal effort at data collection has been too limited and too slow. Given higher education's movement toward a market, the lack of broader data on a timely basis is a serious problem (National Center for Postsecondary Improvement, 2002).

The Risks of a Market in Higher Education

There has been a growing interest among public officials in the United States and around the world in "harnessing the power of the market," as it is often put, to improve the effectiveness, efficiency, and responsiveness of a given sector. Now it is the turn of the higher education sector to feel this pressure. It is not clear, however, that the market as it is now emerging will deliver on the promise that the proponents expect. On the basis of results in other sectors, the hope is for:

- Improved accountability for institutional performance, including greater efficiency and reduced costs
- Improved quality, particularly in terms of learner outcomes
- Greater diversity of institutions and programs

As has been evident from the experience in many sectors where policy makers emphasize greater dependence on market forces, these forces are not easily harnessed to serve public purposes (Stiglitz, 2002). As it is currently emerging, the market in higher education has few incentives toward the public purposes noted here (Collis, 2002).[4] As Stiglitz reminds us, "The examples of

Enron and Global Crossing prove that incentives matter, and that markets do not always provide the right incentives" (Stiglitz, 2002).

With regard to the absence of incentives for serving public purposes, there are several trends that must be overcome if the market is to work. First, the current form of competition among universities and colleges has existed over several centuries. It has been, from the start, focused on prestige. In the last two decades, this competition has intensified, accelerated by the growing prominence of various rankings. But the battle for prestige does not serve the public need for quality in terms of student learning. It will take carefully structured interventions to overcome the current form of competition.

Second, even though one of the most significant public purposes to be served is creation of opportunity for the least advantaged, markets tend to focus on the more advantaged—those with resources and those whose admission to the campus community will help in the battle for prestige. As competition has accelerated, a shift toward the more advantaged students is already occurring. David Kirp and Jeffrey Holman described it this way: "When colleges sell themselves to applicants—and vice versa—fairness falls by the wayside" (Kirp and Holman, 2002). For two decades, federal and state need-based aid has eroded when compared to the rise in college costs. For the last decade, the resources devoted to merit-based aid have increased. The price war that has broken out among institutions and even among states, grounded in the financial aid offered to attractive students, favors the already advantaged. They are also the ones knowledgeable enough about the system to seek out and attract competitive offers.

The competition for better students has, over time, led to students and their families responding by acting more as consumers. This includes bargaining over student aid. More are marketing themselves to the college with the help of consultants. Here again, it is the well-off students who have the family support, the knowledge, and the resources to do this, so the advantage of the already advantaged grows.

The price war also favors wealthier institutions. The distribution of resources is probably more uneven among institutions of higher education than in almost any sector in society. David Collis has pointed out that Harvard, with its huge endowment, could easily offer a full scholarship to the top three students in every state (Collis, 1999). To a degree, this approach to using resources as a competitive weapon has already begun, spurred on by Princeton's move to more generous student aid packages. Other universities, following a typical pattern of the market, have responded, and the effort to attract the better students by offering a more attractive student aid package has spread to a wide segment of higher education. The result is that not just the already advantaged students but also the advantaged institutions are further advantaged.

A third concern is whether the market will encourage diversity or homogeneity among institutional approaches. Experience in other sectors has produced mixed results, depending on how the market is structured. (Think of airline deregulation and how all airlines try to leave LaGuardia Airport at 5:30 P.M.) Given the power of the prestige model, it may take a considerable time for new and diverse organizational forms to emerge from within the traditional public and private nonprofit institutions. There are new sources of diversity becoming more prominent in the form of the new providers—the for-profit, the virtual, and the corporate universities and colleges, some of which use substantially different organizational forms.

Consolidation of the sector is a further concern. This could play out in a number of ways. On the one hand, we have already seen a number of for-profits buying up colleges and universities (such as Career Education Corporation's acquisition of the Whitman Education Group, DeVry University's purchase of Ross University, and the Sylvan Learning Systems network of eight foreign universities; Farrell, 2003b; Blumenstyk, 2003). On the other hand, some institutions that are finding it hard to compete have decided it might be easier to merge than go it alone (Crane, 2003; for an interesting perspective, see Martin and Samels, 2002). In Japan, the education ministry is encouraging mergers because competition for students has become so fierce. The plan is to reduce the number of national universities from ninety-nine to eighty by April 2005 (Brender, 2003). Some merging and consolidating is to be expected, and even welcomed, but too much consolidation will dilute the diversity of institutions available for students. The thought of the University of Phoenix's Apollo Group buying a handful of (or even a hundred) universities worldwide is not overly alarming. But what if AOL/Time Warner buys Apollo and then begins to aggressively purchase, consolidate, and standardize universities around the world?

Many are simply concerned with letting business ideology get too embedded in higher education. As terms such as *outsourcing, privatizing, reengineering, strategizing, branding,* and so on become commonplace, some feel that the distance from the market so long coveted by academics is wearing thin. A number of books and articles warning of the danger have been written (one by the Futures Project, Newman, 2000; see also Benson and Harkavy, 2003). David Kirp, who warns against letting nostalgia for the old—even if the old was not optimal—cloud our vision, still believes that "if outsourcing is carried too far, there's a real danger of turning the university itself into a business, and in the process outsourcing the soul of an old institution" (Kirp, 2002, p. B13).

Meeting the public need with regard to quality will also require confronting the power of the competition for prestige. Unless consciously structured to do so, the market doesn't have the incentive for quality instead of prestige. Markets often have an incentive for prestige over quality (so that a Rolls Royce is more expensive than a Volvo), and prestige often attracts a sizable premium. In higher education, although this effect is generally understood to be the case, this is an underanalyzed question. (Is a Harvard undergraduate education really better than one from Colorado College or Truman State?)

For several decades, there has been a determined effort by individual faculty, teams, and projects to develop new approaches that improve learning—such as learning communities, service learning, or application of technology. All of them, and more, have demonstrated promise. The difficulty has been finding ways to encourage scaling up. So far, there is no evidence that market forces have encouraged the spread of proven ways to raise the quality of learning. For this to happen, the competition must shift, at least in part, from a focus on prestige to a focus on learner outcomes. This implies a need for openly available reports from universities and colleges on learner outcomes. As Susanne Lohmann argues, learning must become "the ultimate bottom line" (Lohmann, 2002).

These problems are further complicated by the atypical nature of the higher education market. In its current form, the market is heavily and unevenly subsidized. The two principal sources of subsidy, state and federal funding and private gifts, both significantly favor wealthier students and institutions. Probably more than in any other sector of society, the institutions that are competing—colleges and universities—bring to the market a stunning range of resources, from small, tuition-dependent colleges with no endowment to Harvard with its $19 billion in endowment and almost a half billion in fund-raising last year. As a result of the public and private resources poured into higher education, the education of most students is subsidized—some students receiving only modest subsidies, some receiving heavy subsidy. These distortions are bound to make any market function unevenly.

Complicating matters further, the nature of higher education as a system has many aspects that are at odds with the usual attributes of a market-based sector (see Graham and Stacey, 2002; and, in particular, Pusser, 2002). The Institute for Higher Education Policy report titled *Cost, Price and Public Policy: Peering into the Higher Education Black Box* notes four special characteristics that "defy the usual 'production function' and cost accounting analyses":

1. Students are both inputs and outputs.
2. The unequal subsidies involved are self-perpetuating, and often "a good student could pay less to attend a 'good' school than a mediocre student pays to attend a 'mediocre' school."
3. There is an "extreme diversity in price and quality" exacerbated by prestige.
4. Higher education produces "interdependent products" (associate's degrees, bachelor's degrees, graduate degrees, research, service) in different combinations that are "difficult to both characterize and quantify" (Stringer and others, 1999, p. 9).

Beyond these anomalies, the working of the market is bound to be affected by deep-seated resistance within the academy to the idea that higher education might even be considered a market. There is a widespread belief on campus that the activities of scholarship and teaching cannot and should not be corrupted by association with the self-interest of the market. The dilemma for policy makers and academic leaders as they face the need to carefully structure the emerging market is that they must preserve the higher purposes of teaching and scholarship while addressing the inroads that a

different set of factors—institutional and personal self-interest—
have made in undermining the ideal of this vision.

In many respects, universities and entrepreneurial colleges do
not operate like a business—and probably should not (Lohmann,
2002; see also Lohmann, 2004). In other sectors, new competitors
with new approaches often create pressure for change. In the U.S.
higher education system, there are few incentives for starting new
public universities or colleges, given the cost and the huge array
of existing institutions. Further, when new and innovative models
have been tried (the University of California at Santa Cruz and
Evergreen State University in Olympia, Washington, are examples),
the attraction toward the prestige of the traditional model has
gradually overcome the commitment to innovation, and the new
soon looks like the old. Some observers question whether the university (even as compared to the community college) has the ability to become more market oriented, given factors such as the
complexity of the university's responsibilities, the extent of subsidies provided, and the fact that the most expensive institutions
have the greatest demand (see, for example, Pusser and Doane,
2001). The Futures Project contends that this doesn't, in fact, pre-
clude formation of a market.

As described earlier in this chapter, a further factor that ham-
pers creation of an effective market is the inadequate information
available. As Gordon Winston has noted, "The perfectly informed
customer of economic theory is nowhere to be seen" (Winston,
1997, as quoted by Pusser, 2002, p. 114). The most obvious need is
for information about the extent and depth of learning, including
such useful surrogates as rate of graduation or degree of engagement with faculty.

Much of what will happen as market forces become more
important is still unclear. When organizations are driven by the
pressures of the market, they often make different decisions than
those they would have chosen in a more regulated circumstance.
In higher education, for example, such questions as whom to
admit when access is limited, or the purpose for which the education is intended, or the character of service provided by the
university or college to the community are almost certain to be
affected by the power of the market. In the operation of markets,
those who have resources tend to get the benefits of the services

and avoid any drawbacks. Services to the community are therefore more likely to focus on assisting local industry than the local library. Students from affluent families will have better information and greater knowledge about how to work the system and will be more attractive to the institutions. It is more likely to be students from poor families who are left out—as happened when health care moved to a market structure. As economist Robert Kuttner noted, "One thing a market society does well is to allow its biggest winners to buy their way out of its pathologies" (Kuttner, 1996, p. 4).

A likely outcome, unless care is taken to structure the market carefully with public policies, is that institutions will be forced to compromise their public orientation. Pressure arising from competition with more focused for-profit institutions will force universities and colleges to devote their time, their intellectual energy, and their resources to the threatened tasks (for instance, education of students in high-volume majors such as business) rather than tasks that are important to the community but forced to exist through cross-subsidies (low-volume majors such as comparative literature, expensive majors such as pharmacy, outreach assistance to help economic development, or the support of cultural events open to the public).

The logical course for many institutions, particularly the for-profit universities that have not evolved from a tradition of service to the public, is to cherry-pick (focus where the money is and where they can gain a competitive advantage). From the public point of view, a number of institutions doing one thing, or a few things, well is not the same as a single university serving a more comprehensive role. While we believe many universities have spread themselves too thin and would benefit from thoughtful pruning, this is not the same thing as destroying the idea of the comprehensive university that plays so critical a role in society.

A Lesson in the Risks from Market Forces: Intercollegiate Athletics

When the organization of a market is poorly structured, the result can be devastating. Intercollegiate athletics is, within the world of higher education, the clearest case in point. Worldwide, athletic competition has the ability to grab the public's attention in an iron grip. The intensity of fans everywhere—for soccer in Latin America, skiing in Austria, tennis in Australia, or football in the United States—has the ever-present potential to spiral out of control. The power of competition and fan interest is made more difficult to control by the huge money flow. Such is the case today in intercollegiate athletics in the United States, where the connected interests supporting athletics have gained remarkable momentum.

It is easy to forget, given the visibility of college athletics in this country, that this is one of the few nations where sports teams are built into the schools and colleges. In most countries, local club teams serve as feeders to professional leagues. The gradual emergence of varsity teams (that is, run by the institution) supplementing club teams (run by students) as the principal mode of intercollegiate competition began in the 1800s, grew in the first half of the 1900s, and exploded in the last half of the 1900s.

The original intent was to provide both social and educational opportunity—to let male students work off excess energy; to teach students sportsmanship, teamwork, and how to handle victory and defeat; and to build a sense of community on the campus. These days, academic leaders have just about stopped talking about these reasons for supporting intercollegiate athletics; though they do continue to support programs with cash, only a few programs, even among those institutions with big-time programs, break even. Their current reasons for continuing to support athletics are closer to institutional prestige, creation of a sense of community on campus, and staying connected with the alumni. These are not small issues. To be in Nebraska for a home football game, or in Connecticut for a women's basketball game, is to see community spirit writ large. But for many schools the athletic department has grown into a huge, unstoppable machine with no core educational mission.[5]

Offsetting any benefits is the enormous magnitude of a problem that has been well documented. The issues can be illustrated by a few examples:

- For big-time programs in basketball and football, head coaching salaries now often exceed $1million per year, and some double that—ten or twenty times what senior faculty receive (Wilgoren, 2001).

- TV and ticket revenues have increased dramatically. The teams participating in the top five postseason football bowls in 2000 received $11.5 million each (Simmons, 2002).
- Under the NCAA revenue distribution formula found in their contract with CBS, an institution will receive $780,000 for each win in the Division I basketball tournament (Barlow, 2001).
- Costs have risen at a rate matching or exceeding the growth in revenue. Only 48 of the 320 schools in Division I have programs that are profitable, with the rest operating at an average annual deficit of $3 million (Hearn, 2002).
- Despite the costs, universities are expanding their facilities. Texas spent $52 million renovating its basketball facilities, Pittsburgh opened an $80 million basketball pavilion, Florida spent $10 million on a practice facility, Xavier now plays in a $45 million center, and on and on (Drape, 2003). Thomas K. Hearn, Jr., president of Wake Forest University, worries that "if the full cost of athletics facilities—including construction and operation—were assessed fully to the athletics department, I suspect that no athletics program in the nation would be solvent" (Hearn, 2002, p. 21).
- With these huge expenditures on basketball and football, there isn't much left for low-profile and women's sports. Defenders of Title IX have observed that if some of the perks and overspending were cut for football and basketball, there would be plenty of money left for other teams. As Selena Roberts, sportswriter for the *New York Times*, commented after describing the four-star hotel that Colorado's football team stayed in before every home game last year, "And imagine, college wrestling coaches have blamed Title IX for the elimination of their sports" (Roberts, 2003a, p. 11).
- Almost every major athletics department has an apparel (shoe, jacket, and so on) contract bringing in millions (see, for example, Adame, 1998; Hagan, 2001).
- Brigham Young University, unable to fit a men's varsity soccer team within the Title IX cap, bought a franchise in a semiprofessional league for the team (Suggs, 2003).
- The University of Oregon rented a billboard outside Madison Square Garden to advertise its star quarterback, hoping to increase his chances for the Heisman Trophy ("Billboard Quarterback," 2001).

- The intensity of competition that forces athletes to commit more and more time (preventing most from playing more than one sport), including off-season weight training and workouts, has spread not only to minor sports such as golf and lacrosse but down to Division III (Suggs, 2002).
- Student attendance at athletic events, despite all the hoopla, is falling. Since the NCAA requires a minimum average attendance to qualify for Division IA football, San Jose State hired a marketing firm, Home Town Sports Group, to develop techniques to attract fans such as throwing parties and giving out free tickets. The State University of New York at Buffalo has gone so far as to pay popular figures such as Tony Hawk, the skateboarding superstar, and Rocketman (who apparently "flew around the stadium in his jet pack") to make appearances (Blair, 2002, p. D1).
- During the 1980s, "more than half (57 of 106) [of the] institutions . . . in the NCAA I-A Division were censured, sanctioned, or put on probation" (Barlow, 2001, p. 36).
- A new study of the men's basketball teams that made it to the round of sixteen in the NCAA tournament showed that their graduation rates were well below those for all male athletes on athletic scholarships and even worse for African American players. At two of the sixteen universities, no African American players graduated during the time period studied. Similarly, 58 of the 328 colleges in Division I men's basketball did not graduate any African American players within six years of beginning college (Litsky, 2003b).
- The parade of rules infractions for everything from corrupt recruiting to falsifying academic records goes on. In just one week of March 2003, men's basketball imploded—with full media coverage.[6] Villanova suspended twelve players for unauthorized use of a university access code to make telephone calls. Georgia suspended its basketball coach, fired an assistant coach (his son), and suspended two players for faking a course to provide fraudulent grades (amid further allegations of illegal payments to players). The head coach was also accused, in a separate case from an earlier coaching job, of sexual harassment and changing players' grades. The president of St. Bonaventure was fired after approving the admission of an unqualified player. Fresno State and Michigan each banned

themselves from postseason play after allegations of academic fraud and payments to players (Drape and Glier, 2003; Roberts, 2003b; Litsky, 2003a).

- A basketball coach, finally fired after years of abusive behavior toward players and officials, was quickly hired by another major university—to the universal praise of the sportswriters (McKinley, 2000; Robbins, 2001).

Universities have long since abandoned teaching responsibility and sportsmanship. *New York Times* sportswriter Harvey Araton describes college sports as "amateur practices that are long dead and a sleazy system that subverts more than serves the integrity of higher education"(Araton, 2003, p. D1). The pressure of ever more intense competition has spread to sports such as lacrosse, down to Division III, and downward to the high schools. Of the fourteen high schools in Guilford County, North Carolina, eleven were recently rocked by scandals revealing that students were participating in athletics despite ineligibility from "low grades and excessive absences" (Jonsson, 2003, p. 17). With a star basketball player, LeBron James, on its team, an inner-city Catholic high school organized a national tour, playing prep schools across the country. The school director, defending against a charge of exploitation, has argued that reports that the school made $1 million are exaggerated—in reality, it was only $400,000 (Longman and Fountain, 2003). Tim Flannery, associate director of the National Federation of State High School Associations in Indianapolis, has commented, "Some of the problems we have now in high school sports mirror the problems they have at the professional and college level. . . . Winning is becoming the most important thing" (Jonsson, 2003, p. 17).

One reason the problems in the intercollegiate athletics market are so intractable is that there is no agency willing to effectively and firmly structure the rules of the market and enforce them. Colleges and universities are ambivalent about restraining themselves. Government is wary about getting involved as legislators and governors recognize the passion of the committed fans and prefer to limit their role to being seen in the school's colors at key games. The result is that despite the hard work of a number of task forces and commissions of truly wise and experienced leaders, no one can find a way to restore sanity.

There are other examples of the risks of market forces. In Chapter Four, for example, we described the evidence that the erosion of public purpose in the area of research has already gone too far. The push for corporate research dollars has led universities to cede significant control of the publishing of research results to corporate sponsors.[7] The question is, Can we prevent other areas of higher education—especially those close to the educational core—from following the same path as athletics?

Creating a Successful Market

When structured skillfully, markets can help; long-distance telephone deregulation has surely resulted in lower cost and better service for consumers. The most obvious example of such success in higher education was the surge in the quality of American university research after World War II. During the 1920s and 1930s, American universities were struggling to narrow the gap with their European counterparts. Having seen how crucial research had become to national survival during the war, leading scientists proposed a radical concept for postwar federal support of research: competitive funding for proposals from faculty members (and their university) judged by teams of peers from that discipline. Within ten years, American universities and their faculty were at the forefront of research in essentially every field. The competitive, peer-reviewed grant process (a market in research) worked far better than either block grants to universities or the general support of federally funded laboratories, techniques used in addition to the competitive grant system in the United States and as the principal systems in Europe.

The key, therefore, is a skillfully contrived structure. If the performance of a research team is poor, new grants are not forthcoming, and the team is dismantled. If the public needs for research shift, the amount of funding and the proposal guidelines shift in response. The large number of granting agencies (twenty-six federal agencies) and the existence of some funding for new and unproven scholars or controversial ideas allow new people and new ideas to break through.

Even with its great success, the research market is not without its own unintended consequences. Over the five decades since its inception, it has had the unexpected effect of generating a focus on scholarly publishing at the expense of good teaching. It has as well encouraged a sense among research university faculty of being independent scholars based at the university more than scholars committed to the university as a community. In sum, the market created by sponsored research has been a great success, with some unanticipated but now evident drawbacks.

The Political Difficulties of Structuring a Market

Creating an effective market is not easy. The rough-and-tumble of the political process is not ideally suited to the careful, analytical planning effort that would help avoid at least some of the unintended consequences that so often accompany moving toward a market structure.

For one thing, legislators are familiar with the process of regulation. Even legislators committed to the ideology of free enterprise find it hard to restrain themselves from a quick, decisive regulatory response when problems appear. Political leaders, particularly at the state level, also often lack necessary information and analysis, forcing them to make decisions on anecdotal information, or what feels right, or—most dangerous—ideology.

Although it is easier to understand regulation and create a coalition of supporters around some regulatory approach, state action that involves incentives usually has a more positive impact. This, however, requires the state to set goals, design the incentive, and then allow the institutions the flexibility to set their own course of action, all of which is difficult to design and hard to sell to fellow legislators.

In these circumstances, term limits hurt (Mackey, 2002). It takes time, measured in years, to master the complexities of education policy. Term limits not only force experienced legislators to leave the legislature but also cause frequent changes in assignments. For example, the still new chair of the education committee might be forced to move up to replace the chair of ways and means who was just term-limited out (or moved up to replace the speaker).

Also complicating the process of thoughtful legislation is the considerable ability of higher education institutions to resist change. Far more than schools—or any other public sector enterprise—these institutions, particularly universities, have considerable capacity to press their case, sufficient independence to challenge the legislature, and a large alumni group ready to come to their support (including some in the legislature). Since institutional matters can easily take over a president's day, broader policy conversations seldom hit the top of the priority list. Robert Atwell and Jane Wellman have commented on how, "accustomed to speaking only on matters of institutional self-interest, most presidents have opted out of the larger policy conversations at both the national and state level" (Atwell and Wellman, 2002, p. 66).

A further complication arises when academic leaders within the same system want different things. For example, in Texas, the chancellor of the University of Texas System, Mark Yudof, pressed for deregulation of tuition setting in early 2003. Sensing a unique opportunity to find a simple solution to budget cuts, legislators took Yudof's plans even further by suggesting giving authority over tuition setting to all of the universities in return for lower state appropriations. That's when the trouble started. The flagship, the University of Texas, was in a comfortable competitive position, and its leadership was confident that the market could bear higher tuitions. But the other state universities, knowing they were in a less lucrative competitive position, were more threatened by autonomy if it meant losing their appropriations (Kay and Jayson, 2003). In the end, the University of Texas prevailed, and the public colleges were given power over tuition setting (Potter, 2003a).

There are also times when the institutions and the political leaders are simply at odds over what to do. The governor of Massachusetts, Mitt Romney, started a major feud over his desire to abolish the system office of the president of the University of Massachusetts. In March 2003, all five chancellors of the University of Massachusetts System refused to attend a meeting convened by Romney (the system president subsequently left, but he was replaced, and the system office remains intact). Such hard feelings are just one indicator of the stalemate between the academic and political leaders (Roy, 2003).[8]

The introduction of market forces also creates another complication: the emergence of unanticipated consequences that can be positive or damaging. In New Zealand, as part of a broader rightward shift, a conservative government removed most regulations constraining competition for both schools and universities in 1988.[9] At the school level, the result over the following decade was almost complete segregation of the schools by socioeconomic status.[10] At the higher education level, three of the institutions ended in virtual bankruptcy (their remaining parts are being absorbed into other institutions) as the better-known and better-financed institutions cannibalized the less well known (see Chapter Seven for a deeper discussion of New Zealand).[11]

When the state moves toward a market-oriented system, it needs a carefully designed plan. It needs as well a political strategy to overcome these obstacles. Academic leaders must step forward and contribute to creating a plan that ensures thoughtful and necessary interventions but avoids old-style regulation lest higher education end up with the worst of both worlds.

The Changing Perception of Quality

For market forces to encourage an effective system of higher education, it becomes ever more important to create modes of measuring how much learning is taking place; what is the quality of the learning experience? Information about the quality of learning is probably the central need in the effort to ensure a workable market. At the same time, all of these changes are beginning to shift the perception of quality in higher education. The traditional battle has been for prestige, and largely a battle of inputs. In this battle, the size of endowments, the research reputation of faculty, the test scores of entering students, the share of applicants rejected, and the attractiveness of the campus determine reputation. Despite the lack of relevance of these measures to student learning, they have still created a condition of intense competition (Frank, 2002). Since little or no information has been available about how much students are learning, parents, policy makers, and the academy itself have been forced to assume that an institution with high prestige must be effective in generating learning as well. This is changing. There is growing pressure, principally from policy makers, to measure learning directly and to measure what students know (not what courses they have taken).

There is pressure from students, too. A recent survey of freshmen indicated that 40 percent reported being bored in class, up from 26 percent in 1985. Increasingly, these students see that technology and better pedagogy can make learning exciting. They are more willing to select a university or college on the basis of information they can find about student learning (and often on the Internet). Once enrolled, they are increasingly willing to look for courses outside their university or college that provide more effective learning. Given far more diverse patterns of attendance—students attending multiple institutions on the way to a degree, or even multiple institutions at the same time—measuring learning outcomes is likely to become more important for universities and colleges as well, since they can no longer depend on the comfortable assumption of quality based on the belief that attending a university with a prescribed curriculum for four years automatically ensures a sound education. Around 60 percent of undergraduates enroll in more than one institution on the way to their degree (Levinson, 2002). There is, as a result, a growing effort to create new ways to assess learning, ways that are made increasingly practical because of technology.

Nonprofit colleges and universities, as the traditional stewards of educational quality, have long considered some of the alternative providers, particularly for-profit institutions, to be no real competition. But as the difference between for-profit and nonprofit institutions has begun to blur, a significant change in public perception regarding the merit of for-profit institutions has taken place. Some have established themselves in traditional academic areas, particularly through offering the kinds of bachelor's, master's, and even Ph.D. programs formerly reserved for traditional nonprofit universities and colleges. The best known of these institutions, but hardly the only one, is the University of Phoenix. By determined efforts to evaluate learner outcomes and improve faculty effectiveness at teaching (far more extensive and effective than any at all but a few traditional universities or colleges), the best of these for-profit institutions have positioned themselves as quality leaders rather than as institutions of questionable reputation.

Some of the new competitors—the University of Phoenix, the British Open University, and others—have demonstrated the effectiveness—in fact, the urgency—of faculty working closely with new partners in creating courses and course materials (Farrell, 2003a).

As a report from the National Center for Postsecondary Improvement has pointed out, "Faculty members, as content experts, find themselves working in conjunction with programmers, graphic artists, course designers, and webmasters to craft learning materials and educational experiences for students" (National Center for Postsecondary Improvement, 2002, p. 15). After literally centuries of faculty acting alone, this requires a new approach to managing academic affairs.

In this new environment, the quality of course work is becoming a more salient issue. As the use of online instruction expands, it exposes the reality that quality depends on outcomes—not surrogates such as seat time. If, for example, introductory math courses are taught in large lectures that give students little chance for practice, if students' only interaction with faculty is with teaching assistants, if freshmen science courses have laboratories with hundreds of students, then the institution—or at the least these courses—will be increasingly at risk. The Internet makes information about alternatives readily available. Students in the past had little capacity to weigh an institution's performance against that of its competitors and were forced to accept its flaws because there seemed to be no choice. They now have options. Some institutions, particularly those unwilling to plan for the future or address their shortcomings and change, will run into trouble and may even fail. One of the benefits of the increased competition may be, as a result, a heightened concern within institutions to address these long-overlooked flaws.

Selecting New Policies to Shape the Market

Policy makers (particularly governors, legislators, commissioners, and state boards of higher education) are increasingly focused on accountability. More and more, they are asking whether market forces might help. They want more effective ways to encourage institutions to be responsive to the multiple needs of society. They want institutions to assess and then be accountable for their performance. Perhaps most important, they want to know how much students are learning and make that information readily available—so students can make intelligent choices, so institutions can improve and be held accountable (National Governors Association, 2002). But for market forces to be helpful and not harmful, government (in this case, state governments) must undertake strategic interventions that create incentives and restraints that channel the working of the market. This requires quite different policies that will restructure the higher education system.

New policies require careful thought. To make the shift from policies designed to support a regulated system of higher education to policies designed to create and properly structure a market system is a major undertaking. A range of policies are needed to create a workable market. This includes rethinking budgeting, the form of financial support, financial aid, and much more.

The Futures Project has looked at policy options tried or proposed around the world to see which hold the promise of creating a more effective and responsive system of higher education. We have particularly studied options in four areas, policies that encourage:

1. More autonomous, entrepreneurial, and accountable institutions (see Chapter Seven)
2. Institutional acceptance of the responsibility for student learning (see Chapter Eight)
3. Academic success and completion of programs for an ever-expanding share of the population (see Chapter Nine)
4. Competitive public funding for services and teaching (see Chapter Ten)

We chose these four areas of policy because they form a coherent basic structure for a market. Taken together, we believe they can have sufficient impact to create a workable market system of higher education.

The best way to start is not to examine each current policy or regulation to see if it should be changed or eliminated but rather to start at the other end and ask what interventions by state government are necessary to make the market work *effectively*. An examination, regulation by regulation, would involve endless debate and political skirmishing. Making the shift away from a regulatory system is not easy; there are literally thousands of regulations. Behind each regulation is an interested individual or group. When, instead, governments have started by asking what the *public needs* from higher education, and what *strategic intervention* by government is required to help ensure these needs are met, a far more flexible and workable agreement has resulted.

Chapter Seven

Autonomy, Accountability, and the New Compact

Any move to greater autonomy and accountability should be accompanied by an effort to renew the broader compact between higher education and the state. Through the process of renewing the compact—a process that is urgently needed—the state clearly defines what society needs from higher education and then, working with the institutions, defines ways of ensuring that universities and colleges are meeting the public purposes of higher education.

Higher education around the world is grappling with what is referred to as the "autonomy-accountability trade-off." In country after country, academic and political leaders have been crafting policies that provide the opportunity and the incentive for institutions to become more autonomous and entrepreneurial while holding institutions more accountable for performance.[1]

In the United States, as academic and political leaders negotiate these terms—more autonomy in exchange for more accountability—it is critical to engage in a serious debate about the most effective means of structuring the relationship between institutions of higher education and the state that governs them so that institutions can operate effectively in today's intensely competitive, market-oriented environment. The Futures Project does not advocate creating a market in higher education; rather, the project's research has led to the conclusion that the market has arrived, and higher education should acknowledge its existence and respond thoughtfully and effectively.

Although many of the policy initiatives that are now being discussed in states—a number of which are outlined in this chapter—are quite new, there is much to be learned from review and analysis of the trends that led to their creation. The Futures Project has conducted an early analysis of available results about these policies and formulated recommendations for one approach to the autonomy-accountability trade-off.

The experience in many states suggests that increased autonomy over day-to-day operations better equips institutions to respond to the new competitive environment. The state does, however, have a fundamental stake in maintaining control over a limited number of key issues, including the roles, missions, and performance of institutions. Any move to greater autonomy and accountability should be accompanied by an effort to renew the broader compact between higher education and the state. Through the process of renewing the compact—a process that is urgently needed—the state clearly defines what society needs from higher education and then, working with the institutions, defines ways of ensuring that universities and colleges are meeting the public purposes of higher education. After a state-level compact has been negotiated, creating institution-level agreements would allow academic and political leaders to determine appropriate institutional roles and missions; new levels of autonomy; and relevant, customized forms of accountability.

Reasons for Seeking New Structures

The new interest in autonomy and accountability stems from the convergence of several trends. First of all, colleges and universities now operate in a competitive, global market. To survive, and certainly to excel, in this new environment, institutions need to be flexible, change quickly, and respond to market pressures. Many academic leaders recognize these pressures and have started searching for ways to make their institutions more entrepreneurial and autonomous. Frequently, these leaders are met halfway by market-oriented lawmakers who are also wary of stifling higher education's creativity and flexibility through overregulation. (See Chapter Two for more detail on the new competition in higher education.)

Academic leaders have also argued for increased autonomy from a state or nation that provides a smaller and smaller share of total institutional budgets. In the United States, although state appropriations have continued to rise (up 60.2 percent from 1993 to 2003), institutional budgets have expanded, and state funding makes up a declining proportion (Grapevine Project, 2003).[2] Arguing that their funding increasingly derives from private sources, academic leaders feel justified in asking for more freedom from state regulations. The 2003 budget crisis in the United States, which has resulted in real cuts in many states and a budget squeeze virtually everywhere else, has emboldened public university leaders to make the argument more aggressively, and it has left public officials more willing to listen.[3] Most other countries do not rely on private funding to the degree the United States does, but a growing trend of privatization is having a similar effect elsewhere. (See Chapter Three for more detail about rising costs.)

Finally, a sense of frustration with the slow-changing nature and flaws in the performance of higher education has led policy makers to seek new ways of using the power of market-oriented competition to achieve greater accountability for performance. The policy makers' hope is that the market will push institutions to be more effective and efficient in a way that regulation has not. This rightward shift toward the market in the United States is evident in a variety of public sectors, from elementary and secondary education to environmental policy and health care. The movement toward the market and accountability can be found around the world. Higher education observers in Europe, for example, have documented "a growing lack of trust in the work and function of higher education," leading to increased interest in contractual relationships that clearly spell out accountability (Gornitzka, Smeby, Stensaker, and de Boer, 2002, p. 2). The secretary-general of the Association of Commonwealth Universities commented that "every university around the world is learning to play in the accountability and value-added stakes" (Gibbons, 2003).[4] See Chapter Three for more on policy makers' orientation to the market.

The result of these trends is that academic and political leaders all across the globe are looking at new ways of structuring the relationship between institution and state, and they seem surprisingly willing to engage one another in serious discussion about the best way of doing so.

The Range of Existing Relationships

A scan of existing relationships between governments and universities around the world reveals a spectrum of funding ranging from guaranteed full public funding to 100 percent private funding. In the United States, one would be hard-pressed to find a public institution that does not receive any private funding, with the exception of the military academies. Even in a country like Germany, with a long history of a centralized, publicly funded system, a small amount of private fees have been introduced.[5]

On the private side of the spectrum, very few U.S. institutions are 100 percent private. Even for-profit universities in the United States receive state and federal funding through their students' financial aid. The handful of American private colleges and universities without any public funding are typically religious institutions that have rejected public funding—including financial aid—to protect themselves from all public influence and accountability. But even for those institutions, if they are nonprofit, their tax-exempt status makes them reliant to a degree on the public's goodwill.

If one were to array these state relationships in sequence, one would see that very few institutions cluster at either extreme of fully private or fully public funding. Most institutions fall somewhere in between, with complex reliance on both public and private funding. Around the world, the relationship between the state and public institutions is changing dramatically as universities and governments react to changes in their environment. One of the most important changes is a worldwide, market-oriented shift toward a greater degree of private funding and a lesser degree of state control in all sectors and, most recently, in higher education, which is pushing institutions in the direction of the private end of the spectrum and blurring the differences between public and private education (see Figure 7.1).

Despite this blurring, a major difference remains in the nature of control: Does the government appoint the board and own the institutional assets? Is the institution subject to laws regarding public expenditures, or public hiring, and so on? Public institutions, regardless of the degree of reliance on private funds, generally operate within a regulated public sector that demands certain tasks in return for its financial support. There are, for example, many states in the United States that supply a comparatively small share

**Figure 7.1. The Range of Existing Relationships,
from Public to Private**

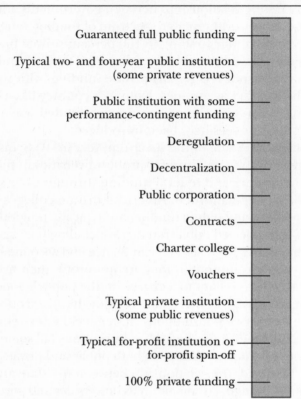

Guaranteed full public funding

Typical two- and four-year public institution
(some private revenues)

Public institution with some
performance-contingent funding

Deregulation

Decentralization

Public corporation

Contracts

Charter college

Vouchers

Typical private institution
(some public revenues)

Typical for-profit institution or
for-profit spin-off

100% private funding

of their higher education institutions' budgets but still have strict and cumbersome regulations in place. As states and nations continue on the path to autonomy and privatization, there are serious questions about how higher education is regulated, how institutions should be held accountable given that they still receive large public subsidies, and how the public good is to be ensured.

Emergence of New Models Around the World

Over the past decade and a half new policy ideas have emerged that represent a radical shift in government thinking about how to govern public universities. Ideas such as performance funding, budgeting, and reporting are now in use in eighteen, twenty-six, and forty-four states, respectively, as well as other countries such as Australia.[6] These policies represent attempts by legislators to reward successful outcomes, make performance more transparent, and build more accountability for performance into the system. They do not, however, grant institutions more autonomy, as a number of other policy ideas—from decentralization to vouchers in higher education—strive to do. More policy shifts are taking place—some radical restructuring, some just tinkering at the margins. More and more public institutions, and sometimes entire systems, find themselves moving toward (or being moved toward) market-oriented models on the private side of the spectrum.[7] This is the early stage of a trend that requires deeper analysis, but here is an attempt to cover what is currently known.

Decentralization and Deregulation: Tweaking at the Margins

When thinking about how to increase the autonomy of higher education institutions, policy makers, academic leaders, and researchers often turn first to decentralization and deregulation. Deregulation and decentralization both result in a shift of the role of government, from having extensive control over higher education to less control and more focus on steering the system. Efforts to deregulate strip away the burden of excess rules and regulations, easing the heavy but protective hand of central legislation. In comparison, decentralization can be defined broadly as "institutional self-governance," which roughly translates to an increase in local control of funding, operating authority, and accountability.[8]

The decentralization of New Jersey's higher education system is often touted as one of the most successful cases in the United States. In 1994, Gov. Christine Todd Whitman announced her intention to dismantle the Board of Higher Education (BHE) and the related Department of Higher Education in favor of a smaller, decentralized governance system. Much of the prior authority of the BHE was transferred to decentralized boards established for each institution and empowered with control over tuition and fees, academic programs, legal counsel, personnel, trustee nominations, and facilities construction, while elements of state-level budget and program review were eliminated. A few concerns have emerged, principally about interinstitutional competition and the need for college presidents to find ways to "submerge individual campus interests" in an effort to advance the common good, as well as the argument by some higher education experts that New Jersey would benefit from increased accountability. However, overall performance of the system has been good. A 1996 interim assessment of the reorganization was largely positive, and New Jersey has performed well on external evaluations such as *Measuring Up 2000* and *2002* (for more on New Jersey, see McLarin, 1994; McMahon, 1997; Martinez and Richardson, 2003; National Center for Public Policy and Higher Education, 2000).

The success of New Jersey has fueled many other experiments with decentralization and deregulation. The governor of North Dakota signed a "flexibility with accountability" bill in May 2001. Under the legislation, institutions were given their appropriations as block grants and received authority to keep their tuition and private donations and grants (Gouras, 2001). Institutions were later given control over setting tuition, within a specific range (Sullivan, 2002). The bill also created new accountability reports designed to "give lawmakers enough information to track the system's performance, because they have much less control over the university system's purse strings" (Gouras, 2001, p. 5B).

A similar attempt to shift control from a central authority has been under discussion in other states. In South Carolina, a bill passed the House but then lost support that would have allowed the University of South Carolina, Clemson University, and the Medical University of South Carolina to break away from the Commission on Higher Education, be released from some regulations, and create a new board that coordinates the objectives of the three research universities (Stensland, 2003a; see also Stensland, 2003b). In Florida, where decentralization attempts in 2002 became highly politicized (see Chapter Three), the universities have brought forward proposals in 2003 and 2004 to gain further autonomy. The universities are seeking contracts with the state that would outline specific outcomes for which they would be held accountable, such as student enrollments and graduation rates. In return, the institutions propose to receive a guaranteed amount of state funding with the freedom to spend it as they see fit to meet their goals (Yeager, 2003; John Hitt, personal communication, July 23, 2003; Yeager, 2004). In Colorado, Metropolitan State College of Denver was spun off from the state colleges in the Colorado System and given its own board in June 2002, and Fort Lewis College was made independent of the Colorado State University System and given its own board as of August 2002 (S. Kaplan, personal communication, 2002; see also Metropolitan State College of Denver, 2003).

The move to increase autonomy is spreading across the globe. A new law passed by the Slovak Parliament in February 2002 has added full economic autonomy and individual governing boards to the academic autonomy instituted by law in 1990 (Mederly, 2002). Indonesia is shifting toward greater academic and financial autonomy, with four universities expected to achieve substantial autonomy by 2005. As autonomy is implemented, the universities will set up their own boards, receive public funding through block grants, and have the authority to set and collect fees (Beerkens, 2002). Between 1992 and 1998, state support in Russia for higher education decreased significantly because of a declining economy. The state in turn granted universities more freedoms. Institutions were given autonomy in areas such as program approval and generation of external revenues (Bain, 2002; see also Morgan, 2002a).

Creating Public Corporations

These examples of decentralization and deregulation are important means of improving governance. There are, however, other approaches, such as conversion of universities to "public corporations" or "state enterprises," that have the potential to result in more radical change. A useful definition of a public corporation or enterprise is "a corporation with a public body as the major stockholder" (Armajani, Heydinger, and Hutchinson, 2001). When the Oregon Health and Science University (OHSU) became a public corporation in 1995, the legislation offered this definition:

> "Public Corporation" means an entity that is created by the state to carry out public missions and services. In order to carry out public missions and services, a public corporation participates in activities or provides services that are also provided by a private enterprise. A public corporation is granted increased operating flexibility in order to best ensure its success, while retaining principles of public accountability and fundamental public policy. The board of directors

of a public corporation is appointed by the Governor and confirmed by the Senate but is otherwise delegated the authority to set
policy and manage the operations of the public corporation. [S.B.
2, as quoted in Hibbard, 1997, p. 3; see also Oregon Revised
Statutes, ORS 353.010, Title 30, *Education and Cultural Facilities,*
Chapter 353, Oregon Health Sciences University]

As a public corporation, OHSU separated from the state higher
education system and is now governed by its own board of directors ("OHSU: An Historical Chronology," 2003; Hibbard, 1997).
The university's goal was to become more efficient and responsive
to the market by reducing bureaucracy associated with state agencies while maintaining its public service mission (Kertesz, 1995;
Kohler, 1996). In persuading the state to make the university a public corporation, OHSU officials emphasized that in addition to
teaching and research, OHSU had a particular health care mission
that required increased flexibility and autonomy (Hibbard, 1997).
Furthermore, the state provides less than 10 percent of the university's operating budget (OHSU Foundation, 2001). Evaluations
of OHSU's change to a public corporation have been positive, citing its ability to secure private donations; improvements in human
resources services, salaries, and pension plans; improved efficiency
and financial planning; and innovative collaborations that help the
institution deliver more effective care (see OSHU Foundation,
2001; Kohler, 1996).

In 1995, similar legislation was passed granting Oregon's entire
higher education system a fair degree of autonomy, making
the Oregon State System of Higher Education (OSSHE) a "semi-
independent agency," status just shy of public corporation (Novak
and Johnson, 2001; Hibbard, 1997). As a semi-independent agency,
OSSHE was liberated from many rules and regulations, though it
did not receive all of the autonomy it was seeking. In its new status,
the system was granted control over purchasing, contracting, and
personnel management in return for a promise to serve an additional two thousand resident undergraduates without requiring
more state support (Novak and Johnson, 2001; Lively, 1995). The
government developed "parameters" to guide campus decision
makers, and "postaudits" provide accountability (Hibbard, 1997).

An evaluation of the system's autonomy declared the change a success, citing that the system met its increased enrollment goals by fall 1997, the system saved $5.8 million in the first two years thanks to new procedures in facilities contracting and procurement, and some processes have been streamlined and improved. Further steps toward autonomy have followed the original legislation, including a shift toward funding driven by performance and enrollments and an expedited academic program approval process (Novak and Johnson, 2001). Even so, the academic leaders in the state continue to argue for more autonomy. In a letter written in July 2002, the presidents of Oregon's public universities told the State Board of Higher Education, "If the state is going to withdraw its support, it also has to withdraw the handcuffs and shackles that keep us from operating efficiently in an environment where we have to earn most of our revenue" ("Colleges Want to Sever Ties with State," 2002, p. C2). The Oregon presidents then proposed a trade-off, informally called "the deal," that would have contractually outlined a stable funding equation and a set of flexibility initiatives for the universities in return for improved performance in areas such as enrollment, research, graduation rate, and cost ("Universities Ask for Freedom . . . ," 2003).

In 1999, the Maryland General Assembly voted to make the University System of Maryland a public corporation, "thereby granting the USM the management flexibility it needed to pursue national eminence in a time of rapid changes in higher education" (University System of Maryland, 2001a). The effort to transform the system was stimulated by concerns shared by the governor, legislators, and the institutions that the system had become too bureaucratic and that the public colleges and universities were unable to be responsive and competitive (Hill, 1999a; see also Schmidt, 1998, 1999; University System of Maryland, 2000; "College Presidents in U. System . . . ," 1998; Hart, 2001). The thirteen member institutions of the University System of Maryland were freed from many state reporting requirements and were given in particular more freedom to create new programs (Hill, 1999; see also University System of Maryland, 2002). The legislation reduced the authority of the Maryland Higher Education Commission over public universities' budgets and mission statements (Hill, 1998; University

System of Maryland, 2001b; "Governor, Leaders Support Greater College Autonomy," 1999).

Charter Colleges

Transformation of an existing public institution into a charter college requires institutional and state leaders to rebuild the relationship between the institution and the state from the ground up. This rebuilding, which involves intensive discussion about the institution's role and mission, is a key advantage to the charter process since it allows academic and political leaders (groups that don't often talk constructively) to start with a clean slate and begin a discussion about what the state needs from higher education. The result is that the institution's role and mission are refreshed and redefined, and areas of new autonomy and accountability are negotiated and spelled out in detail in the charter. The term *charter* conjures up the contentious battle in K–12 over creation of public charter schools, but the models are different enough that the terms of the debate in K–12 do not cross over to higher education.[9]

Undoubtedly the most famous and most scrutinized charter college is St. Mary's College of Maryland. In 1992, the leadership at St. Mary's negotiated with the governor and the legislature to increase the autonomy of the institution (Berdahl, 1998). St. Mary's secured a lump-sum budget and more control over areas such as employment and procurement. In return for this freedom, the leadership agreed to recycle a portion of new tuition revenues into need-based aid to maintain access for low-income students, take responsibility for more external fund-raising, and accept a cap on state support (Berdahl, 1998). The college is held accountable for meeting its role and mission through presentations to the legislature and through Managing for Results, a program that oversees the performance of state agencies (Torre Meringolo, personal communication, Nov. 25, 2002; see also Berdahl, 1998; "Managing for Results . . . ," 2002). External evaluations, conducted by Robert O. Berdahl, professor emeritus at the University of Maryland, found that the change in status has been positive for St. Mary's, and praise has come from other sources, including accreditation teams and the press (Berdahl and MacTaggart, 1996; Berdahl,

1998; Naughton, 2001). However, in the years since Berdahl's last evaluation, St. Mary's has seen a drop-off in enrollments for students of color. First-time, full-time freshmen who were African American dropped from a peak of 14.1 percent in 1994 to 6 percent in 2000, and the number of all freshmen of color fell to 12.5 percent.[10] The leadership at St. Mary's reacted quickly to this turn of events by seeking out new recruitment approaches, and there has been progress; in the fall of 2002, the percentage of entering students of color had risen to 17.1 percent. The charter worked; the leadership worked to improve in an area for which they knew they would be held accountable (namely, enrollment of students of color). But the college has a long road ahead if it is to create a student body representative of the state; students of color make up 39 percent of all enrollments at four-year public institutions in Maryland (see "Almanac 2002–3," 2002).

In 2001, the Colorado legislature created the nation's second charter college when it granted the Colorado School of Mines "exemplary" status, which gave Mines a lump-sum budget and more control over tuition and academic programs. It is also exempted from the higher education commission's system for assessing and reporting performance. Accountability is governed by a performance agreement that defines the criteria upon which performance of the institution will be judged. Performance criteria include strength of transfer agreements with community colleges, increase in graduation rate, response to employer surveys, and pass rate for the Fundamentals of Engineering examination.[11]

The Massachusetts legislature followed suit in June 2003, creating a "new partnership" with the Massachusetts College of Art. The legislation grants MassArt tuition retention for a five-year trial period and further directs the Board of Higher Education to negotiate increased fiscal autonomy for MassArt along with a performance contract unique to MassArt's role and mission (Massachusetts College of Art, 2003; Katherine Sloan, personal communication, June 30, 2003).

Models that look like charter colleges are not limited to the United States. The Chalmers University of Technology in Sweden became an endowed semiprivate foundation—a status akin to a charter college—in 1994. Chalmers has its own board, which oversees a fifteen-year contract with the government that stipulates performance goals such as the number of students to be educated and relationships with the community. Unlike other Swedish universities, the Chalmers board is authorized to appoint its own vice-chancellor, build relationships with corporations, conduct fund-raising, and hire and fire employees. Although all Swedish universities were initially offered the opportunity to apply for the new status, the only other institution that converted to a foundation is Jönköping University. Chalmers and Jönköping have performed well on external and government assessments and have attracted international attention for their entrepreneurial character (Clark, 1998).[12]

Chalmers also served as a model for transforming the Technical University of Denmark (DTU) into an "independent foundation" in December 2000. The new Danish law established a board of seven members for DTU, and the minister implemented an accountability system, referred to as "development contracts." The contracts set out strategic guidelines for the university, including such items as increasing recruitment of students; completion rate; and number of publications, citations, and patents. The changes at DTU were designed to be a pilot for the entire Danish system, and the minister of science, technology, and development has proposed a new law that will enact similar changes at all universities.[13]

Austria has essentially transformed all of its universities into charter universities. Under the New Organization Act of 2002, the universities became independent of the state and were transformed into public corporations with their own boards. Performance contracts were instituted to assist the ministry with oversight, and the ministry will be less hands-on. Universities have full authority in the areas of employment, academic programs, and resource allocation. Funding is allocated through three-year lump-sum budgets, and the universities have complete autonomy over budget categories (Sporn, 2002).

Contracting for Performance

Similar to the idea of charter colleges, there have been implementations of contracts between institutions and the state. These are, in essence, semicharters; there is not much of a distinction. On the basis of research of the Futures Project, we have concluded that the main difference is in spirit. Creation of a charter college, as we envision it, requires a process of redefining the mission and charter of the institution as well as the philosophy behind what the university is to be held accountable for compared to what the university has authority over. These discussions should take place before deciding on the obligations that will be contractual.

In France, the system was highly centralized until the passage of the Savary Law in 1984, which granted French universities financial, administrative, academic, and teaching autonomy. Then, in 1988, a system of "funding through negotiation," which instituted four-year contracts and lump-sum budgets, was implemented. The idea was to encourage the universities to analyze their priorities and create plans for the next four years and then to negotiate with the central administration for resources to support those priorities. The contracts affected only about 5 percent of total budgets, they were not legal documents, and they did not hold institutions accountable, but they held important symbolic value. A study of the contracts revealed that they were, for the most part, respected and that they engendered a higher level of trust and goodwill between the ministry and the universities. However, their weak legal status led to their demise when a new ministry, coming into power in 1993, refused to honor some parts of the contracts (Henkel and Little, 1999; see also "Structures of the Education and Initial Training Systems," 1995; "The French Education System," 2003).

Contracts have emerged as a market-oriented approach to organizing higher education systems in the Nordic countries. Danish universities, which already had a block grant funding system, in 2000 started negotiating four-year development contracts with the ministry that set out performance goals in teaching and research. The contracts are voluntary and not directly tied to funding, but they do influence funding, and all institutions participate. Sweden began a general decentralization of authority to the institutions in 1993, including a program of three-year contracts negotiated with the ministry and explicitly tied to the funding system. The contracts contain criteria such as the number of degrees that institutions are required to award, in which fields of study, and to how many students. In 1998, the Finnish ministry began negotiating with each institution a three-year contract that outlines objectives and funding. The funding, which is awarded as a lump sum, is based upon criteria such as the number of degrees awarded, institutional size, and special funds for exceptional research or teaching (Gornitzka, Smeby, Stensaker, and de Boer, 2002).

The First Voucher Proposals

Moving even further toward the privatized end of the spectrum are vouchers for higher education, a tool designed to put state appropriations into the hands of students. Lawmakers in both Texas and Minnesota have considered this idea before, but no action has been taken in either state. Colorado has taken this idea the furthest, introducing it into legislation and seriously pursuing it in 2003 but then tabling the idea until the 2004 legislative session (Burdman, 2003; Prah, 2002; Amacher and Meiners, 2001; Jordan, 2002). The goal of the legislation was that the funding subsidizing the institutions directly would now be shifted to vouchers that students would carry to the institutions. The vouchers were not designed to cover the full costs of attendance, only to funnel state appropriations directly to students to create increased competition among the institutions. This approach would also help institutions skirt the Colorado Taxpayer's Bill of Rights, which has restricted tuition increases since 1993. Rep. Keith King (R-Colorado Springs), who sat on the blue-ribbon panel and drafted the legislation, made his interest in competition clear when he proudly asserted that this proposal "puts a market economy into the process."[14]

Proponents of vouchers in Colorado believe they will make college more affordable for low-income students. The blue-ribbon panel was influenced by focus groups indicating that low-income students found the voucher idea appealing. Tim Foster, executive director of the Colorado Commission on Higher Education, posited that "the interesting dynamic is that you convert the state subsidy to their money. It increases their stake. It's a psychological sea change" (Burdman, 2003, p. 4). Opponents of the plan, however, liken it to a shell game, just moving money from here to there with no real improvement for low-income students. Donald Heller, associate professor at the Center for the Study of Higher Education at Pennsylvania State University, warns that the actual increases in sticker price will deter some students (Burdman, 2003).

Miami University of Ohio's board of trustees has also approved what they are calling a "tuition restructuring plan," which looks quite similar to the Colorado vouchers. The plan would more than double the current cost of in-state tuition, bringing it to the same level as nonresident tuition in the fall of 2004. All Ohio students would then receive an "Ohio Resident Scholarship" that rebates $5,000 of the increase in tuition. A second set of scholarships, known as the Ohio Leader Scholarships, would then be rewarded on a discretionary basis for financial need as well as merit. The plan has been criticized for raising the sticker price so high that low-income students will feel priced out and for including merit—instead of focusing on financial need—in the strategy for the Ohio Leader Scholarships. Joni Finney, vice president of the National Center for Public Policy and Higher Education, warns that "other universities that have raised tuition ostensibly to make higher education accessible to poor students have instead used the increased revenues to provide scholarships to talented students whose attendance will increase the university's prestige."[15] Miami's experience will be closely watched by higher education experts eager to determine the impact on participation, especially for low-income students.

Encouraging For-Profit Institutions

A major area of privatization activity has been the purposeful addition of private institutions into the mix of higher education. Some countries, such as Germany, have encouraged private institutions to consciously create competition for the traditional state system in the hope of creating more responsive state universities. Others are opening up their systems and encouraging privates to enter to meet a demand for higher education that far exceeds the capacity of their present higher education systems. China's public higher education system, for example, enrolls fewer than 7 percent of high school graduates, and only 15 percent of qualified students are admitted to Malaysia's system (Doyle, 2000; *The Star,* 1997). Faced with high demand for access to postsecondary education, governments have seen little choice but to encourage the growth of private institutions to increase enrollments while minimizing the public investment.

In Central and Eastern Europe, for example, there were no private universities prior to 1989 (Lewis, Hendel, and Dundar, 2002). Private higher education in the Czech Republic, Hungary, Poland, and Romania grew at an average annual rate of almost 60 percent between 1990, when fewer than 12,000 students were enrolled in the private sector, and 1997, when 320,000 students were enrolled (Giesecke, 1999). By 2000–2001, Poland had 195 institutions enrolling 30 percent of the total student population, and Romania had 83 institutions enrolling 29 percent of students (Lewis, Hendel, and Dundar, 2002).

Although this trend is especially prevalent in developing countries, every government in the world is struggling to educate a growing share of its population. Private institutions have been encouraged in a variety of countries, among them the United States, Germany, Egypt, Chile, Oman, New Zealand, and Singapore (Farag, 2000; Suroor, 2000; Hashim, 2000; Wan, 2000).

- Nearly 80 percent of Brazil's higher education institutions are private, enrolling 60 percent of students (Cavalcanti, 2000).
- The number of authorized private higher education institutions in Benin (formerly Dahomey) jumped from zero in the early 1990s to twenty-seven by 1998, capturing 16.72 percent of all higher education enrollment (Guedegbe, 1999).
- In Malaysia, private higher education institutions rose in number from 156 in 1992 to 564 in 1999 and experienced enrollment growth from about 15,000 students in 1985 to 127,594 by 1995 (Lee, 1999).
- Twelve hundred private institutions of higher education enroll approximately 60 percent of Indonesia's tertiary students (World Bank, 2000).
- Even the Iranian Parliament has approved the entry of both private and foreign universities—a first since the Islamic Revolution (Uvalic-Trumbic and Varoglu, 2003).

Some of the new institutions are nonprofits with philanthropic intent, others are for-profits established by entrepreneurs who see a profitable market, and still others are branch campuses established by foreign institutions seeking a revenue stream. Though the exact breakdown of nonprofit versus for-profit in these private institutions is not known, the general consensus seems to be that they are primarily for-profit. Even the foreign institutions that are nonprofit in their home countries are seeking out new markets with "for-revenue" intentions, if not for-profit.

Purposeful addition of private institutions will undoubtedly help to meet a short-term need for more postsecondary education. It should not be forgotten, however, that the ultimate effect is to further privatize the system and create competition for students between existing public institutions and new, private institutions that may not be focused on fulfilling the public needs. The backlash is already evident as countries are beginning to realize the threats to quality, access, and the public system wrought by this increased privatization and competition. In South Africa, rapidly growing private providers came under fire for not sharing the public sector's "commitment to access, equity, quality" and for "'cherry picking' financially lucrative courses," threatening the public system's ability to cross-subsidize more expensive disciplines such as medicine and engineering (MacGregor, 2000). Ultimately, they were seen as such a threat to quality and the viability of the public institutions that new regulations were instituted, and the number of private providers was reduced from 202 in 2000 to fewer than 100 now (Uvalic-Trumbic and Varoglu, 2003).

Opening the System to a Market: New Zealand and Australia

The most extreme cases of educational systems that have been opened to the market can be found in New Zealand and Australia, as part of a wider effort to introduce free-market principles to all of their public sectors. Analysis of these two cases shows why using the market as the *only* means of regulation in higher education is not the right answer; sensible regulations are needed to control for negative side effects.

A danger inherent in greater competition is that, rather than creating pressure that causes all institutions to improve, the result is pressure toward winners and losers. This has, in fact, been the result in New Zealand after market forces were unleashed in the late 1980s. New Zealand began cutting funding to higher education, introduced student fees, and based government funding on enrollments, making it demand-driven and competitive. At the same time, institutions were given freedom over setting tuition fees and spending their funds, and the growth of private institutions was encouraged.[16]

New Zealand higher education has reaped some benefits including increased overall participation, more entrepreneurial universities, and more choice for students. But this aggressive move to a higher education market, without adequate regulation to protect against the downside of a market, also brought problems in its wake. Tuition fees skyrocketed. To help students cover the costs, the government introduced a highly controversial income-contingent loan scheme. There has been ceaseless debate about equity of participation and the debt level of students.[17] Inadequate quality assurance regulations allowed low-quality programs to grow. Three public institutions found themselves unable to compete, effectively went bankrupt, and were in the end merged with other institutions.[18] Many would argue that weak institutions should be allowed (even encouraged) to close, but these three institutions represented close to 8 percent of all public higher education institutions in New Zealand. By way of comparison, in the United States that would be the equivalent of a closure of 135 public institutions of higher education.[19]

Meanwhile, in primary and secondary education, market-driven reforms proved a marked failure. Enrollments became sharply polarized around race, ethnicity, socioeconomic status, and student performance. By 1998, the education ministry began conceding that the market system failed for all but the more elite K–12 schools (Fiske and Ladd, 2000a, 2000b). In 2000, the government began seeking ways of reasserting its control over the whole education sector (higher as well as primary and secondary) and considering how to roll back many of the market reforms.

New Zealand's experience can be seen as a shot across the bow for other countries considering market reforms. There are benefits to be had, but policy makers must ensure that adequate policies are in place. In an analysis of New Zealand's reforms, Maureen McLaughlin, education manager for Europe and Central Asia with the World Bank, while studying as a Fulbright New Zealand scholar came to the conclusion that "providing information for informed decision making, building in safeguards for accountability, and helping institutions with governance and capacity building are important components of a competitive, demand-driven model. The original National proposals to unleash market forces neglected to pay enough attention to these factors as they opened the system up to new rules and ways of operating" (McLaughlin, 2003, p. 24).

A new Labour government, elected in 1999, has been working hard to "maintain many of the competitive aspects of the current system but do so within a more centrally steered and regulated approach," but once market forces take hold, it is difficult if not impossible to change course (McLaughlin, 2003, p. 6).

Australia adopted market-based policies for higher education in the late 1980s. In 1987, the government began to introduce student fees, which encouraged private funding of higher education. The Higher Education Contribution Scheme (HECS) was created to allow students to defer fee payments until they had the financial ability to pay after graduation (Nelson, 2002). Universities were encouraged to attract overseas students, who would pay the entire cost of tuition. The theory behind these changes was that "students who pay for their education will demand more from the provider of that education; institutions that compete for the revenue derived from the students will be more responsive to student demands, and the quality of the tertiary education experience for the student will improve" (Scott, 1999, p. 193).

Higher education received increased financial autonomy in the 1990s, and there has been growing pressure for universities to become more managerial. For example, the title and duties of vice-chancellors are being transformed into those of chief executive officers, and councils are being called boards of governors (Meek, 2002). The reforms have extended far beyond the user-pays principle to a new model of an entrepreneurial university, guided by incentives and not mandates, where revenue generation is necessary for the university's continued existence (Gallagher, 2000).

Australia's market reforms did not go as far as New Zealand's, but they continue and, if anything, are being reinforced by the current government (Nelson, 2003). Many parties are disgruntled with the change, but there is no real push to revert to the system in place prior to the reforms, as found in New Zealand. Participation rates have increased, and initial evidence suggests that equity has actually improved for some underrepresented groups

(Meek, 2002). There have, however, been some issues. Many academics decry a loss of quality and diversification of mission in the system as institutions focus more on revenue and less on education and students (Meek and Wood, 1997; Gilbert, 2000). Another concern is that those institutions that had already amassed wealth and prestige before the transition to market forces possessed a great advantage over those that had not; when public funding was reduced, the gap between established, prestigious universities and lesser-known institutions widened (Scott, 1999).

Comparison of Australia and New Zealand leads to the conclusion that the market does not always deliver what society needs. Although there are benefits to market-oriented approaches, such as increased student choice and improved efficiency, thoughtful regulations that protect educational quality and student access are necessary to steer higher education systems through the market.

Autonomy in the Face of Budget Cuts

Autonomy initiatives in the United States gained momentum in reaction to the nationwide economic slowdown of 2002–2003 and concomitant budget cuts. These proposals are typically the fruit of discussion between academic presidents who want something in return for lower appropriations and state legislators who are willing to soften the blow of lower appropriations by easing regulations. As one state senator in Illinois who is exploring ways of giving more autonomy to universities in the face of budget cuts described the dilemma, "We can't on one hand say, 'Here's a budget cut,' then tie your hands by saying you can't increase revenue" (Josephsen, 2003, p. A6). These initiatives are new, so keeping track of the proposals is like shooting at a moving target as they move through various stages of approval. A review of these initiatives reveals that they cross over the types of ideas outlined here; some look like decentralization, others are more like charters, and still others are similar to public corporations.

Officials at the University of Colorado System argued that because of the limits imposed by TABOR (the 1993 Colorado Taxpayer's Bill of Rights, which restricts tuition increases), they needed greater flexibility to attract and retain high-quality faculty, build better academic programs, and use their money more efficiently.

They proposed a trade-off involving the university receiving a decreasing proportion of its revenues from the state (less than 10 percent of its budget) and in exchange becoming a "state enterprise" with greater control over such issues as purchasing and tuition setting (Hoffman, 2003; see also Burdman, 2003; Hebel, 2002). The legislation was vetoed by Gov. Bill Owens, who feared that CU would raise tuition too high and focus mainly on wealthy out-of-state students who can pay higher tuitions ("Owens Ties CU's Purse Strings," 2003; Martinez, 2003).

Budget cuts in Wisconsin have led to discussion of granting greater freedom from state government to the entire University of Wisconsin (UW) System and privatizing UW-Madison completely. The governor's proposed budget as of April 2003 cuts $250 million from higher education, with a quarter of those cuts hitting UW-Madison. UW System president Katharine Lyall has floated the idea of transforming the system into an independent authority with its own governing board, assuming more control over areas such as purchasing, personnel, and budgeting. The familiar complaint emanating from Madison is that, despite the state paying a declining share of the system's budget, "politicians continue to boss the university as if they were running a fully funded arm of state government" ("Don't Dismiss UW Privatization," 2003; see also "Among Offered Budget Ideas: Privatize UW-Madison," 2003).

There are too many other examples to list here in detail. The Washington state legislature is considering creating compacts between the state and the institutions. The details have not been worked out yet, but the idea is that the compacts would grant institutions greater autonomy in operational areas while stipulating new forms of accountability.[20] The University of Arizona, Arizona State University, and Northern Arizona University are involved in a plan known as Changing Directions, which would give the three universities more autonomy in the areas of tuition setting and admissions standards while asking them to differentiate their missions to better meet the state's needs (Cavanagh, 2003). The University of Virginia, Virginia Tech, and the College of William and Mary introduced a plan for more autonomy in decision making, purchasing, hiring, and capital spending as a result of drastic state budget cuts that have left the universities short about $385 million a year. The institutions have ceded to political pressure to not pursue this change in 2004, but it is likely to come up again next year (Sizemore, 2003; see also Edds, 2003). The Iowa Board of Regents has been encouraged to consider the idea of making the state's three Regent universities "independent agencies" (Charles, 2002). In Texas, legislation has passed to deregulate tuition. The plan has been pushed by Chancellor Mark Yudof, who describes the idea as allowing the regents to "create markets and use an entrepreneurial attitude" in their financial decisions (Potter, 2003b, p. A23; Potter, 2003a; Kay, 2003a; see also Drosjack, 2003; Kay, 2003b).

Discussion about changing the regulatory structure of higher education systems is, ultimately, a political discussion. It is worthwhile to note that sometimes those initiatives starting with level-headed negotiations getting less media coverage and resulting in less partisan bickering can result in more autonomy, whereas we can see from an example such as Florida that the more politicized an initiative becomes, the less effective it may be in the end.

As this overview of policy options makes clear, the differences between policies are often difficult to discern. The charter of a charter college might look quite similar to a contract, compact, or performance agreement in another state.[21] Despite the widespread confusion about terminology, one thing seems clear: institutions, states, and nations are searching for ways of injecting more autonomy into the system after decades of building regulations (Berdahl and MacTaggart, 2000). Benno C. Schmidt Jr., former president of Yale University, chair of the City University of New York's Board of Trustees, and chair of Edison Schools, brushes over definitions to champion the idea of greater autonomy: "Whether one calls the idea charter colleges or uses some other nomenclature, the movement toward greater operational and resource autonomy, coupled with higher accountability for results, is here. . . . And, in my judgment, it will only build in the future" (Hebel, 2000, p. A34).

Policies for a Workable Trade-Off Between Autonomy and Accountability

Our examination of these alternatives has led us to conclude that elements of all of these approaches are valuable and should be incorporated as a part of a new policy framework for public institutions in the United States. The public debate, however, should not be as simplistic as whether to regulate or deregulate, whether to centralize or decentralize. Instead, constructive discussion must first take place about the state's overriding interest in mission and performance accountability. Key questions include "What does the state need from its higher education system?" "What does higher education need from the state?" and "How can we ensure that students—especially underrepresented students—are served well by any new policy changes?"

Creating a Statewide Compact to Link Higher Education to Society's Needs

To answer these questions, the Futures Project recommends development of a statewide compact. The goals of the compact are to articulate the main objectives of the state in supporting a higher education system and to design a new form of governance that balances an appropriate amount of autonomy with relevant and customized accountability for performance. A useful analogy is an argument made by Michael Gibbons, secretary-general of the Association of Commonwealth Universities, for a renewed "social contract" between science and society. Gibbons has argued that since the Second World War universities have provided research and teaching in the sciences in return for funding and autonomy, in "an arrangement built on trust which sets out the expectations of the one held by the other, and which—in principle—includes appropriate sanctions if these expectations are not met" (Gibbons, 1999, p. C81).

The Futures Project is arguing for a similar concept for state systems of higher education. Every state must define its own needs and institutional roles. Among the few states that have addressed this are North Dakota, in its flexibility-with-accountability relationship, and West Virginia, in its "Compact for the Future of West Virginia" (see, for example, North Dakota University System, 2001; West Virginia Higher Education Policy Commission, 2003). It is critical to think through the process of how to create a statewide compact before starting. For example, how can the state collect data and opinions on what the public wants from its higher education system? There are other process-related questions: Who should be included in the process? Who should oversee the process and later maintain the compact? How will the compact be reviewed and approved by the public or elected representatives? How will the compact be introduced into the mainstream?

The proposal given here, a skeleton model of a compact, is merely a starting point for state-level discussion, illuminating some of the performance standards the public has a right to expect from its higher education system. Some areas of the compact may not be relevant for a state's needs; others may be missing, and each area of the compact needs to be further developed, with specific goals delineated, the means of assessment outlined, and plans for continuous improvement described (see Chapter Four for further detail on higher education's performance in addressing these societal needs):

- Access is not enough. Access to higher education is vital to the future of this country and must be extended even further. However, we can no longer afford to allow public policy to stop at questions of access. We must now broaden our goal to include *academic success* for an ever-expanding share of the population, which includes adequately preparing students and then retaining them once enrolled.
- Taking responsibility for efficient use of resources. As stewards of the public trust and significant taxpayer investment, state colleges and universities must pledge to spend public funds in a way that most effectively responds to public needs, which includes turning an eye to efficiency and finding out how to improve quality while reducing cost.
- Teaching and learning do matter. Higher education has hidden teaching and learning under a veil of secrecy, suggesting that what goes on in the classroom is too sacred for scrutiny. Institutions now need to do more than provide the opportunity and resources that allow learning; they must take responsibility for learning.
- Preserving the integrity of scholarship. The lure of corporate sponsorship of research cannot be allowed to supersede the integrity of scholarship. Higher education must turn to full disclosure of all financial interests held by researchers and institutions, and universities must maintain control over publication and review rights.

- Preparing students for tomorrow's democracy. Higher education has worked diligently to engage students in community service. This effort has successfully bolstered student volunteerism, but it has not translated into greater participation in the political process. Higher education must work harder on encouraging the civic education of today's students to ensure the efficacy of tomorrow's democracy.
- Deepening outreach and service. Colleges and universities have found many ways of giving back to their communities through activities such as outreach programs to local students, service learning programs, and application of faculty research to community needs, but there remain significant areas where higher education must become more engaged—most notably in its support of elementary and secondary education.[22]

In addition to defining the state's needs, the compact should address the needs of the institutions by describing a broader philosophy about what the relationship between the state and its institutions should look like:

- Which decisions would best be made centrally?
- Which decisions are best left in the hands of the institutions?
- What types of autonomy might help institutions be more effective?
- Which regulations are overly bureaucratic?
- What priorities does the state have an interest in continuing to regulate?
- What form of accountability is the most effective, given conditions in this state?
- How can each state and institution develop a stable, long-term relationship?
- What expectations are reasonable given the level of the state's support of and investment in the higher education system?

A statewide compact will not solve all of higher education's many problems, but it is a step in the direction of clearly stating responsibilities and priorities for all of higher education's constituencies—from the governor and legislature to the taxpayers and students to the institutions themselves. The center point of the policy framework resulting from these discussions should be the concept of greater operating autonomy for public universities and colleges. In return for this freedom, there should be a clear agreement between the state and each institution outlining the latter's differentiated mission, public responsibilities, and means for measuring and reporting its performance. The state, in short, trades autonomy for clear mission and accountability, allowing the institution considerable flexibility in how it operates while keeping a strong voice in the public purposes the institution should pursue (Figure 7.2).

Establishing Institutional Agreements: Unique Roles, Responsibilities, and Freedoms

After the state's broader goals are defined and communicated in a statewide compact, the next task at hand is to determine how each institution fits into the bigger, state-level picture. To accomplish this, the state and each public institution should negotiate an institutional agreement. This requires each institution's leaders to engage in constructive discussion with state leaders about its unique role and mission; the kind of autonomy needed to thrive in the future; and the types of accountability that are appropriate, effective, and mutually acceptable. These are the broad categories that the Futures Project recommends including in an institution-level agreement:

- *Mission agreement.* A clear definition of the institution's unique public mission should be negotiated directly between institutional leaders and state representatives. A key part of this process is to build conscious diversity into the system so that the sum of the institutional missions, when viewed from the system perspective, meets society's needs. Though this sounds idealistic, a number of institutions have already been through it, and anecdotal evidence suggests this is a healthy process that refreshes the institution's mission and rebuilds relationships between academic and political camps.
- *Procedural autonomy.* Robert O. Berdahl, professor emeritus at the University of Maryland, argues that states should grant procedural autonomy to institutions while maintaining control over role and mission (Berdahl, 1998). Such autonomy would be best managed by public institutions with their own governing

Figure 7.2. Finding the Right Balance of Autonomy and Accountability

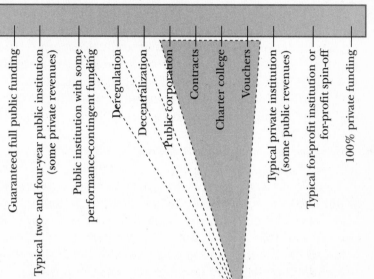

Guaranteed full public funding

Typical two- and four-year public institution (some private revenues)

Public institution with some performance-contingent funding

Deregulation

Decentralization

Public corporation

Contracts

Charter college

Vouchers

Typical private institution (some public revenues)

Typical for-profit institution or for-profit spin-off

100% private funding

Mission agreement: A clear definition of the institution's unique public mission should be negotiated directly between institutional leaders and state representatives. A key part of this process is to build conscious diversity into the system, so that the sum of the institutional missions, when viewed from the system perspective, meets society's needs.

Procedural autonomy: Robert O. Berdahl, professor emeritus at the University of Maryland, argues that states should grant procedural autonomy to institutions while maintaining control over role and mission. Such autonomy would be best managed by public institutions with their own governing boards.

Mission accountability: A multiyear performance agreement should be worked out between each institution and the state that clearly defines what the institution will be held accountable for, and how that accountability will be instituted and periodically assessed. There are two statewide measures for which all institutions would be held accountable:

- Institutional responsibility for student learning
- Academic success for an ever-expanding share of the population

The Futures Project: Policy for Higher Education in a Changing World
www.futuresproject.org

boards. The Futures Project argues for a form of procedural autonomy that frees institutional leaders from the bureaucratic regulations that impede their ability to operate efficiently in a competitive higher education climate, including but not limited to line-item budgeting, centralized tuition setting and distribution, state procurement procedures, onerous and lengthy academic program approval processes, and centralized employment practices.

- *Mission-focused accountability.* Because each university or college will have a unique mission, accountability measures need to be unique as well. A multiyear performance agreement should be worked out between each institution and the state that clearly defines what the institution is held accountable for and how that accountability is instituted and periodically assessed. Depending on the type of institution and its mission, accountability measures might cover research productivity, relationships with local businesses, or community service. There are, however, two statewide measures on which all institutions should be held accountable: institutional responsibility for student learning (see Chapter Eight on this topic) and academic success for an ever-expanding share of the population (see Chapter Nine for more detail).

It is critical that, in the negotiations between the institutions and the state, the legislature makes its expectations clear. Academic presidents often feel that the legislature sends mixed and contradictory signals. Past research has shown that states making their expectations clear receive better performance from their institutions.[23]

Accountability is a controversial topic. Critics suggest that accountability is overly bureaucratic, that it forces all institutions to meet the same standards regardless of unique mission, and that given the quality of the higher education system, it is not necessary. We at the Futures Project argue, instead, that there are forces pushing for accountability that won't be easily stopped. Rather than getting run over by accountability solutions designed by higher education's critics, a smarter route is for each institution to be involved in developing accountability that suits its role and mission. If colleges and universities want to engage in constructive negotiations with the state, it must be acknowledged that there are flaws in higher education's performance that need to be addressed. Furthermore, given the level of public investment in higher education, it is appropriate that institutions be held responsible for meeting the needs of the state so that institutional interests do not dominate. This perspective echoes that of Aims McGuinness, a higher education analyst with the National Center for Higher Education Management Systems, who commented, "I've never seen a case where the sum of the individual institutional goals equals the sum of the public goals" (Stensland, 2003b, p. B1).

The forms of accountability typically used now do not work well, and a one-size-fits-all solution will never be right for higher education. Instead, individual agreements that describe an institution's unique contributions, and how that institution will be held accountable in a way that is flexible, customized, and mutually acceptable, is the right choice for the future.

The Benefits of Institutional Agreements

Higher education across the globe is moving toward a market-oriented structure. In the face of a market, academic and political leaders must decide on a structure for the system that delivers public benefits and serves the public good. Budgetary pressures and a desire for marketlike competition have pushed leaders on both sides—political and academic—to begin arguing for increased autonomy at the same time that accountability has gained new prominence in higher education vocabulary. We are, as a result, witnessing serious discussions about an autonomy-for-accountability trade-off that is unprecedented.

The institutional agreements described in this chapter offer new promise in the era of the trade-off. First of all, they require academic and political leaders to come to the table for constructive discussion about the needs of the state and how higher education fits into those needs. The negotiations allow these leaders to start a fresh conversation and create a state-institution relationship that matches the needs of the time without renegotiating every extant regulation. They also force a written, mutual understanding of the institutional role and the state role as well as the responsibilities of each, reducing misunderstanding and setting the stage for a more constructive relationship. Because agreements are tailored to each institution, there is an opportunity to encourage diversity of role and mission among the institutions. This model also allows the state to pilot this approach with only one or two institutions, gaining experience and building acceptance before tackling the whole system.

By building agreements from the ground up, institutional leaders can argue for the procedural autonomy that makes the most sense for their institutions, instead of trying to work through the arduous process of scaling back regulations already in place one by one. Institutional agreements also allow academic leaders to have a powerful role in creating accountability measures, instead of having ideas forced upon them by the legislature (as has happened in several states and other countries). Academic leaders tend to shy away from accountability, arguing that it adds a layer of bureaucracy. There is truth in this argument, but the reality is that accountability is coming whether academic leaders like it or not.

An important advantage that flows from creation of a state compact and individual institutional agreements is greater public understanding of higher education's roles and responsibilities as well as acknowledgment of the flaws in higher education's performance and the expectations that must be met. As noted in Chapter Five, the public is unclear about these issues. There is, however, rising public concern. This is the time for higher education to address these concerns and build a new level of understanding and support.

The trade-off between autonomy and accountability leaves all parties feeling that they get something out of the deal. Academic leaders get autonomy, and political leaders gain leverage for reinforcing public needs. Most important, this new relationship creates the conditions for a higher education system that is flexible, entrepreneurial, customized, accountable, and able to meet the state's needs.

Chapter Eight

Who Is Responsible for Student Learning?

The issue is not one of either institutional responsibility or student responsibility; it is the need for both.

If higher education is to meet the public need for graduates with the skills, knowledge, and capacity to create the progress that society needs, a fundamental change must take place. Colleges and universities must take responsibility for student learning.

Currently colleges and universities operate on the assumption that, although they furnish classes and instructors, libraries and books, computers and an Internet infrastructure, the student has the responsibility to turn opportunity into learning. For successful learning, the student must take responsibility, but so must the institution. For learning to be successful for the greatest number of students, there must be clear learning goals, not just with regard to content but as to the intellectual skills and capacities to be achieved.

Three examples make plain the willingness of institutions to provide an array of learning opportunities but leave the students with the responsibility as to whether learning actually reaches the quality that society now demands:

1. Almost never do institutions set out a clear statement of what the student is expected to learn in terms of knowledge, intellectual skills, competencies, and attitudes in order to become a well-educated graduate—a statement that could and should serve as a guide to students, faculty, administration, staff, and every other party to the learning process.

2. Despite the centrality of learning to the mission of every college and university, these institutions (with a small number of notable exceptions) do not know and do not try to find out how much learning is taking place. Instead, they accept as assurance of learning the completion of a required number of courses—despite extensive evidence that students can, and regularly do, pass courses without mastering the skills and knowledge that will be required.

3. In those cases where the instructor of a course, the faculty of a program, or the leadership of an entire institution decides to align the curriculum and the mode of teaching with the learning goals, so as to assess actual learning and embark on an effort to alter the mode of teaching and learning to improve results, the gains are dramatic.

We are, in other words, falling well short of what society needs in terms of educated graduates, despite the growing body of research that shows we can improve significantly if we so choose. Even if higher education were addressing each of these issues, there is a further demand to be met: the powerful changes under way in society demand new learning goals, new intellectual skills, new knowledge.

The issue is not one of either institutional responsibility or student responsibility; it is the need for both. The more institutions accept their responsibility, the more students will. Where institutions are clear as to the expected learning outcomes, where there are meaningful assessments of student learning, and where these assessments guide continuous efforts to improve the quality of learning, the student's sense of responsibility for truly mastering learning soars. Instead, in most settings there is an unspoken, comfortable conspiracy between faculty and students not to bother each other too much; mediocrity reigns.

The goal for each program and each institution surely should be far higher. It should, at the very least, include development of an approach to learning that is so interesting and satisfying that almost all students complete their program of study. Currently, only half of students do. But being intellectually challenging and interesting enough to excite students is only part of the task. In the twenty-first century, citizens need greater (and different) skills and capacities than ever before. Today, in our rhetoric if not our practice, it is widely recognized that more than content—that is, knowledge of subject—is needed. Business and academic leaders alike agree on the need for the ability to communicate effectively, think critically, and solve problems. Even mastering these specific abilities is becoming more demanding. Thinking critically in today's technology-infused society requires more effective emphasis on quantitative reasoning.

Beyond these widely discussed (though not widely achieved) skills, the new society needs more profound ethical awareness and the capacity for independent, moral judgment; the capacity to take initiative; the capacity for creativity; the ability to work with others; global awareness and multicultural respect; and, perhaps most important, civic responsibility and efficacy.[1]

The ultimate goal should be creation in each academic setting of a learning-centered climate that maximizes learning and meets the new and higher standards that society now needs.

What Does a Learning-Centered Institution Look Like?

Each academic year, faculty members design (or redesign) courses and begin teaching. Students select among the array of offerings and start listening to lectures, taking notes, and reading books. Research over many decades has shown that this traditional process does create an intellectual growth for most college-level students significantly greater than what takes place with individuals of comparable ability who do not participate in a college experience. It does not, however, take advantage of several decades of new research about how students learn or new approaches to pedagogy that increase learning significantly. It does not, in other words, come close to maximizing the quality of learning either in terms of how much and how deeply students learn or how enthusiastic and committed students become regarding the process of learning.

The failure to take advantage of our growing knowledge of how to improve learning represents what Russell Edgerton describes as the "lost opportunity" of the last two decades. Edgerton describes what will be needed for a twenty-first-century education:

> The curtain has risen on the 21st century. A 20th century education, rooted in the industrial-era view of teaching as telling, is no longer adequate to prepare undergraduates for the challenges ahead.

Three developments have occurred, largely in the last thirty years, that have transformed both what undergraduates need to learn and how this learning can best be facilitated. First, the character of American society has changed, raising the qualifications for performing numerous roles. Second, dramatic advances have taken place in our knowledge about how people learn, how this learning can best be facilitated, and the organizational contexts that are most effective in supporting this learning. Third, new technologies have been developed that provide new ways to leverage student and faculty effort. A 21st century education is an education that takes these developments to heart [Edgerton, 2003a].

Typically the further one moves on the spectrum away from the supposed best students—those who easily fit the typical student mold or those who were raised with educational advantages—and toward those with different learning styles or those who have enjoyed less educational advantages—the "lost opportunity" becomes more dramatic. In part this reflects the far greater resources, variety of learning experiences, and support structures that are devoted to the best students. In part this reflects the ability of the best students to benefit from a traditional teaching style, even though it is largely focused on lectures and abstract discussion. The exciting prospect is that, if advantage is taken of all that is already known and proven in exemplary settings, the quality and amount of learning can be greatly increased for all students but particularly for the least advantaged.

Building on the work of Arthur Chickering and Zelda Gamson, Kay McClenney has outlined six characteristics of a learning focused institution: "clearly defined outcomes for student learning; student participation in a diverse array of engaging learning experiences that are aligned with expected outcomes and designed in accord with good educational practice; systematic assessment and documentation of student learning; emphasis on student learning in processes for recruitment, hiring, orientation, deployment, evaluation, and development of personnel; priority given to improvement of student learning in institutional planning and resource allocation; and focus on learning consistently reflected in leadership, key institutional documents and policies, and action to build a culture of evidence" (McClenney, 2003, pp. 6–8). These six characteristics exemplify an institution that is taking responsibility for creating a climate where students choose to persist in their studies and succeed academically.

1. *"Clearly defined outcomes for student learning."* Although colleges and universities often assume that there is, somewhere, an understanding as to what their students should learn by graduation day, at almost all institutions it is in fact only a vague assumption. When pressed, the institutions cannot produce a clear, explicit, and compelling definition of learning goals (the knowledge, intellectual skills, competencies, and attitudes that each student is expected to gain). Each student should know what the overall learning goals are and what he or she is expected to gain. Each faculty member should know what the overall learning goals are and what his or her course is intended to provide toward those goals. Each faculty member should understand and be committed to the overall goals so as to ensure that teaching and counseling focus on helping students reach those goals.

2. *"Student participation in a diverse array of learning experiences."* The majority of teaching uses the lecture mode; some studies estimate up to 85 percent of class time is devoted to lecture. Skilled lectures can accomplish much, but a growing body of research has made plain that it is the least effective approach when the goal is deeper understanding, the ability to apply knowledge gained, the capacity to think critically, and remembrance over a long time. Generally, researchers conclude that students gain more as the teaching mode moves from lecture to class discussion, to learning activities that involve active participation (such as a simulation exercise or a team project), and to learning by teaching others. Each mode has its advantages; using several modes helps. Selection of the appropriate mode needs to be aligned with the desired learning outcomes. But a growing array of research has made one point clear: when students are actively involved in the learning process rather than sitting passively and listening, they are more likely to move beyond memorization to deeper understanding (National Research Council, 2000; Gardiner, 1998; Brent, 1996).

3. *"Systematic assessment and documentation of student learning."* Without this, there is no way for the student, faculty, institution, or society to determine whether learning is meeting the expected goals and no way for the student, faculty, and institution to improve. Assessment, to serve these purposes, cannot be simplistic. To be practiced every day, it cannot be cumbersome. A growing array of institutions have put in place their own systems of assessment, demonstrating both that it can be done in a practical way and that significant learning improvement results. The Council for Aid to Education is now working with a test group of sixty institutions to refine a computer-based assessment system. This has the advantage of greater sophistication coupled with lower cost. It also encompasses the convenience of Internet use to allow assessment at multiple sites.

4. *"Emphasis on student learning in the recruitment, orientation, deployment, evaluation, and reward of faculty and administrators."* What is surprising is not that there are flaws showing up regularly in the quality of student learning. It is amazing that the teaching process works as well as it does, given that almost never are the results measured and given that faculty who take the time and trouble to establish effective modes are not rewarded—and in real terms are often penalized.

5. *"Institutional and individual reflection about learning outcomes leading to action aimed at improvement."* It is here that formative assessments become critical. To chart student and institution progress, assessments are required.

6. *"Focus on learning consistently reflected in key institutional documents, policies, collegial effort, and leadership behavior."* Learning goals should be articulated clearly in terms of the expectations not just of students (for example, in terms of graduation requirements) but for faculty and staff and expectations for the entire institution.

Assessment of learning outcomes is not a simple process. But there are two things to bear in mind. First, there are many examples of institutions that have successfully developed meaningful ways of measuring and reporting on student learning. It can be done. Second, experts have amassed a great deal of evidence about what works, how to get started, and pitfalls to avoid. The process exists. One need not start from scratch. Again, it can be done.

Assessment experts Catherine Palomba and Trudy Banta, for example, have described the characteristics essential for useful assessment, characteristics that can be used as guidelines when developing a system for an institution (Palomba and Banta, 1999, p. 16):

- Asks important questions
- Reflects institutional mission
- Reflects programmatic goals and objectives of learning
- Contains a thoughtful approach to assessment planning
- Is linked to decision making about the curriculum
- Is linked to processes such as planning and budgeting
- Encourages involvement of individuals from on and off campus
- Contains relevant assessment techniques
- Includes direct evidence of learning
- Reflects what is known about how students learn
- Shares information with multiple audiences
- Leads to reflection and action by faculty, staff, and students
- Allows for continuity, flexibility, and improvement in assessment

Creating an Organizational Culture of Quality Learning

If an institution is to change and become learner centered, if it intends to implement the changes noted above, tinkering at the edges won't do it. Several basic shifts in the organizational culture are essential.

Moving from Rhetoric to a Focus on Actual Performance

No college or university sets out to teach poorly. If one listens to the institutional rhetoric or reads the catalog, one finds that teaching is the most important task, a special and revered responsibility. In practice, rhetoric and reality part company.

The National Center for Postsecondary Improvement conducted extensive interviews with 378 faculty members. They were asked questions about productivity and quality. Here are two typical responses:

> Educational quality is not something that we discuss explicitly. We assume that each person is trying to keep up with the materials in all the various areas that they teach in. Our faculty work reasonably hard and want to stay current, so we don't really have a concern about quality [Massy, 2003, p. 152].

> Educational quality does not come up as an issue in the department because it is closely aligned with course content and we generally don't discuss course content. Everyone here is doing a good job [Massy, 2003, p. 152].

As these quotes indicate, faculty tend to equate quality in teaching with skilled coverage of the content of their discipline. The course assessments—examinations and term papers—also focus on content. Missing is an emphasis on more profound learning goals.

Faculty generally do not think about their course design or about more effective ways of engaging students in the teaching and learning process. As William Massy states, "It's the pressure to conduct research that inhibits faculty intellectual activity; otherwise it would be probably occurring spontaneously" (Massy, 2003, p. 160).

Massy points to Hong Kong, the United Kingdom, Sweden, Denmark, Australia, and Singapore as countries that are gaining ground because they are thinking and working hard on educational quality issues: "I think with another generation of our standing pat people won't be calling the U.S. system the best in the world anymore" (Massy, 2003, p. 161). In some respects, this is already happening.

Massy suggests that institutions should embark on a kind of academic audit in pursuit of "quality work," outlining seven education quality principles that help institutions develop a culture of quality:

1. Define education quality in terms of outcomes
2. Focus on the process of teaching, learning, and student assessment
3. Strive for coherence in curriculum, educational process, and assessment
4. Work collaboratively to achieve mutual involvement and support
5. Base decisions on facts wherever possible
6. Identify and learn from best practices
7. Make continuous improvements a top priority [Massy, 2003, p. 186]

Moving from Denial to Acceptance of Responsibility

From time immemorial, institutions have put the lion's share of the responsibility for learning on the student; if the student has not learned it, it is because he or she has not studied hard enough, has not thought hard enough, has not wanted to learn, or is not prepared well enough.[2] The tendency is to assume that any problems or disappointments are the fault of the student. If a student drops out, for example, the usual response—if the departure is even noticed—is, "We probably shouldn't have admitted that student in the first place." Randy Swing states, "Institutions want to blame students for not studying more, or blame high schools for not sending better-prepared students" (Shapera, 2002, p. 16).

If there were one, or just a few, students dropping out or failing to gain an adequate education, if there were no colleges or universities able to succeed with such students, perhaps this attitude would make sense. It is not, unfortunately, a few students for whom the experience is less than successful. A majority of students drop out; many return but drop out again.[3]

Yet there are institutions that have achieved remarkable success educating students who arrive academically deficient. Xavier University in New Orleans and the University of Texas at El Paso, to mention two examples, have educated students whose backgrounds and educational experiences would lead other institutions to deem them underprepared and too much work to educate successfully. Among others of their type, the Community College of Denver and Valencia Community College achieve higher success rates (in terms of graduation or transfer) than institutions with comparable students (CCSSE, 2003; Florida Department of Education, 2002). The key in each case is acceptance of responsibility, including a determined effort to collect the data necessary and use them to improve performance.

Moving from a Focus on Prestige to a Focus on Learning

There has been for centuries an assumption that the prestige of the college or university equates to the quality of learning enjoyed by its students. Recently there has been growing realization within the higher education community and among policy makers that the current indicators used as surrogates for quality (magazine rankings, reputation, endowment, selectivity of students, library holdings, and so on) tell little, if anything, about the actual quality of learning taking place at an institution.[4] Ernest Pascarella and Patrick Terenzini have shown through a review of educational research on teaching and learning that "there is little consistent evidence to indicate that college selectivity, prestige, or educational resources have any important net impact on students in such areas as learning, cognitive and intellectual development" (Pascarella and Terenzini, 1998, p. 592). Yet when the new rankings from *U.S. News & World Report* (which are based on measures of selectivity and prestige) are published, everyone clamors to see where their institutions and peer institutions are ranked.[5] This is usually followed by a push to capitalize on the rankings or to adjust the factors that improve the ranking. Meanwhile, those institutions that do not do well—and even many that do—continue to argue that the rankings are badly flawed. It is, to say the least, irrational.

More important, higher education needs to move beyond the assumption that prestige equals quality. The notion that because one goes to an elite college or university one receives an excellent education is misleading. There are two clear advantages to going to an elite college or university. First, students learn as much from each other as from faculty, so it is helpful to associate with bright, well-connected students who themselves expect to succeed and whom the institution expects to succeed. Also, elite institutions have extensive facilities for learning—libraries, technology, and so on—and alumni networks that help career development.

Why, then, is there so much resistance from the best to find out the reality of how much their students are learning? Peter Ewell notes that "Harvard and Williams wouldn't look bad on NSSE [National Survey of Student Engagement] but a lot of schools might look as good without having their reputation" (Shapera, 2002, p. 6).

One piece that bolsters an institution's ranking, and ultimately prestige, is the misleading use of SAT, GRE, and LSAT scores. Despite popular assumptions, high scores do not guarantee a student's ability to learn or to become an active, engaged member of the campus or, after graduation, of the larger community. Further, these test scores do not predict future success in the student's chosen career, which is, after all, the basis on which the admissions office is purportedly attempting to make selections (Perez, 2002). Although institutions rely upon these scores as an important determinant for admissions, high scores do not tell us anything about the quality of learning or intellectual discourse taking place at an institution that high-scoring students are attending. Standardized tests are being used to help make decisions that are based on information the tests are not capable of providing. The principal thing these tests are good for is driving up (or down) a university's prestige. The simple truth is that we do not know which institutions provide the so-called best education in terms of value added.

New Pressures for Change

The tradition of simply assuming that a high level of learning takes place in college courses rather than attempting to measure any results has a long history, dating back in this country to 1636. It is supported by well-rehearsed rhetoric. Seldom has it been challenged, except by researchers troubled by specific failures to produce the needed learning results. When it has been, the challenge is largely ignored. Today, new pressures are pushing higher education toward raising, in a serious and sustained way, the question of what students are actually learning.

The Market

As higher education becomes more market oriented and as competition intensifies, there is a natural demand for more information about who is learning what. Information tends to drive markets; in this sense, higher education is no different. For example, several of the best-known, for-profit universities, most notably but not only the University of Phoenix, have recognized the need to create a better reputation for quality and have developed and promoted their use of extensive systems of assessment. They have used the availability of student learning outcomes for all of their courses as an argument supporting application to the various states for the right to give degrees, comparing the availability of their information to the lack of information about learner outcomes at traditional universities or colleges. Their presence has often forced traditional institutions to begin collecting data themselves.

The Political Environment

Increasingly, policy makers at the state and federal levels are concerned with higher education's unwillingness to address accountability, the business community is calling for better-educated graduates, and the public is seeking information that would be helpful in weighing options in higher education (U.S. House Committee on Education and the Workforce and U.S. House Subcommittee on 21st Century Competitiveness, 2003).

Policy makers' frustration with the growing call for more autonomy by academic leaders was loud and clear in a series of focus groups that the Futures Project held in the 2001–2002 academic year. State legislators made it plain that academic leaders would not receive more autonomy without increased accountability. They called for assessments of learning. "We have a good system of higher education," said one legislator, "but we don't know what we want from it. What I want is a clearly articulated plan where we can define the outputs and then measure how we are doing. At that point we can incentivize the universities for performance." "I like the idea of an assessment culture," said another (Immerwahr, 2002, p. 16).

Whether higher education leaders want to acknowledge it or not, state and federal policy makers are intent on demanding more explicit measures of performance from higher education in return for greater operational autonomy. In a recent report released by a joint congressional committee, two of the five recommendations were to "improve market information and public accounting" and "deregulate higher education"(U.S. House Committee on Education and the Workforce and U.S. House Subcommittee on 21st Century Competitiveness, 2003).

If higher education leaders do not take notice and begin to answer the public's and policy makers' questions, they could find themselves in a position similar to elementary and secondary education, where policy makers have firmly defined the modes of setting standards and assessing performance.

Illinois offers an interesting example of what can happen when state leaders and academic leaders do work together to create an environment that is committed to "determining what students know and are able to do as a result of completing a unique program of study" (Performance Indicator Advisory Committee, 2002,

p. 1). The goal is to furnish meaningful evidence of the quality of student learning while also providing feedback to improve the quality assurance process and accountability. To this end, on February 4, 2003, the Illinois Board of Higher Education approved mandatory assessments, designed by the institutions, at the end of the sophomore and senior years. The assessments are not high stakes and can take the form of portfolios, tests, lab work, internship, or some combination. The main thrust is to assess the level to which students are learning and, where necessary, improve upon the depth of learning taking place.

Illinois also serves as a reminder that the question is not, "Are students learning?" The right question is, "Are they learning as much as they should be, could be, and need to be, and are they learning the right skills and knowledge?" Given the demands of individual states for the skills to meet the needs of their economy and the skills needed for full participation in society, a broader set of learning goals is required.[6]

The state of Florida, for example, is considering imposing high-stakes assessments that would hold public institutions accountable for what students learn—or more accurately, do not learn—during their enrollment. Students will be asked to take an examination before entering postsecondary education and another before graduating. The state is looking to measure value added. Governor Jeb Bush wants to "dramatically and fundamentally change how we have funded higher education . . . he [Governor Bush] wants proof for a return on investment." Under the proposed plan, a "significant portion of each university's funding" would be tied to the test results ("College FCAT? . . . ," 2003). The colleges and universities that make up Florida's public system have a big stake in taking the lead in creating assessments in which they believe.

Policies to Improve the Quality of Learning

The goal of state policy should be to generate the motivation for institutions to create a campus culture that focuses on defining, measuring, and improving learning—that is, creation of a learner-centered environment. Policy should not inadvertently throw up roadblocks or inhibit the rise of a culture of quality. For colleges or universities to take advantage of what we already know works, a commitment from faculty, administrators, and students is critical to move teaching and learning to the center of the institution where all share in the responsibility for student learning. The role of policy is to help create that sense of shared responsibility for learning; it is not an easy task and not one that lends itself to traditional forms of state regulation.

The academic community has an important stake in helping policy makers create appropriate and effective modes of accountability. Higher education leaders have frequently argued that the assessments taking place in elementary and secondary education at the direct instigation of state policy makers are too dependent on simplistic testing and do not measure the real goals of education (critical thinking, the ability to apply concepts to real-life problems, and so on). If academic leaders do not take the lead in creating meaningful assessments—assessments that capture the fundamental intellectual skills, knowledge, capacities, and attitudes that are essential to society—as well as other measures of accountability, policy makers will impose them upon the institutions, much as states have done in elementary and secondary education and as has been inherent in the federal legislation of No Child Left Behind, with the ever-present danger of new policies creating a counterproductive bureaucracy.

Asking the Right Questions

One key role for policy leaders is to ask the right questions of their education system and its leaders. State policy makers and institutional leaders might begin by asking some questions that help frame the issue:

- What knowledge do we expect students to acquire to be productive and effective in the workforce and as citizens? What does it mean to say students are prepared for successful participation in the economy and society?
- What skills and knowledge are necessary for all students regardless of major?
- What knowledge and skills do our students currently have when they leave college?
- Which teaching methods are used, and are they producing successful learner outcomes for all students?

- What role can technology play in improving teaching and learning? What role can it play in assessing learning?
- What assessment measures should be used to demonstrate mastery of agreed-upon academic goals and knowledge levels?
- What are the priorities and appropriate balance of the faculty role at each institution among research, teaching, advising, and service?
- Which institutions are succeeding in achieving high levels of learning? Which state policies have helped, and which have hindered?

Adopting Policies to Encourage Responsibility for Learning

Once a thoughtful and meaningful discussion begins, states and institutions can move on to adopting policies and practices that ensure students are gaining knowledge and learning the skills that are fundamental to success in today's world. State legislators can opt for a number of methods, ranging from incentives to mandates, that move institutions toward developing a culture that values, supports, promotes, and assesses student learning and makes public the results. The Futures Project advocates that state policy leaders not attempt to implement a cookie-cutter approach but rather work as closely as they can with academic leaders to develop policies that reflect diverse institutional missions and student bodies. Academic leaders need to come to the table willing to admit their institution's flaws and be ready to act as part of the solution.

In general, the Futures Project believes the most effective avenue for state policy is a focus on (1) creating effective modes of assessing student learning and (2) public reporting of the results. There are several policy levers for doing so.

The first is mandatory (or financially encouraged) participation in the National Survey of Student Engagement (NSSE) or Community College Survey of Student Engagement (CCSSE) and public reporting of results. NSSE measures the degree to which students are engaged with their institution, using five benchmarks: level of academic challenge, active and collaborative learning, student-faculty interaction, enriching educational experiences, and supportive campus environment. CCSSE's organization is slightly different, focusing on the benchmarks of active and collaborative learning, student effort, academic challenge, student interaction with faculty, and support for learners. The survey results help institutions understand how effectively they contribute to student learning by measuring the level to which students are engaged with the institution, the academic process, the faculty, and with other students. The results aid in improving all campus offerings and activities. Although NSSE and CCSSE do not measure student learning directly, prospective students and their parents are given better information about how seriously the institution focuses on the learning experience. Of particular importance is attention to engaging low-income students as a means to counter their low rates of graduation and attainment. In 2003, 437 four-year colleges and universities participated in the national survey; roughly 348,000 freshmen and seniors were sampled for NSSE (National Survey of Student Engagement, 2003). For CCSSE, more than 65,300 community college students were sampled from the ninety-three participating community colleges in 2003 (CCSSE, 2003).

Given the success of NSSE and CCSSE to date, the Futures Project suggests creating a matching National Survey of Faculty Engagement that uses comparable techniques to measure and report on faculty engagement in the learning process.

The second policy lever is requiring or encouraging institutionally developed assessments of learning and public reporting of assessment results. As measures for assessing learning are developed, transparency is critical so that prospective students, parents, the business community, and the public will know what type of education the student is given and what they can expect their tuition and tax dollars to support. One simple example is the federal government's requirement that colleges and universities make public the graduation rate of athletes. Public reporting of the results helps to put pressure on colleges and universities to continuously improve.

Third is making available a system of public information about learning. The goal should be to produce a variety of assessments that, taken together, create an incentive for improving institutional performance in a far better way than a single simplistic institutional ranking. The swissUp system is an example of a useful way to make information available to the public. SwissUp offers an interactive Website (http://www.swissup.com) that allows the user to rank the universities of Switzerland by discipline according to each user's criteria: "It is designed for students and prospective students seeking comparative and differentiated information on education offerings in Switzerland." SwissUp also ranks these universities in multiple ways by the criteria it deems most important: student satisfaction, attractiveness, staff-to-student ratio, duration of studies, and efficiency. The developers recognize that no one ranking system in itself is comprehensive and that quality is very difficult to interpret: "Based on selected indicators, it [swissUp] allows a comparison of education streams within universities. The ranking does not allow designation of 'the best university in Switzerland.' Nor does it allow one to say which is 'the best training' in a specific field. For a set stream and a set indicator, the ranking permits a comparison of universities according to the selected indicator and its interpretation" ("The swissUp Ranking," 2001).

Fourth is establishing competitive grants for teaching. Another basic approach that governments can use is to create a competitive grant program that supports improvements in pedagogy. There are two broad purposes that the Futures Project believes can be met by a carefully structured grant program. The first is to encourage proven modes of learning such as problem-based learning, multi-discipline learning, service learning, internships, and collaborative learning. The second is to encourage effective and efficient use of technology for improving learning as well as for cost-effective course delivery. These two approaches are, of course, potentially interactive.

In addition to fostering encouragement and the means for introducing more effective modes of teaching, competitive grants have the great benefit of rebalancing the faculty reward system. The goal is not to reduce the incentive for faculty to do high-quality research and scholarship but to create an equally powerful incentive to do effective teaching. (See Chapter Ten for a detailed description of a competitive grant concept.)

The fifth policy lever is improving accreditation. The government can exert influence on accrediting agencies, encouraging a heightened level of self-regulation that includes assessment of learner outcomes. Several regional accrediting agencies have already begun emphasizing the need for clear, public evidence of learning, most notably the Western Association of Schools and Colleges and the Southern Association of Colleges and Schools. The Council for Higher Education Accreditation, the umbrella body for accrediting agencies, has also incorporated the drive for learner outcomes into its mission. The principal difficulty is that well-established universities and colleges simply do not fear that they will lose their accreditation. As a result, the principal leverage is with new or marginal institutions. A possible corrective would be to make the accrediting team's report public so that the desire to put forward the best possible face in a competitive world would serve as an incentive to improve performance and respond to criticism. As recent developments in several countries—United Kingdom, Hong Kong, and Sweden, for example—have demonstrated, more powerful and effective forms of academic auditing (a more involved step than the American approach of accrediting) can be developed that produce a substantially greater focus on the quality of learning (Massy, 2003).

The government does have the ability to influence accreditors. The accreditors are independent agencies answerable to universities and colleges, but they depend in many ways on government for their power. For example, in a recent exercise of that power, several years ago the federal government insisted that public members be appointed to the agency boards.

The sixth lever is creating a higher education NAEP. The National Assessment of Education Progress (NAEP) serves a valuable function for elementary and secondary education: it allows states to see how their students who have taken state assessments compare to students in other states. If colleges and universities are to create their own assessments, a national mode of comparison would be critical.

Two problems with a higher education NAEP are obvious. First, the NAEP exams are voluntary. Getting college students to volunteer to take the exams is far harder than getting third graders to do so. Second, convincing universities and colleges to allow information about their students' performance to be made public takes work. To make this policy practical requires some hard effort and new ideas.

Taking Responsibility

The U.S. higher education system is still, in many ways, the best in the world. That does not mean there is no room for improvement. The goal must be to create a system that elevates teaching and learning to a high level, to at least the same status as research and publishing. The system must ensure that a degree or certificate means the student is not only more knowledgeable than when he or she entered higher education but can also think critically, apply concepts across disciplines to solve complex problems, work effectively with others, and continue to learn how to learn. Until institutions accept their share of responsibility for student learning, this will not happen. Policy makers at the federal and state levels are demanding assurance of learning, supported by employers and, increasingly, the public. Unless institutions want to be burdened by high-stakes mandates, they need to come out from behind their rhetoric and face reality.

Chapter Nine

Expanding Access and Success

After a long history of improving social mobility through ever greater access to higher education, major flaws have emerged that threaten this great American tradition.

There is today widespread agreement throughout society that the economy demands more skilled and knowledgeable workers. Blue-collar jobs are shrinking in number, while jobs requiring a college education are growing. The change in the workforce is not the only impetus for a higher level of education. Participation in the community and in the political system also requires improved education. The complexities of civic life, like those of the economy, demand more knowledge and skills. For America to prosper and thrive, its citizens—all of them—need to be engaged. A college education today is as significant as gaining a high school diploma was in the 1950s; it is now the pathway to social mobility, personal prosperity, and civic engagement.

Opportunity is at the heart of the social contract America has made with its citizens. For this to be meaningful, a greater share of the population—particularly students from low-income families and students of color—need to enter and successfully exit the doors of America's colleges and universities. After a long history of improving social mobility through ever greater access to higher education, major flaws have emerged that threaten this great American tradition. While there is still widespread discussion among policy makers, academic leaders, and the public about the need for further gains in access to higher education, recent shifts in state and federal policy are actually moving in the opposite direction. Coupled with the growing reliance on market forces to structure higher education, and changes in institutional strategies, these changes are slowing and in some cases reversing the growth in access. Beyond this, recent studies have made plain a major flaw. For a strikingly large share of students, particularly low-income students of color, access has led to disappointment, dropping out, and failure to gain the needed education and degree. Access, it is now clear, is not enough.

The failure to perform against the promise of access is disturbing not only because of its obvious importance but also because the knowledge of how higher education can succeed at this task is at hand. A number of programs have demonstrated conclusively that universities and colleges can educate an ever-expanding share of the population, including low-income students, successfully and without sacrificing quality or the rigor of the curriculum.

The Demands of the New Workforce

The new economy demands a highly skilled and knowledgeable workforce. Over the last forty years or so, the demand for a college degree has increased dramatically for better jobs. For example, in 1959, only 20 percent of "prime" jobs required at least some form of postsecondary education; in 1997, the number of these jobs increased to 56 percent (Judy and D'Amico, 1998, p. 6). Since 1973, the portion of clerical workers with some form of postsecondary education rose from 25 percent to 54 percent; even the portion of blue-collar workers with college experience increased, rising 11 percentage points from 17 to 28 percent (Carnevale and Fry, 2003).

Political, business, and academic leaders and increasingly the public now see that for future prosperity this country needs more citizens with the high ability and skills that jobs now require. Even employers who once regularly hired high school graduates, such as municipal police departments, increasingly require applicants to have a college diploma.[1] The Council on Competitiveness expects the number of jobs requiring technical skills to grow by 51 percent by 2008. Another estimation is that by 2008, of the twenty million "new jobs" that will be generated, fourteen million are going to require some form of postsecondary education (Carnevale and Fry, 2003).

In addition to serving as the ticket of admission to these job opportunities, a degree opens the door to further possibilities. Because the American workforce is changing so rapidly, more and more individuals find it to their advantage to return to higher education in some form (to a campus program, online instruction, or corporate university) to develop new skills and often a required certification. Those without a degree, or at least some successful higher education experience, are too often frozen out of these opportunities.

The Even Greater Demand: Social Mobility

What is at stake in the admission to higher education of low-income students and students of color is far more than a diverse campus, even more than having citizens with the skills needed for the workforce. What is at stake is the fundamental concept of our democracy—a concept based on widespread civic participation and social mobility. Today, social mobility is increasingly dependent on gaining a college education. For America to function as a fair and open society, an ever larger share of its citizens must continue education through to completion of a college degree.

For this to happen, academic leaders and policy makers now have to focus their attention and invest their energy and resources on this issue. The state and the institutions need to see that *all* students who enter the doors of higher education exit with a degree in hand, not only because it is the right thing to do but for other reasons as well. Those with a degree in hand have higher income, better health, and greater civic engagement than those with just some college. When students succeed, taxpayers get more from their investment.

For higher education to serve society and constitute an avenue to social mobility, access must lead to achievement. This entails the expectation that essentially all students, given an effective program, can become astute learners. There already exist successful outreach and retention programs, proving that this can be done. But these exemplar programs must change from being an anomaly, from being isolated programs serving a limited number of students, and move into the mainstream of higher education.

Income

According to a study done by the Commission on National Investment in Higher Education, "the single most important factor in determining level of income is level of education" (Council for Aid to Education, 1997). This can be seen by comparing level of education to change in income. The wages of men with a college education kept pace with inflation from 1976 to 1995; the wages of men with some college dropped 14 percent, those with only a high school education dropped 18 percent, and earnings of high school dropouts decreased by 25 percent (Council for Aid to Education, 1997).[2]

The small but growing black and Hispanic middle class makes plain both the importance of a college education in terms of income level and how much more needs to be done. Despite the gains that have been made by blacks and Hispanics in socioeconomic status (one indicator of social mobility), a large gap remains. Education is essential to any effort to close this gap and create a meaningful opportunity for full participation in society. Twenty-six percent of all whites age twenty-five and over have graduated from college, but only 16.5 percent of African Americans and 10.6 percent of Hispanics (Harvey, 2002).[3] When looking at new worth by race, one can see that the divide continues to grow. In 1995, black household net worth was $7,400, Hispanic household net worth was $5,000, and white household net worth was an astounding $61,000 by comparison (Phillips, 2002, p. 136).

If college admissions and completion continue as they are today with academic success far more likely to be gained by wealthier, white students, society will further stratify. Those who have access to the growing number of skilled jobs will remain prosperous and thrive; those who are underprepared will have access only to shrinking low-skilled jobs and remain trapped, increasingly cut off from opportunity.

Civic Engagement

There are as well difficult-to-quantify but important social benefits of a college education, such as civic engagement, life of the mind, and better health. Research has shown that college graduates vote, work on political campaigns, and volunteer at higher rates than those with a high school diploma or less. Colleges and universities, recognizing the importance of these issues to the national life, have sought to increase student interest in community service and strengthen their institutional commitment to working closely with the surrounding communities. Since its founding in 1985, membership in Campus Compact, a national association of college presidents working to promote civic participation and community service on college campuses, has grown to include over 900 institutions. Record numbers of freshmen now volunteer.[4] A survey conducted for the Panetta Institute found that 73 percent of college students had recently done volunteer work, with 41 percent having volunteered on at least ten occasions (Clymer, 2000). A college education also results in greater political participation. According to the Committee for the Study of the American Electorate, in the 1996 election:

- Forty-nine percent of eighteen- to twenty-four-year-olds with four years of college voted.
- Thirty-nine percent of students in that age group with one to three years of college voted.
- Twenty-two percent of high school graduates aged eighteen- to twenty-four voted. (Clymer, 2000)

Health

A strong correlation among income, education level, and health has also been observed. Within specific income ranges, people with a higher level of education self-reported being in better health than those with a lower level of education. The percentage of the population over twenty-five in 1997 who reported being in excellent or very good health rose with the level of education across all income ranges:

- Less than high school: 38.7 percent
- High school diploma or equivalent: 57.8 percent
- Some college: 67.6 percent
- Bachelor's degree or higher: 79.7 percent (U.S. Department of Education, 2002)

The Unfinished Problem of Access: Attainment

The late 1960s brought a renegotiation of America's social contract. The previous century had seen a long, slow history of expansion of access. The 1960s saw a marked acceleration of this trend. The process of dismantling racial segregation as well as gender and class discrimination was aided by opening the doors of higher education to a broader spectrum of students. Political and academic leaders focused their attention on increasing access to those who previously had been both formally and informally barred.

However, as political and public support for increased access grew, and as the number gaining admission rose, a basic disconnect developed: access was increasing, but academic attainment and degree completion were lagging badly. Today, three and a half decades later, even though the attention focused on access needs to continue, it must now include a focus on attainment. Access means little without attainment. There is a growing realization that opportunity is sharply limited when students begin but do not complete a degree.

Completion rates for low-income students and students of color are abysmal. Among those students from the least advantaged backgrounds, the results are far worse. Of black students who gain access, 29 percent drop out in their first year (U.S. Department of Education, 2000); for Hispanic students, the figure is 31 percent. Only "one in 10 Hispanics graduates from a four year college or university" ("Hispanic Students Bring New Challenges," 2003).

Tom Mortenson, a higher education policy analyst, found that "by age 24 a person whose family income falls in the top quartile is ten times more likely to have received a bachelor's degree than is another person whose family income falls in the bottom quartile" (Mortenson, 1995, p. 1). What is most startling about this is that, over the last two decades, the difference has worsened. In 1979, "before the redistribution of higher education opportunity began, the difference was four times" (Mortenson, 1995, p. 1).

So, although the opening of access has been a truly stunning achievement, a massive problem remains: access to what? As a college education becomes ever more essential for success, with the opening of each new academic year in September and with the closing graduation marches every May, America becomes more segregated along class and color lines.

Mobility Deferred

The impact of this failure of ensuring that access leads to attainment has been profound on this country's social structure. For social mobility to be real in the twenty-first century, more students from low-income and minority backgrounds must gain access to higher education. Those who do gain access need to complete their program and gain a degree. For too many Americans, the dream of social mobility is simply that—a dream.

The United States, the wealthiest of nations, has become the country in the developed world with the most unequal distribution of income. Every year that goes by, income disparity grows. According to the Congressional Budget Office, between 1979 and 2000, the wealthiest 1 percent of Americans' average after tax-income increased by 201 percent—$576,000. During the same period, the income of the poorest fifth of the population showed an increase of just 9 percent, $1,100. Figures for a slightly earlier period, 1977–1994, reveal an actual decline in after-tax income. The lowest quintile experienced a 16 percent loss in after-tax income, and the second lowest quintile after-tax income declined 8 percent (Phillips, 2002). In 1999, the median household income for a high school graduate was $42,995, for an associate degree holder it was $56,602, and for someone with a bachelor's degree it was $76,059 (Mortenson, 2002). Furthermore, between 1973 and 1999, the median family income for a high school graduate decreased by 13.1 percent, while for someone with four years of college it increased by 9.9 percent (Mortenson, 2002).

The median household income of people of color is still far behind that of whites. In 2000, at $30,439, black median household income was still at least $15,000 below the median household income of non-Hispanic whites ($45,904). Similarly, Hispanic median household income, at $33,447, remained far behind that of non-Hispanic whites (Center on Budget and Policy Priorities, 2001a). Providing students of color with access and ensuring their degree completion is the best way—arguably the only way—to decrease this disparity, especially when one takes into account the growing demands of the new economy.

As *New York Times* writer Edmund Andrews pointed out, "People who start out in poor families move up more slowly than others while people in wealthy families drop back more slowly" (Andrews, 2003, p. C1).

Barriers to Access and Attainment

The belief in the American dream and the notion of society affording the opportunity for those who are motivated to pull themselves up by their bootstraps is a powerful image, one that often stands in the way of furnishing the means necessary for the success of many students. At the center of this belief is the notion that if one works hard enough, he or she will make it—will graduate and go on to be successful in life. This is just not so for many students. Opportunity is not simply opening the door; real opportunity is putting in place programs ensuring that hard work will lead to a degree. Unfortunately, working hard sometimes is not enough to overcome the barriers faced by low-income students. Everyone needs support, like the boost more affluent students get from years of music lessons; test preparation programs; rigorous high school curricula; and high expectations from their parents, teachers, and community. Research has shown the culture of low expectations of and for low-income students and students of color, along with a lack of access to rigorous high school curricula, undermines their chances to enter higher education prepared and ready for college-level work.

Preparation

Preparation is often one of the biggest barriers to success in college. The type of academic courses that students take in high school has proven to be a crucial factor in keeping students on the path to college. For example, students who take a rigorous high school mathematics curriculum are much more likely to enroll in college than those who do not. In fact, of those students whose parents' education did not extend beyond high school, 64 percent who took math beyond algebra II enrolled in a four-year institution, whereas 34 percent of students who stopped at algebra II enrolled in a four-year institution (Choy, 2002).

Today, more than 70 percent of students of color attend predominantly black or Hispanic elementary and secondary schools.

Despite four decades of efforts at desegregation, black and Hispanic children overwhelmingly reside in poor school districts, more so than at any time since 1968 (Orfield, 2001). Poor school districts often resort to larger class size and a higher proportion of novice teachers to meet budgetary constraints. Linda Darling-Hammond reports that "majority minority" schools typically have larger class sizes than predominantly white schools, and a greater percentage of teachers teaching out of subject (Darling-Hammond, 1998).

Poor schools often lack the ability—grounded in resources, mission, and will—to prepare students for participation in today's new economy. Inner-city school curricula more often than not lack the requisite rigor. Students from these schools who are tenacious enough to pursue their education beyond high school often find themselves entering a community college needing to take developmental or remedial courses. This, too, can be a roadblock as research has shown that students who enter at four-year institutions complete at a higher rate.

Financial Roadblocks

The correlation between income and college attendance is clear. Whereas "85 percent of high school graduates from families earning more than $75,000 go to college, only 53 percent of graduates from families earning less than $25,000 do so" (Burd, 2002a, p. 2).

Currently, families of low-income, college-qualified high school graduates face an annual unmet need of $3,800 that is not covered by the current financial aid system. A new study has shown that over the last five years, the unmet need of students from the two lowest-income quartiles has grown substantially, while it has actually *decreased* for students from the two higher-income quartiles, in part a result of student aid being diverted from "need" to "merit." The financial barrier effectively prevents about half of low-income students from attending a four-year college. As a result, more than 400,000 qualified high school graduates, with the credentials to attend college, will be unable to attend a four-year college; 170,000 of these low-income students will attend no college at all (Stephens, 2002). This table shows the percentage of postsecondary students who received a bachelor's degree in 1996 (five years after enrolling) by socioeconomic status (Advisory Committee on Student Financial Assistance, 2001):

Quartile	Percentage
Lowest	6.1
Middle two	18.7
Highest	41.1

Campus Culture

Campus culture is often another obstacle for students of color. There remain too many documented cases of racism on college campuses, ranging from fraternity and sorority members who mock lynchings in black face, to parties ridiculing the civil rights movement, to racist and hate-filled messages exchanged on university and college e-mail systems.

A study gauging the role that campus climate plays in access and achievement of black, Latino, Asian, and Native American students at "feeder" schools for the University of Michigan Law school found that generally "campus racial climate has been shown to be a major determinant of academic outcomes for students of color" ("Expert Report of Walter Allen and Daniel Solorzano," 2002, p. 6). Specifically, this research has shown that "hostile or non-supportive campus climates are associated with poor academic performance and high drop out rates among Black and Latino students" (2002, p. 6).

Students of color have also reported feelings of alienation during selection of study groups, in student-to-student interactions, while using student services, and participating in campus activities. They often talk about feeling discouraged, alienated, and suspicious of their professors: "It's not fair on the African American students to be on guard every time I go in to talk to a professor. Every time I go in and talk to the advisor. Every time I go and talk to anybody. I'm like, 'Are they here really to help me or are they going to lead me down the path that I don't want to go down?'" (2002, p. 42).

There are limited visible signs of black and Hispanic success on campus—signs white students often take for granted—such as white faculty, portraits of former white presidents, and celebrated alumni and donors. Black and Hispanic students often arrive without the support of friends and family or the experience that comes with having a family member who has graduated from college. There are too few symbols of academic success in America's inner cities that reinforce the value of education. Consider this comparison of the percentage of postsecondary students who received a bachelor's degree in 1996 (five years after enrolling) by race or ethnicity (Advisory Committee on Student Financial Assistance, 2001):

Race or Ethnicity	Percentage
Black, non-Hispanic	16.9
Hispanic	17.8
White, non-Hispanic	27.3

First-Generation Status

First-generation students face many barriers to college, including lack of family support and lack of knowledge of the admissions and financial aid processes. Typically these students know "nothing about financial aid and have difficulty following the application process; most parents were of little help" because of their lack of knowledge about the system (Macy, 2000, p. 15). A series of focus groups with low-income students conducted by the Futures Project made plain that the lack of information as to how the system works—financial aid, course requirements, and so on—is a major inhibitor to academic success.

Only 36 percent of first-generation students aspire to a college degree, whereas 78 percent of students whose parents have a college degree aspire to the same (Education Resources Institute and Institute for Higher Education Policy, 1997). As a result, far too few take the necessary steps that lead to enrolling in a college or university. Only 45 percent of first-generation students take the necessary entrance exams (SAT or ACT) compared to 82 percent of students from college-educated families (Education Resources Institute and Institute for Higher Education Policy, 1997). Even fewer apply to a four-year institution (26 percent of first-generation versus 71 percent for those students whose parents have a college education; Education Resources Institute and Institute for Higher Education Policy, 1997). First-generation students are also more likely to delay enrolling; only 29 percent enroll right after high school compared to 73 percent of non–first-generation students. When first-generation students do enroll, more often than not it is as part-time students, which decreases the chance of attainment (53 percent enroll part-time compared to 38 percent full-time; Education Resources Institute and Institute for Higher Education Policy, 1997). Only 44 percent of these students attain a degree within five years compared to 56 percent of non–first-generation students (Education Resources Institute and Institute for Higher Education Policy, 1997).

Demography

Expanding access and increasing completion rates for low-income students and students of color are critical for many reasons, but none more than the need to consider demographic projections. Looking ahead at the demographics of California, Texas, and Florida offers a glimpse of what is to come as the majority of their schoolchildren are in the demographic groups that need the greatest support. Anthony Carnevale and Richard Fry have projected that nationally the eighteen- to twenty-four-year-old population will expand by 16 percent between 2000 and 2015. Eighty percent of these prospective students will be nonwhite, and almost half will be Hispanic.

A recent Rand research study conducted for the Hispanic Scholarship Fund showed that approximately 50 percent of Hispanics now living in the United States were schooled in their native country, where familiarity with and devotion to formal schooling is often low. An increasing percentage of this growing Hispanic population has entered the United States with "low levels of education . . . [and] never entered American schools" (Vernez and Mizell, 2001, p. vii). In 1998, "only 50 percent of foreign-born

Hispanics had high school diplomas compared with 80 percent of native-born Hispanics" (p. vii). One challenge will be to get these prospective citizens into the education pipeline. Higher education systems, primarily in California, Texas, New York, and Florida, will shoulder the lion's share of educating poor, first-generation, and underprepared Hispanic students. (It should also be noted that the three states with the highest share of Hispanic students—Florida, California, and Texas—have banned affirmative action.) By the year 2010, the number of Hispanic children who "will be living in families in which both parents have less than a high school education" will rise by 20 percent (Vernez and Mizell, 2001, p. viii), and nearly 45 percent of these same children will be living in poor families (Vernez and Mizell, 2001, p. viii).

The fact remains that race, socioeconomic status, and parents' educational level strongly correlate to life chances. There are barriers unique to each group, but there is overlap. Access to information, grant aid, outreach and retention programs, and participation in a rigorous high school curriculum increase the graduation rate.

Dangers of the Market

The shift in organization of the higher education sector toward a market is likely to make the problem of access and completion even worse (see Chapter Three). Information about college preparation, college admissions, and financial aid too often flows principally to middle-income and upper-income families. The intensifying competition for students with higher test scores, or students from wealthier families, has resulted in an increase in honors programs and honors colleges and increasing use of merit-based financial aid programs. At the very time that society needs more low-income people entering and exiting the gates of higher education, the market is, as currently structured, pushing colleges and universities in the opposite direction. Even those colleges and universities that typically are seen as open-door institutions have begun to shift their attention and their resources from low-income students and students of color to the more affluent and easy-to-educate students.

The Retreat from Affirmative Action

Since the passage of California's Proposition 209 in November 1996, there has been organized and determined opposition to affirmative action. Over the last couple of years, that opposition has made strides in its attempt to dismantle affirmative action through referenda and court action. The Center for Individual Rights, the American Civil Rights Institute, and the Center for Equal Opportunity have argued strenuously that quotas must be eliminated and that outreach, retention, and summer programs exclusively for students of color violated title VI of the Civil Rights Act of 1964 and must now be opened to white students or eliminated. The result of this assault has been slow erosion of affirmative action as colleges and universities have chosen (or been ordered) to eliminate or amend programs and scholarships that are targeted at students of color. Polls show that the public, by a sizable majority, is opposed to formal quotas for affirmative action. However, an even larger majority favors programs of support for the least advantaged (that is, low-income and minority students) to help them gain an education. A 2003 Pew Research Center nationwide survey found that "in order to overcome past discrimination," 63 percent favored affirmative action programs "designed to help blacks, women, and other minorities get better jobs and education" (Pew Research Center for the People and the Press, 2003, p. 1). Fifty-seven percent of respondents supported affirmative action programs that "give special preferences to qualified blacks, women and other minorities in hiring and education."

Foundations are also backing away from funding programs targeted at black students. The *Journal of Blacks in Higher Education* (JBHE) reported that in 1993, the five largest foundations combined gave more than $30 million for such programs. In 2001, the top five foundations combined gave $5 million. JBHE has concluded that today "foundations . . . may be less willing to target grant money to race-specific programs for fear that their federal tax exempt status may be challenged in court" ("Weekly Bulletin," 2003). The result is that a broad public understanding of the need to address affirmative action is being thwarted by a determined minority.

It is clear that what is needed is a debate aimed at creating a course of action for maintaining, and, in fact, improving, access to colleges and universities. The recent ruling on the University of Michigan cases before the U.S. Supreme Court, *Grutter v. Bollinger* and *Gratz v. Bollinger,* has begun to energize universities to take the necessary steps to create such a debate—one that is long overdue.

New policies and a new debate are needed that expand the share of the population able to take advantage of access to higher education and help to ensure greater success by all students once access is achieved.

The Struggle to Find New Approaches

As legal wrangling over affirmative action with regard to admissions escalates, a number of states have searched for new approaches that are acceptable. Some have tried to address access issues by implementing percentage plans where the top percentage of graduates in each high school (in some plans, the top 10 percent) are admitted to the state's flagship university or universities. However, percentage plans alone, like the Top Ten Percent Law in Texas, are not likely to result in minority enrollments equal to the minority share of the population or even close to what previously existed. Even the authors of that plan have publicly stated their opposition to percentage plans replacing affirmative action: "As the authors of the first such state plan, we do not agree that it is possible to use such plans as substitutes for considerations in admissions" (Rios, 2003, p. 1).

According to a study of the Texas program by Princeton professor Marta Tienda, preliminary results demonstrate that the law benefits both minority and nonminority groups, but even with the percentage plan, the proportion of minorities enrolled in the state's public universities is still far below their percentage of the total population. Also, the success of any percentage plan is dependent on continuation of segregated high schools. Mary Francis Berry, chair of the U.S. Commission on Civil Rights, has pointed out that percentage plans must be combined with outreach programs and financial and academic support to work well for the students who do gain access. The Civil Rights Project at Harvard University examined the feasibility of percentage plans as an alternative to race-conscious admissions policies. Author Angelo Ancheta noted another limitation: "Percent plans can only operate at large state-run university systems, and cannot be employed by private universities, small institutions, national institutions, or graduate or professional school programs" (Ancheta, 2003, p. 17).

Nationwide, there are examples of successful programs that can be models for the future. Some states are working to change campus culture by adopting comprehensive programs that support low-income or first-generation students and as a consequence often also help students of color. In 1990, the Indiana state legislature created the Twenty-First Century Scholars Program to help low-income students enroll in and graduate from college. Since 1995, when the first group graduated from high school, almost fifteen thousand students have received college scholarships (St. John and others, 2002). The program also provides tutoring, mentoring, college visits, activities for parents that help them understand the college-going process, and other support and information services.

In 1998, the University of Wisconsin System launched Plan 2008 to build a racially diverse applicant pool and ensure graduation for at-risk students. Plan 2008 differs from retention programs at most colleges and universities because it is comprehensive and systemwide; it layers program efforts to expand the pool of qualified low-income and minority applicants; and it ensures their academic success with overlapping outreach, preparation, remediation, and retention programs. Plan 2008 is built on seven goals ("University of Wisconsin System," 1998, pp. 15–19):

1. Increase the number of Wisconsin high School graduates of color who apply, are accepted, and enroll at UW system institutions.
2. Encourage partnerships that build the educational pipeline by reaching children and their parents at an earlier age.
3. Close the gap in educational achievement, by bringing retention and graduation rates for students of color in line with those of the student body as a whole.
4. Increase the amount of financial aid available to needy students and reduce their reliance on loans.

5. Increase the number of faculty, academic staff, classified staff, and administrators of color.
6. Foster institutional environments and course development that enhance learning and a respect for racial and ethnic diversity.
7. Improve accountability of the UW system and its institutions. This will be done through the Multicultural/Disadvantaged Annual Report and the annual Accountability for Achievement report.

The University of Wisconsin System has shown success in meeting these goals ("University of Wisconsin System Minority and Disadvantaged Student Annual Report," 2002).

Institution-Based Programs

There are, across the country, a growing number of programs demonstrating that successful education of low-income students is possible. Since 1968, the University of Rhode Island's Talent Development program (TD) has been providing disadvantaged students with support and guidance. Talent Development boasts a 70 percent graduation rate; many of its alumni are doctors, lawyers, entrepreneurs, and teachers. Ed Givens, assistant director of TD, was himself a participant more than fifteen years ago. Givens, an African American first-generation college student, credits TD with helping him graduate from URI and going on to pursue a master's degree: "Without Talent Development, I am not sure I would have ended up graduating. I hit a point in college where I stopped going to class. I only ate, played football, and slept. Advisors from Talent Development came to my room and talked to me. Found out what the problem was. They helped to get me back on track. The advisors got to know me beyond my academics and always voiced their belief in me" (interview with E. Givens, conducted by J. Scurry, Jan. 7, 2003).

Similarly, Joanna Ravello, a first-generation college student whose parents are from Trinidad, attributes her academic success both at URI and in a master's program to TD: "Talent Development is really a great program. I would not have gone as far as I have without it. TD helped to make the transition from high school to college so smooth. They taught me how to handle problems, navigate the system, and empowered me to deal with majority students. It [the university] is a very complex system. TD helped to take the guess work out" (interview with J. Ravello, conducted by J. Scurry, Jan. 7, 2003).

As successful as programs such as URI Talent Development are, they remain a special effort aimed at a specific group of students. The goal should be a broader attempt at creating a learning environment across the entire college or university. Just as TD forces attention to the actual learning and personal needs of a selected group of students, a learning-centered environment can do the same for the entire student body. One benefit would be improvement in the interest, satisfaction, and graduation rates of the entire student body.

A successful example of this is the Community College of Denver (Colorado). Close to 60 percent of the student body take at least one remedial class (Hebel, 1999) compared to 18 percent of Colorado's community college statewide student body (Colorado Department of Higher Education, 2001). CCD has learned how to help these students succeed. CCD students who have taken a remedial course are more likely to graduate and/or transfer to a four-year college than their classmates (Hebel, 1999). The portion of CCD graduates who are minority has increased from 13 percent in 1986–1987 to 47 percent in 1999–2000 (McClenney and Flores, 1998). The reasons for this remarkable record are straightforward: a belief that the students can succeed and a determination to provide whatever academic and personal support is necessary.

CCD houses all remedial and developmental education efforts within one central department, creating a coherent and organized effort that has been found in numerous studies to be a pathway to success.[5] The "one-stop" Academic Support Center (ASC) offers English as a second language, GED, literacy, math, writing, and speech learning services, along with TRIO* services, in one location. CCD also offers online math and writing labs. The multiple arms of the ASC converge around the shared, identified goals of facilitating faculty-student communication, enhancing student

---

*A series of programs established by Congress to help low-income students gain access to and graduate from college. Programs are funded under Title IV of the Higher Education Act of 1965. Programs are designed to aid students in triumph over all the barriers to higher education.

self-esteem (crucial to success), focusing instruction on students' individual needs, and creating a sense of community and connection to the college. The fact that the college has identified these goals in writing reflects proactive campuswide commitment to remedial education.

La Familia, another innovative CCD program, creates learning communities for entering first-generation, low-income students. These learning communities establish a supportive learning environment in which members take linked classes, are matched with peer mentors, and receive career and academic counseling. La Familia participants enroll in their second year of study at a rate of 80 percent compared to a 62 percent second-year return rate for all first-generation CCD students (Hebel, 1999).

Two components of CCD's success have been identified as a qualified faculty dedicated to the education of less advantaged students and commitment to and embracing of diversity (Hebel, 1999). An extensive peer and faculty tutoring system also ensures that any student wanting quality one-on-one assistance can get it. CCD performs systematic evaluation of its remedial programs and responds to its findings, which helps "defend its programs against budget cuts and keep them from being outsourced to private entrepreneurs" (Hebel, 1999).

LaGuardia Community College in New York established a New Student House Program to create small learning communities for students identified as underprepared. Participating students take four of six basic skills courses together; the program employs group learning, class meetings, "improvisatory theatre pedagogy," a required speech course, and computer-based learning (Tinto and Riemer, 2001). The learning community meets together periodically with a staff member who works as both a "course facilitator and a student counselor" (Tinto and Riemer, 2001),[6] creating a link between students' academic and extracurricular experiences.

Rather than isolating remedial education students, the LaGuardia concept of learning communities integrates these students into the general curriculum while creating a source of support, thus allowing them to earn credit at the same time they acquire the requisite skills and content to thrive in for-credit classes. The system has flexibility so that students may switch levels as their learning needs change. Retention experts Vincent Tinto and Stacey Riemer have shown that this approach lends itself to far greater levels of academic success and graduation. Tinto and Riemer describe learning communities as "a kind of co-registration or block scheduling that enables students to take courses together, and help each other" (Tinto and Riemer, 2001).

Creating a Culture of Attainment

Higher education has made great strides over the years, but it is not ready for the new wave of students who are in need of a college education. Successful programs such as those noted here have already demonstrated that low-income students and students of color can achieve at the same level as their more affluent, white counterparts. But to meet the needs of society for a more effectively educated population, more than a handful of successful programs are needed. Not only are more such programs needed, but the programs that lead to academic success must be spread across the entire institution, not kept as an isolated island of concern. Academic leaders and policy makers must work to ensure that the whole of the current system of higher education is more accessible, affordable, and easier to understand and navigate.

The Futures Project believes that *each* institution—not just those that serve primarily low-income or minority students—must reexamine its mission and use multiple types of outreach and retention programs to ensure the success of all students. While the success of wealthier, majority students is far greater, the overall graduation rate is still far from satisfactory. Successful outreach and retention programs must become an integral part of how institutions think about and deliver education. There are a number of approaches institutions can use in creating a culture of attainment that works:

- Outreach programs to middle and high schools that raise students' expectations, encourage them to take the right courses, and help them plan for attainment
- Early college high schools, such as those pioneered by LaGuardia Community College, that enroll disadvantaged high school students in courses on the college campus
- Bridge programs that provide transition support from high school into higher education

- Joint enrollment programs that allow high school students to take college courses even as they are enrolled in high school and encourage these students to begin believing they can go to college and prepare themselves academically
- Remediation programs that are effective
- Posse group admission (admitting a group of disadvantaged students all from the same high school) to help students have peer support
- Targeted financial aid for the most in need
- Four-year degree programs offered by universities on the community college campus
- Academic support for students once enrolled
- Mentoring support for students once enrolled
- Analysis, and strategic use, of student performance data
- Case management approach to ensure that the most at-risk students stay on course

These programs allow institutions to create a culture that not only supports students through to graduation but fosters lifelong learning, creating pathways for low-income students or students of color to earn a graduate degree. Higher education, for example, should be encouraging these students to enter the professions, including the professoriate, and provide the opportunities to do so. This is an integral step in diversifying the faculty.

An institution can begin by asking a set of questions:

- Where are there roadblocks in the admission process for less advantaged students?
- Are there outreach programs in place that reach disadvantaged students as early as middle school and draw them into the pipeline?
- If there are, how effective are these programs? How do they compare with similar programs at colleges and universities? Are there ways to make existing programs more effective or efficient?
- To what degree do the current financial aid system and increasing use of merit aid impede access? Can a better balance between need-based aid and merit aid be achieved?
- How can diversity be ensured in the current legal climate? Which institutions are succeeding on this front?

- Is the campus welcoming for all? Does the campus climate support students of color? Do staff and faculty reflect the color of the students?
- Does the campus foster a climate that encourages success for all students, with particular attention to those most needing help?
- Which students are being lost, and why?
- Has the campus examined the most effective and efficient remedial and retention programs across the country? What can be gleaned from these programs? Can they be replicated?

The Role of State Policy

As has been described in earlier chapters, the environment in which higher education is now operating is far more competitive than ever before. One of the biggest drawbacks to markets is that they serve those who have the financial resources to participate, leaving the rest of the population to fend for itself. In a higher education system that has always struggled toward—but never achieved—the goal of equal opportunity to gain an education, this particular threat from a market is especially daunting. Against this backdrop, the need for thoughtful and effective state policies, focused on extending participation and academic achievement to an ever-expanding share of the population, is all the more urgent.

The Futures Project believes that each state system must approach access and achievement as a holistic process, creating a system that is manageable and navigable for all students. There are examples of institutions and systems that have mastered the art of providing meaningful access and high levels of achievement. The common thread is that those institutions and systems have designed a process for their students, thinking about what is needed for success at every stage of the game. Affluent students, or students who have parents or role models who have gone to college, are born into a network that teaches them the process of success, instructing them at each step on how to apply for financial aid; how to seek out faculty mentors; how to obtain necessary help from deans, advisors, and counselors; and fostering a belief that they will succeed. The goal of our policy recommendations is to recreate that process for *all* students.

A Navigable Process

Ensure and Improve the Availability of Need-Based Financial Aid

States must take steps to reduce the erosion of need-based financial aid we have experienced in recent years. Merit aid programs are shifting resources away from those who need it most. Our financial aid system, once a matter of pride in our democracy, has taken on the tone of reinforcing advantages for those who have the most advantages already, making it easier for those who were going to college anyway, but ultimately denying opportunity to those who stand to benefit the most. The lynchpin of a state's navigable process will be its commitment to providing need-based aid to its low-income population and reducing the barriers to financial aid for part-time and working adult students.

Draw More Students into the Higher Education Experience Through Outreach Programs

The path to higher education begins in middle school *at the latest.* The more advantaged and affluent begin telling their children at a very young age they are going to college and take steps that will put their children on that path—trips to museums, college-prep curriculum, visits with guidance counselors, and increasingly even consultants for college admissions.

State policy can create an environment that puts students on the path to college as well. Policy can provide the appropriate incentives and support for institutions to offer outreach programs that encourage students in middle and high school to aspire to attend college and to prepare academically. The federal government, for example, already funds several such programs, including the federal TRIO programs. Outreach programs have proven their worth. Their delivery of more students to higher education is their payoff.

Create a Supportive and Welcoming Campus Environment

Once on campus, all students need assistance as they work their way through the complex systems of registration, advising, financing, and socializing that combine to create an intimidating and confusing environment. State policies need to support funding for campus-based programs that help to make students astute navigators of all this complexity. At a bare minimum, advising programs, for example, should not be optional. State policy can ensure that all students have access to an advisor who helps them to make academic decisions and seek academic assistance.

Support Remedial Programs

The argument that remedial programs "*should* not be necessary because students *should* arrive in higher education prepared" is an argument that is not based in reality. Whatever one's political beliefs about remediation, the simple fact is that many students need extra preparation. The states have made massive efforts to improve elementary and secondary education, with some resulting improvements. However, until schooling has been changed to adequately prepare all students, remediation will be necessary.

Some states prohibit institutions from using state funds for remedial programs on the grounds that the state should not be asked to pay twice for educating remedial students. Until the preparation gap is eliminated, states should support remedial programs but insist that the institutions focus on the use of the most effective programs and assess their progress.

Align the Preschool, Elementary, Secondary, and Higher Education Systems Through P–16 Programs

Higher education cannot make an impact on the level of preparation of incoming students without an effective relationship with the preschool through secondary system in the state. The goal of a seamless system is not to create a council. It is to create an environment that works: pushing preschool, elementary, secondary, and higher education to address issues together; forcing higher education to do a better job of preparing teachers; aligning state standards for high school graduation with college admissions standards; smoothing the transition from high school to college; creating the opportunity for students in high school to take college courses; and instilling the idea of lifelong learning in children from a young age. The various levels of education should no longer be allowed to operate in separate spheres.

Improve Transfer and Articulation Policies

The American system of higher education is lauded for its diversity of offerings. Other countries have started creating community colleges to replicate the ideal of open access to a higher education.

But the system does not live up to the ideal. Far too many students who enter community colleges with the intention of transferring to four-year institutions do not make the transition. Public policy can smooth the wrinkles, facilitating the process of learning about educational opportunities, getting advice while changing institutions, accumulating and transferring credits, and entering as transfer students on a level playing field with those who started at four-year institutions. States should insist upon clear, workable, comprehensive transfer policies. Again, the various types of institutions should no longer be allowed to operate in separate spheres.

Encourage or Mandate the Assessment and Reporting of Learner Outcomes

A critical, though often overlooked, aspect of attainment is the quality of the learning experience. Students who are bored, discouraged, not engaged with the learning process, or failing are less likely to stay in higher education and graduate. State policies that require the assessment and reporting of the quality of learner outcomes will focus attention on improving the rate and quality of learning taking place in our institutions, resulting in not only higher rates of graduation and retention but higher-skilled students overall.

Encourage Decision Making Based on Data

State policy should mandate or encourage the collection and reporting of data that help the state to make wise decisions about its system, that help students make wise decisions about their education, and that help institutions to make wise decisions about their daily operations and future. Data elements would include rates of retention, graduation, transfer, learner outcomes, course passage rates, and so on. Many of the institutional presidents who have created successful learning environments for underserved students are the strongest proponents for relying upon data to chart their progress, identify obstacles, and understand what works. Such a system should be available to all leaders at all levels of the system and institution. Directors of advising should know, for example, how many students are leaving the institution and why so that advising processes can be improved.

Bring These Policy Initiatives Together as a "Navigable Program"

Each of these initiatives should not be pursued in isolation. They should be grouped, linked, and seamless, creating a policy environment that looks at all the needs of all the students.

Higher education should be the great equalizer for this nation. But current trends are discouraging. If higher education leaders and policy makers do not work to reverse the trends, remove the barriers, and focus their attention on access through to completion, this could be the first generation of students not to surpass their parents' educational gains. Institutions must accept the responsibility of creating a climate of attainment. Thoughtful policies foster incentives for institutions to do what is right and needed. The task is not just to expand access but to ensure that students of color and low-income students attend, succeed at, and graduate from college. If not, the American dream will fail to be realized for millions of young people.

Chapter Ten

Competitive Grants for Teaching and Institutional Service

The goal of proposing the policies laid out here is to apply the lessons learned in research funding, as well as in operation of other federal and state competitive grant programs, to the teaching and service responsibilities of higher education so that responsiveness and quality can be enhanced even as institutional autonomy grows.

Over the long life of higher education there has been one constant: the argument that more funding is needed. Much less attention has been focused on what *form* of funding would best serve higher education in executing its responsibilities. Surprisingly little attention has been given to the use of competitive grants for these purposes, despite their striking effectiveness in at least one field, research.

Competitive peer-reviewed grants (where grant applications to the various federal agencies that support research are reviewed by committees of researchers active in the field) for sponsorship of research performed by universities have proven remarkably successful. After the development of a program of federal sponsorship of such grants in 1945, the United States moved from a second-rate center of research to leadership in essentially every field. American universities responded to the federal government's efforts to create an effective, competitive market in research at first hesitantly, then enthusiastically and certainly skillfully (Mazuzan, 1994).

What the successful effort in research demonstrates is that a carefully structured system of competitive grants encourages innovation, enhances institutional autonomy, and still responds to public needs. Too often the emergence of a competitive market in a sector of society leads to a shift from public purpose to private purposes. The federal research system has shown this need not be so.

Surprisingly, few attempts have been made to apply the same concept to the other two domains of higher education: teaching and service. (By *service*, we mean the effort by a university or college to use its expertise to assist communities with their problems.) What the Futures Project believes is needed now are policies that provide public funding for these two additional areas through competitive, peer-reviewed grants. The goal of proposing the policies laid out here is to apply the lessons learned in research funding, as well as in operation of other federal and state competitive grant programs, to the teaching and service responsibilities of higher education so that responsiveness and quality can be enhanced even as institutional autonomy grows.

The Advantages of Competitive Grants

What is it about the process of competitive grant funding that makes it so effective? The National Research Council, in examining a range of competitive grant programs, listed three advantages:

1. They are "responsive and flexible," allowing programs to change as public needs change and as new opportunities emerge.
2. They attract a range of participants from different institutional types and encourage the participation of leading scientists.
3. They attract a variety of ideas well beyond those that granting agencies might have traditionally proposed (National Research Council, 1994, p. 2).

Competitive grants have other advantages as well:

- By updating the proposal guidelines, public authorities can steer institutional efforts toward public purposes without micromanaging or creating bureaucratic entanglement.

- The process encourages, rather than inhibits, creativity and a sense of ownership.
- Particularly when a carefully structured peer-review system is used, quality is enhanced. In the traditional laboratory system, the organization receives a yearly appropriation or block grant. In such a system, it is difficult to close down a poor-performing unit. In a peer-reviewed competitive system of funding, poorly performing teams and poorly conceived projects fail to get the next grant; the teams dissolve, and their manpower is dispersed.
- The system constantly moves to the cutting edge. Old, no longer relevant areas of activity are phased out. Operating in new and more effective ways is valued.
- Grants serve as a powerful motivator for institutional change, empowering those within the organization who advocate for improvement.

These attributes—the ability to attract innovative people and innovative ideas—show up as well in grant programs in areas other than research. The success of the competitive grant approach has been demonstrated well beyond the field of research, though not on the same scale. To cite just two examples, competitive grants have helped the expansion of community service through grants from the Corporation for National Service, and they have been critical to the push for school reform through competitive grants from dozens of private foundations.

Other examples have emerged outside the borders of the United States. The European Union is now working on expanding the use of competitive grants for university research to help make European research more effective in order to compete with the United States (Gould, 2003). To aid the task of overcoming the wide difference between the have and have-not nations of Europe, one program calls for each advanced nation to partner with a nation where research is still at a low level (Etzkowitz, 2001). Research funding in Chile has grown to four times what it was in the early 1980s under a competitive, peer-reviewed model (Bernasconi, 2003). The British government, which already has had some success with a competitive grant program for university research (Gould, 2003), plans to concentrate its research grants in fewer universities so as to allow that smaller number to compete more effectively with American universities (Centre for Higher Education Research and Information, 2003). African nations have established a multinational agency (Association for Strengthening Agricultural Research in Eastern and Central Africa, or ASARECA) to foster collaborative research across national boundaries by grants to multinational teams. Recently, the organization has begun moving away from open-ended institutional support to "performance-based" or competitive grant funding to improve the impact of each grant ("About ASARECA," 2003). In 1989, Australia began to pursue a new policy that would allocate research funds on a competitive basis. The intent was that institutions would "increasingly be funded according to what they do rather than according to an arbitrary classification based on institutional title," directing research funds to "those institutions, research groups and individuals best able to make the most effective use of them" (Gallagher, 2000, p. 8).

Creating Competitive Grant Programs

The experience with competitive grant systems makes plain some of the ground rules for effective programs. There is, for example, an advantage in multiple funding agencies. (In research in the United States, about twenty-six federal agencies make grants; Brainard, 2001.) Every granting agency develops its own personality, procedures, and contacts. Having multiple agencies helps keep the door open to new ideas and new people. Similarly, things work better when there are a large number of applicants; no one applicant, or group of applicants, has sufficient political clout to interfere with the fairness of the process.

There is also an advantage in ensuring both geographic and political distance between grantor and grantee. Federal grants have worked more effectively than state grants. Research universities have enough influence to suggest improvements to the federal system and mitigate unwelcome or unnecessary bureaucracy but not enough to undercut the fundamental competitive nature of the program. On the other hand, the universities and colleges in a given state have historically banded together to push for shifting the money from competitive grants to formula funding, ensuring that all institutions will get something and destroying the competitive structure in the process. This has happened in essentially every case where states have created a competitive grant program (A. McGuinness, personal communication, May 24, 2003). States can, with careful attention to program rules, create effective competitive grant programs in partnership with the federal government. Many have done so in the field of community service, where funding for the state grants flows from the Corporation for National Service to the state and where there are many small applicants that do not have the political influence of the universities. Similarly, federal funding flowing through state grants has worked in the Library Services and Technology Act (see, for example, "Funding: Texas State Library and Archives Commission," 2003). In these cases, the federal government provides both the core funding (often state matched) and the program structure, making the program safe from local pressures to do away with the competitive nature of the funding.

All of these safeguards are important in creating a program that maintains the faith of the political leaders, the institutions of higher education, and the public. The National Academy argues that four criteria are essential to preserving belief in competition: quality, fairness, relevance, and flexibility (Committee on an Evaluation of the U.S. Department of Agriculture National Research Initiative Competitive Grants Program, 2000). To make these criteria meaningful, they must not only be inherent in the program's design, but performance against them must be measured regularly. This in turn monitors program improvement as well as encourages careful efforts to prevent the distortions that undercut the basic aims of the program.

The Success Story: Competitive Grants for University Research

The inspiration for creating the competitive grant system in research that has proved so successful came from the experience of a group of scientists who played a leading role in the Allied effort in World War II. There had never been a war in which fundamental science played such a profound role—including hundreds of developments such as the proximity fuse, radar, and of course the atomic bomb.

American scientists were painfully aware of their dependence on European science and European scientists, many of whom had been driven from or fled Nazi control. Recognizing the urgency of addressing the problem for the postwar period, the scientists (led by Vannevar Bush) arranged to have Pres. Franklin Roosevelt ask them for a plan. The resulting report, in 1945, called "Science, the Endless Frontier," spelled out in prescient detail the concept of a competitive grant system based on universities. It envisioned a single federal foundation, controlled by the science community and responsible for research in all fields.

After a five-year battle between Pres. Harry Truman and Congress, two points of controversy were resolved. The research foundation would be responsible to the president and Congress, and other federal departments would also make grants. Thus, the National Science Foundation (NSF) was created. Both decisions turned out to be critical. By 1950, when the NSF began operations, other government agencies, including the National Institutes of Health, the Atomic Energy Commission, and the Office of Naval Research, were already well under way and making research grants based on the principles spelled out in "Science, the Endless Frontier" (Newman, 1981).

The research program was funded only modestly at first, but its success became readily apparent. Compared to almost all other countries, most of which turned to national laboratories funded on an annual appropriation, American research moved steadily to the forefront in field after field. The United States created national laboratories as well, but it was universities that quickly came to dominate the world's research. As the benefits of research became more and more evident—to political leadership, to the business community, and ultimately to the public—political support and funding grew. Today, federal support for university research, not including the large national laboratories left over from World War II and run by a number of universities, totals about $20 billion ("President's Fiscal 2001 Budget . . . ," 2000). There is now growing pressure to apply the proven peer-reviewed competitive grant system to those areas of research where it has not been employed and where research has been less effective. For example, the National Research Council has strongly suggested its use in the field of education research (Olson, 2003). The U.S. Department of Agriculture, under pressure to improve the effectiveness of its research, has been shifting funding from formulas to competitive grants (Committee on the Future of the College of Agriculture in the Land Grant University System, 1995).

For the other two purposes of higher education—service to the community and teaching and learning—the Futures Project believes that funding can be structured so as to enhance the impact and public purposes of higher education by using competition, with federal funding of university research as the model.

Competitive Grants for Improving Service

One new approach would be to provide expanded federal and state support for outreach and service to the community—a major expansion of the land grant concept—but available to *all* public universities, colleges, and community colleges. (A case could be made for including all nonprofit private universities and colleges. The Futures Project believes that by focusing funding on public institutions there will be a greater impact, and it will help preserve the useful difference between public and private.) Presently, most outreach and community service, both individual and institutional, is funded by internal reallocation of institutional resources, with modest support from the federal and state governments. The lack of a comprehensive system prevents higher education from reaching its full potential in this work.

Although the programs of community support provided by higher education are, taken as a whole, enormously valuable, there is little attempt to examine the impact, effectiveness, or efficiency of individual service projects. Similarly, it is hard for the public to encourage a change in service programs to reflect changed public needs. In addition, future funding from internal reallocation of resources is likely to become harder as broader competition among colleges and universities heats up and institutions are forced to allocate their funds to crucial academic program needs. External funds that are dedicated to service, particularly funds obtained through competitive grants, can ensure both continuation and improvement of outreach services.

The idea of an institutional responsibility for service has been present since the founding of the first American college in 1636. Not until the Morrill or Land Grant Act of 1862, however, was the expectation of employing the fruits of institutional scholarship and expertise to help with the practical problems of community need spelled out in specific terms. The expectation and funding of the Land Grant Act has been focused on specific institutions (the 105 land grant universities and colleges) but also on specific fields, described originally as "agriculture and the mechanic arts" (Eddy, 1957, 1962).

The result of the Land Grant Act was a set of universities far more engaged in the process of community development and support than had been typical in the United States, and far more than is still the case elsewhere in the world. In 1966, the Sea Grant Act added a new source of support for service in the marine field for a set of institutions, the sea grant universities. In 1987, another act of Congress created the Space Grant program (Earls, 2003).

A recent report by the National Association of State Universities and Land Grant Colleges (NASULGC) made plain the impact that these programs have had on their communities.[1] Most important, the land grant institutions have helped transform the basic nature of American society. The most striking and celebrated success has been the transformation of American (and, over time, world) agriculture. Land grant outreach now operates in many fields: economic development, homeland security, biotechnology, and information technology, to name only a few. Approximately two-thirds of the land grant universities have a business park and some form of incubator to help in starting up new businesses (Earls, 2003; see also Kellogg Commission on the Future of State and Land Grant Universities, 2000).

A Kellogg Commission report of 2000 proposed a Higher Education Millennial Partnership Act aimed at renewing the "covenant" between the land grant universities and the public. Operating under a new covenant, the institutions would support, among other things:

- Equal access "without regard to race, ethnicity, age, occupation, or economic background"
- Enhanced civic engagement by "preparing students to lead and participate in a democratic society"
- "Conscious efforts to bring the resources and expertise at our institutions to bear on community, state, national, and international problems in a coherent way" (Kellogg Commission on the Future of State and Land Grant Universities, 2000)

The Futures Project proposes a somewhat different approach aimed at funding and expanding the service function. We propose a major federal, peer-reviewed competitive grant program for which all public institutions, from research universities to community colleges, would be eligible. All of these institutions already perform community service of some sort, and for many public but non–land grant institutions, service is an integral part of their activities. Funding would be available in targeted programs, such as economic development, sea grant, technology development, space, agriculture, and so on. Funding would come from multiple federal agencies (funding already comes from several federal agencies, among them the Department of Agriculture, the National Institutes of Health, the Corporation for National Service, Housing and Urban Development, and the National Aeronautics and Space Agency) with partial matching required by states (perhaps three federal dollars to one state dollar), but its impact would be greatly enhanced by a new structure. State support has been modest and vulnerable to budget cuts (Earls, 2003). The requirement to partially match or lose federal funds would help ensure program stability. Funding in the range of $3 or $4 billion, much of which could come from existing federal and state programs, would make a major difference.

The requirement to compete for grants would help ensure that service programs are constantly improving, constantly at the cutting edge. Faculty engaged in service who receive grants would gain in status. The focus of the service programs would shift as the public's need for service shifted. The result, we believe, would be a substantial expansion and improvement in quality of service by higher education institutions—service that is critical to the improvement of American society in many aspects.

Competitive Grants for Improving Teaching

There is already evidence that competitive grants for improving teaching and learning can lead to significant gains if universities and colleges simply take advantage of what is already known about pedagogy and if they attempt to measure learner outcomes. The federal government already has an agency devoted to making such grants, the Fund for the Improvement of Post Secondary Education (FIPSE). Congress created FIPSE in 1972. It was consciously designed to deliver the benefits for teaching and learning that had already become evident in research, and it was modeled on NSF. There were a number of questions as to whether this format would work for the teaching side of higher education. Would or could faculty be as entrepreneurial about teaching as about research? Would there be enough proposals to justify the concept? Would it be possible to judge the innovative value of various proposals?

As it turned out, FIPSE was a rousing success from the first request for proposals. More than two thousand were received in the first year from all types of universities and colleges. What became instantly clear was that the competitive grant process can be a powerful force in improving teaching and learning, just as it is in research (National Center for Public Policy and Higher Education, 2002). A 1978 study of FIPSE, conducted at the request of the Office of the Assistant Secretary for Planning in the Department of Health, Education, and Welfare (HEW), found that FIPSE had "achieved substantial success in accomplishing its mission to encourage improvement in postsecondary education. To those familiar with evaluations of other federal education programs, this finding may be a pleasant surprise. . . . Yet, when judged by any of a number of criteria, the Fund should be considered a success" (National Center for Public Policy and Higher Education, 2002, p. 3). The report's findings:

- Though grants were generally small (the average annual amount, renewable for three years, was around $80,000; Cobb, 2003), the projects they supported had a large effect.
- The structure of the proposal process encouraged risk taking, creativity, and networking.
- Though FIPSE had a small staff, it was skilled and willing to share its knowledge with those writing proposals and with grantees. FIPSE regularly gathered the grantees together, effectively creating a community of innovators. A surprisingly high share of the institutions whose proposals were turned down still found ways to move ahead with their plans.
- FIPSE grants gave a sense of legitimacy to innovators on their campuses.
- The proposal process, with broad categories, was open enough to respond to field interest (National Center for Public Policy and Higher Education, 2002).

In short, it was clear that the concept and the particular design of FIPSE worked. Despite its spectacular success at using competitive grants to improve teaching and learning, FIPSE's impact has been modest because of its small size; over the past few years, FIPSE's annual appropriation has ranged between $25 and $28 million (Fund for the Improvement of Postsecondary Education—Comprehensive Program, 2004). Subsequent to the development of FIPSE, NSF also developed a competitive grant program for higher education focused on teaching math and science. Although it has been a success and is several times the size of FIPSE, it has not had nearly the impact of improving teaching and learning that FIPSE has. It is, however, a valuable resource, a program that can be modified to draw closer to the FIPSE model.

What FIPSE has demonstrated, as the studies have shown, is that the concept of competitive grants works and that a skillfully designed grant program can be more effective at generating willing involvement in the hard work of improving learning than a regulatory approach. Our estimate is that a grant program of $1 billion (a sum equal to roughly 5 percent of total research grant funding and less than 1 percent of the total amount spent by colleges and universities on teaching and learning) would transform teaching in American higher education. The process of generating proposals in itself focuses the attention of the institution and encourages the creativity of those involved.

The Broader Benefits of Competitive Grants for Teaching and Service

If the funding that supports these two areas—outreach and service as well as teaching and learning—or, more accurately, a modest share of the funding in these two areas were altered so that it flowed to the institutions through peer-reviewed competitive grants, then all three areas of university and college activity—teaching, research, and service—would find it essential to improve performance in order to gain funding. One need only observe the extraordinary success of university research, as well as its flexibility and responsiveness to public needs, to see the potential of having competitive grants in all three areas so as to create a more entrepreneurial and performance-oriented spirit in universities and colleges.

Competitive funding for teaching and learning and for service would also help restore the balance in the interest of faculty among teaching, research, and service. In the current university structure, the attention of the faculty is principally focused on research and scholarship, in part because the faculty reward structure reflects the importance of success in obtaining competitive grants. Before creation of the federal grant programs, which in turn spurred emergence of true research universities, teaching was the dominant faculty concern. Today, it is research and publication, even in four-year institutions not considered research universities. Rebalancing is needed, and a competitive grant system can help. Success in gaining a grant in teaching or in service, even in the limited amounts currently available, does bring prestige to the faculty member and department. One other advantage of competitive grants as a mode of funding is that it provides the public, through the appropriate arm of government, some broad say in the priorities for education and for service, as is currently true for research, while still leaving institutions free to make daily operating decisions and set institutional strategies.

Compensating for Distortions

As is true for any set of forces strong enough to bring about institutional change, competitive grants also have the possibility (even the likelihood, if not well constructed) of bringing serious distortion of purpose in their wake.

The most readily apparent distortion is the tendency of a grant program to overconcentrate resources at a few highly regarded institutions. In research, for example, there is the constant danger that a small number of top-rated universities will attract the very best researchers and the bulk of the grants and thus will come to dominate the research, particularly in the sciences. Will the result be to freeze out researchers or universities of promise who have not yet established a track record?

In the debates after establishment of the NSF in the late 1940s, this was a real fear (and in the earliest programs, the reality). In its first years, competitive grants for research and for support of graduate students very quickly became concentrated at the best-known research universities. Then, under pressure from Congress, the foundation began to develop programs that, although keeping the essential elements of peer-reviewed competition, managed to disperse funding to a wider array of institutions, individuals, and programs. One such approach was grants set aside for promising researchers.

The tug of war between "quality" and "dispersion" continues, however. The U.S. Senate has recently raised the issue that funding from the National Institutes of Health discriminates against rural universities (Brainard, 2002). A recent report from the congressional General Accounting Office notes that those institutions serving minority students lack the resources to compete effectively for competitive grants from the Department of Agriculture (U.S. General Accounting Office, 2003). Another report found that 51 percent of the patents issued in the United States originated from only ten geographic areas, giving these areas a great advantage in job growth ("Universities Can Play Important Role in Innovation, Economic Development," 2003).

When the concentration of grants seems unreasonable, there is a tendency for Congress to intervene and earmark research funds for certain projects and universities, but this undercuts the basic nature of the competitive grant program (Brainard, 2002). Still, by using multiple federal agencies to make grants and by creating programs that open opportunities more broadly (such as the Experimental Program to Stimulate Competitive Research, open only to states that have received 0.7 percent or less of total NSF research funds over the preceding three years; "Investment Strategy: Who's Eligible," 2003), the United States has created a remarkable array of research universities. Today, the number is so large that the danger of concentration is diminished.

Another potential area of distortion is the risk that the competition for funding (and for the prestige—both individual and institutional—that flows from research success) will lead to greater secrecy. The growing value of patents that flow from federally funded university research compounds this danger. University research, in contrast to industrial research, has had the great advantage that its results have been open, allowing the entire scientific community worldwide to share ideas, confirm hypotheses, avoid dead ends, and move forward far more rapidly (Gould, 2003). As university-industry collaboration grows, and as patent income becomes a major source of university revenue, the threat to openness grows.

Another distortion is that success in attracting grants may create a financial and organizational burden on universities. Because the competition for grants is so intense, the federal government has been able to reduce the overhead, or administrative costs, it is willing to reimburse and move to cost sharing. When the volume of grant funding is small, as it was in the early days of research and is today in many grant programs outside the area of research, the grant is a net gain, and little added organization or facilities are needed. Grant funding in research has long passed that point; for the long-run success of the research grant programs, the federal government must strike the right balance of reimbursement that avoids both wasteful practices and damage to the university's functioning ("Need Grows for More Federal Financing of Research Facilities," 2003). The danger is particularly acute in medical research, where grant funding plays a dominant role in funding medical schools.

Another source of distortion is the public perception of which subjects should be allocated available funds. One great advantage of the competitive grant model is that the government, acting on behalf of the public, can steer research into the most needed areas; one disadvantage is that public and political pressures do not always coincide with national needs. Some subjects are simply more attractive in terms of public concern or are championed by an effective lobby. In medical research, for example, cancer research is far better funded than research on Alzheimer's and other forms of dementia, despite the latter's widespread effects and heavy personal and governmental costs. There has simply been relatively little organized public support for a major Alzheimer's effort (no "war on Alzheimer's") compared to that for cancer.

Still, despite these problems, the use of competitive grants for numerous purposes in a variety of settings continues to grow. To be truly successful, higher education must be at the forefront of knowledge in research, service, and teaching—constantly improving in each area in a restless quest to be at the highest level of performance. Competitive grants can help make the case.

Chapter Eleven

College and University Strategies for the New Era

*For each college and university, strategic planning is
crucial to meeting today's challenges. However, the type of
strategic planning typically undertaken by colleges and
universities does not come close to what is needed to
address the current issues.*

As the new world of higher education emerges, leaders of universities and colleges face three demanding tasks:

- How to ensure that their university or college succeeds in a higher education marketplace characterized by intense competition
- How to help policy makers construct a workable higher education system as market forces become the primary means that governments use to structure higher education
- How to make certain that the result for both the system and their institution is serving public purposes

Although the second task, helping policy makers structure the higher education system, is of more immediate concern for public institutions, all institutions—public and private, universities and colleges, for-profit and nonprofit—must face these tasks; all will be deeply affected by the structure of the higher education market that emerges.

For each college and university, strategic planning is crucial to meeting these challenges. However, the type of strategic planning typically undertaken by colleges and universities does not come close to what is needed to address the current issues. For example, most planning has yet to address the profound changes that will occur as competition accelerates and market forces play a large role. There is a body of knowledge available from other fields about how to structure markets. There is as well a great deal of experience with creating organizational strategies for succeeding in a newly competitive climate—some is about higher education but most is about other sectors (Brewer, Gates, and Goldman, 2002).[1] As yet, however, this information has received little attention from academic leaders.

For decades, academic leaders have been wary about engaging in the type of serious discussion with policy makers that is necessary to rethink structure, the proper role of government, and the balance of institutional autonomy and accountability. They fear that such attention will only lead to limitations on their autonomy. They need to put that wariness aside and create a constructive debate, as has occurred in the past (for example, in developing the Wisconsin plan in the early 1900s, the California Master Plan in 1960, or in expanding science capacity during the cold war—all occasions where academic and political leaders worked together to create a new and constructive approach).

Little attention has been paid to the slow-but-steady erosion of public purpose. The growing pressure to restructure higher education presents an opportunity to address the issue of public purpose before the damage is irreversible. Most important, institutional leaders (not just presidents but deans, department chairs, faculty, student leaders) must ask themselves some hard questions. How can the university or college create a plan designed to move away from protecting the status quo and move toward engaging the campus in the work of the future? How can the entire organization accept the challenges of setting expectations, assessing performance, and beginning the never-ending task of improvement?

What follows are suggestions for creating a successful institutional strategy. They are not rocket science; some are familiar proposals. Most leaders in higher education will agree with these recommendations. But doing it, moving a university or college to create and implement a strategy of the type described, is hard work and so far rare.

Why Is Strategic Planning So Hard to Do?

The experience in sector after sector has been that moving from a regulated structure to a market (even a partial market structure) requires clearly thought-out strategies. The mind-set of the higher education community has resisted thinking of the academic world as a market structured by government. Recently, a growing number of presidents, principally from flagship state universities, have begun to recognize that the change toward the market as an organizing strategy is in progress; they have begun to argue for greater autonomy to allow their institutions to face the changing demands.

Beyond this, higher education has its own special characteristics that make realistic strategic planning hard to do. For one thing, there is a strong sense that the role of the administration is to protect the campus not only from political interference but also from the influence of any external forces, including the marketplace (a task roughly comparable to that facing King Canute at the shoreline).

The "collegial" nature of the campus militates against assessment of performance and hard decisions. There is a need to end the long drift into a tradition of governance whose principal effect is to produce gridlock, a tradition of what Susanne Lohmann calls "defects and defenses" that flow from faculty devotion to "deep specialization" in the academic disciplines and a sense of separation from the day-to-day work of society (Lohmann, 2004). But effective governance can be pursued.[2] In their work *A New Academic Compact,* Linda McMillin and William Berberet give both practical advice and actual examples of creating a restored sense of institutional commitment by faculty (McMillin and Berberet, 2002). In another example, Brown University recently completed a reorganization of its academic governance that meets the two tests—encouraging meaningful faculty involvement and improving the timeliness and effectiveness of decision making. The new administration and faculty officers worked together to rethink the demands on governance, reduce the number of committees, establish clear ground rules for operation, and clarify expectations. The reconstruction trimmed down the involvement of 237 faculty members in governance to a more manageable 115 members, replacing the existing forty-four faculty committees with twelve committees and nine new advisory boards that pull faculty and administration together as peers (Nickel, 2002).

The lack of any focus on performance improvement, in all aspects of institutional activities but most notably in the performance of teaching and learning, makes strategic planning and improved performance difficult. The absence of performance assessment has caused serious problems for some time. Now, in a world of intense competition, growing demand for accountability, rapid change, and high risks, this lack is not simply annoying but dangerous.

For a long time, it has been clear that the incentives for faculty and administrators are often counterproductive to an institutional effort to improve. As Dominic Brewer, Susan Gates, and Charles Goldman asserted in their study *In Pursuit of Prestige,* "Traditional institutions are governed largely by administrators or tenure-track faculty members, who reap the benefits of prestige if the institution is successful, but bear few of the costs" (Brewer, Gates, and Goldman, 2002, p. 134). Most significant, it has proven difficult to change the faculty reward structure to value high-quality teaching. Criticism of faculty for focusing on publication rather than effective teaching and engagement with students is rampant, but it is a logical outgrowth of the current reward structure. These issues have been the subject of extensive comment within and about the academy. What is needed now is action at each individual institution.

There is as well a lack of focus on a new and subtle problem: the rising difficulty of drawing a clear line between acceptable and unacceptable activities, exacerbated by the acceleration of competitive pressures. This, in the long run, may be the most dangerous of these problems. As competitive pressures mount, the temptation to gain new revenue or to advance in the rankings at the expense of time-honored values is hard to resist, particularly since each step is incremental. Does a corporate grant for research carry with it a restriction on the freedom to publish that goes just too far? Does the contract for a university-brand credit card begin to erode the belief that the institution is fundamentally different from those credit card companies that bombard us all with weekly solicitations featuring a skilled blend of attractive offers and unattractive fine print? Will the establishment of a for-profit subsidiary to market courseware originally developed for the institution's own teaching erode the basic nonprofit nature of the institution?

Why Things Are Unlikely to Stay as They Are

Higher education has a well-deserved reputation for stability over the decades, even over the centuries. Despite this, change is already happening. Several factors make staying the same unlikely. Within the policy worlds, both state and federal, there is rising concern about the need to address critical issues that affect the performance of higher education. Increasingly, this concern is matched by a willingness to force higher education to address these issues:

- Concern over the lack of information about what and how much students are learning continues to build, spurred in part by criticism on the part of employers about the skills of graduates.
- The cost of instruction continues to rise at a rate typically three times that of inflation and with it the cost to the student, the cost to the state, and the cost to the federal government. Coupled with the recognized need for an expanded share of the population to gain a college education, this means that the total resources required by higher education from all sources must continue to rise at a dramatic—and unsupportable— rate. For political leaders, this looks similar to the problem that is already confronting the country with the rise in health care costs.
- The competition among institutions of higher education continues to intensify, which alters and increases the demands on each university and college. A growing array of new competitors—virtual, for-profit, corporate—simply add to this pressure.
- In the rest of the developed world, the determination to compete with American universities is increasingly vigorous and outspoken. The United States still has significant advantages in quality, flexibility, and use of English as the language of instruction, but with its high costs, lack of attention to flaws, and abundance of hubris, higher education is a candidate to repeat the saga of the American loss of place in such American icons as automobiles and jet aircraft.

All institutions will be affected. Some will fail to respond and fall by the wayside. For those institutions that are prepared to respond, create effective strategic plans, and implement change, this is a time of opportunity.

What Must Institutions Do to Face These Changes?

The experience of other sectors makes plain certain organizational needs that are amplified by a shift toward market forces and intensified competition, most specifically the requirement of more skilled leadership and organizational mastery of change. There is a large and rapidly growing literature on both of these subjects, with little to be gained by our repeating here what has been learned. It is, however, a literature with which university and college administrators should become familiar.

In every sector facing change and competition, there is an issue with regard to leadership. There are, however, some concerns specific to higher education that deserve attention. To begin with, the nature of the search process in widespread use in higher education favors candidates who are unlikely to rock the boat. Few candidates on their visit to campus find it wise to raise the issue of a mediocre rate of graduation, the lack of any meaningful measures of student learning, or the logic of closing marginal departments. As universities and colleges are buffeted by the winds of change, the search process and the desires of search committees and boards are likely to change toward favoring more dynamic, proactive, and effective leadership. But the change toward recruiting stronger leaders tends to lag the need for better leadership.

Higher education, facing change and high risks, is in need of new and better leadership now—not just in the presidency but at all levels. Leadership is not something that should be hoarded; it is not a zero-sum game. The goal must be to expand the number of leaders and the total amount of leadership. This means that institutions must make a continuous effort in two critical areas. The first is to improve the search process. The second is the need for leadership development—a subject that is not addressed at all on most campuses, leaving higher education as one of the few sectors of society that does not focus on a constant effort to find and develop leaders.

Since a crucial task in times of change and high risk is to ask hard questions about the institution's strategy and the effectiveness of efforts to implement that strategy, leadership of the board is critical. But what is needed from the board is leadership, not management. Does the board, for example, ask if the institution knows whether students are learning, and if so, how does it know? Does it track not just how many students apply but how many graduate? The role of such questioning is not to tell the administration what to do but to ensure that the administration is focused on the right issues, developing a plan, and tracking the plan. Does the board regularly raise critical questions about the direction and success of administration efforts? Does it insist on creating a clear, focused strategy? Does it support plans for change and thoughtful risk taking?

Colleges and universities also have a special need to practice the art of leadership with skill, since it is through watching academic leaders at work that students begin to see firsthand what organizational leadership can and should be. In a report for the Kellogg Foundation, Alexander and Helen Astin make this case:

> Even though the United States is generally regarded as having the finest postsecondary education system in the world, there is mounting evidence that the quality of leadership in this country has been eroding in recent years. . . .

> This is both an individual and an institutional challenge. Students will find it difficult to lead until they have experienced effective leadership as part of their education. They are not likely to commit to making changes in society unless the institutions in which they have been trained display a similar commitment. If the next generation of citizen leaders is to be engaged and committed to leading for the common good, then the institutions which nurture them must be engaged in the work of the society and the community, modeling effective leadership and problem solving skills, demonstrating how to accomplish change for the common good. [Astin and Astin, 2000, p. 2]

With regard to change strategies, much of the literature focuses on the business community, with some focused on the art of bringing change to government. To be useful, it must be adapted to the world of higher education, with its emphasis on faculty involvement. What is needed is not elimination of an active faculty role.

On the contrary, the new and expanding literature on the leadership of change stresses participatory processes. For the academic world, this means active participation, but not the hardened, veto—prone processes so frequently in use on the campus.

It is possible, under the right circumstances, to break through this reluctance to change and get institutions to acknowledge a problem and do something.[3] Rosabeth Moss Kanter, the management theorist whose work *The Change Masters* helped American business leaders regroup to overcome the challenge of the Japanese and German business assault of the 1970s and 1980s, notes the continuing relevance of Arnold Toynbee's description of the rise and fall of nations as challenge and response (Kanter, 1985). A young nation is confronted with a challenge for which it must create a response. If it responds skillfully, it then grows and prospers. In time, the nature of the challenge changes. If the nation continues to make the same response that was successful in earlier times, it will begin to decline. So far, most universities are using the same response in 2003 as served them so well in the 1960s and 1970s.

Creating—and Implementing—a Different Strategic Plan

The need is for each institution to create, and implement, a strategic plan and then constantly monitor performance against the plan. This requires a strategic plan clear and specific enough that it can be implemented and visionary enough that it will matter if it is implemented.

Specificity

Many colleges and universities have created what they call a strategic plan. The large majority simply do not serve the current need. Simply put, they are too vague and general. What is too often missing is a strategy that spells out in understandable terms how the institution will move forward, claim its place in the sun, develop its unique character, and attract its clientele.[4] It must amplify and clarify the mission, making it specific and realistic. Instead, institutional strategies have tended toward vague generalities (for example, "the Harvard of the South" or a "great regional university") that tend to end up meaning "sort of like everyone else." The values and goals of higher education institutions are often so general that a study of Chicago-area higher education institutions showed significant similarities of stated purpose among the private University of Chicago, the public University of Illinois–Chicago, the for-profit universities DeVry and Cardean, and Hamburger U. (McDonald's corporate training institution; Kirp, 2000). The mission has to be specific to the institution and clear about the implications for future action.

Mission

The mission statement should be clear and crisp, a short and practical statement of the vision for the institution that can be referred to by one and all. It should differentiate the institution from others, making plain the institution's special nature while also espousing those essential values shared by all of higher education. Determining what the mission *is* is important. Deciding what it *isn't* is equally important. What clientele will not be served? What program areas and activities are outside the mission?

Public Purposes

The strategy should describe clearly the institutional commitments to public purposes. What is the mission that policy makers expect the institution to pursue? Does it include commitment to help society promote real social mobility by creating access and academic success for students of color and students from low-income backgrounds? If so, does the strategic plan describe the expectations, including the background and number of students the institution expects to attract, the programs it must mount to ensure academic success, the target rate for graduation, and the resources this entails? At every institution, are the learning expectations for all students spelled out clearly and communicated effectively so that faculty, students, and the public know what skills, knowledge, and attitudes graduates are expected to master? Are the faculty and officers of the institution fully aware of where students are failing to meet these institutional expectations? Is there clear, transparent information made public about learning? Is there a plan for the institution to support and align its efforts with elementary and secondary education? Is there a clear plan for outreach activity to help the community with assigned priorities and resources, or is this simply left to the interest of individual faculty and administrators? When priorities are set, does the incentive and reward structure match the priorities? For example, if the plan calls for significant improvement in the ability of graduates to use mathematical knowledge to solve practical problems (currently a major failing at almost all institutions), is this matched by a reward structure that makes it rational for a faculty member to spend time on creating new approaches to teaching math using technology that addresses the problem?

Does the plan spell out in clear terms the ethical borderlines within which the institution will operate? Such guidelines simplify the task for faculty and administrators by setting the borders in advance rather than focusing on cleaning up problems after the fact. Has the institution joined with its peers to create a published set of ethical standards to help contain the issue?

Choices

The strategy must recognize the hard questions facing the institution, pose them clearly, and offer answers or create the means to derive answers. Is the institution going to enter the arena of educating older students or the arena of online education? Is it truly an institution devoted to graduate education, or should it focus its talent and resources on undergraduate education? Is the institution "going global"? Would this serve the institution's mission? If so, is it prepared to make a major commitment? It has become painfully clear that, in the current climate, whatever the institution does it must do well. Doing so requires the commitment of adequate resources and attention. As those universities that entered the arena of for-profit online education found out, the day of casual commitment is past.

Focus

The strategy must be clear about what the institution is and will do but also what it is not and what it will not do. One glaring weakness of most university and college strategies is an unwillingness to focus—to devote energy and resources to what the institution must do well and to eliminate activities that are marginal. At any time, but particularly in a competitive and demanding climate, institutions need to concentrate their resources on those activities that are central to their strategy, activities where they propose to do well, not disperse their efforts over activities of marginal interest. The Association of Commonwealth Universities warns, "As more providers compete for public and student funds, institutions must identify a specific focus and not try to be 'all things to all people.' Rationalization should be undertaken to focus on activities catering for the niche in the marketplace" (Association of Commonwealth Universities, 2001, p. 13).

The result must be focus and coherence. This requires making hard choices. Is a review of all programs—academic and nonacademic—being carried out periodically to determine which programs are no longer central to the institution's strategy? Is there an assessment process that has the capacity to measure the contribution of a program? Are new proposals tested against the template of the institution's strategy? Is the institution prepared to cut marginal departments, centers, programs, or activities?[5] Robert Dickeson of the Lumina Foundation for Education, in two recent works, has laid out the case and a straightforward approach to reallocating resources from low-priority to high-priority activities (Dickeson, 1999, 2002).

For many institutions, creating a meaningful focus is not easy. For colleges or universities that wish to excel at the liberal arts, the decisions as to which academic programs to provide are subjective and may well seem arbitrary. The opportunity for differing conclusions is boundless. One need only think of the prolonged debate that the leadership of Washington University endured over the decision to eliminate sociology. Still, focus is essential, and decisions must be made. In some cases, collaboration with other organizations may make more sense than the institution operating its own programs or designing its own software (Martin and Samels, 2002).

Sharing

The strategy and the basic mission of the institution must be shared—that is, understood, and understood in the same way by all of the constituencies. The various constituencies of a given institution often have vastly different perceptions of the institution's goals and different ideas as to what the strategy should be for reaching them. In the past, there was usually enough slippage in the loosely coupled management of the institution so that everyone simply went his or her own way, following their own nonunderstanding of the mission as well as their strategy for pursuing their own interests. Given the more demanding environment, that approach won't work anymore.

Dynamism

Because society continues to change, and because the nature of the competition continues to change, the strategy must be dynamic and flexible, with mechanisms built in for continuous updating. Few colleges and universities have thought seriously about this.

Entrepreneurism

Universities and colleges, particularly community colleges, have shown a great deal of entrepreneurial capacity in certain areas such as adult education, job training, or virtual programs. These activities tend to share some common characteristics. They are add-ons, they bring in new resources, and they do not threaten the regular faculty or traditional programs. On the other hand, the innovations made in these entrepreneurial programs do not have much influence on the traditional program, the central academic core, which often remains bogged down defending the status quo. In his study of five European universities that "made a valiant effort . . . to become more enterprising," Burton Clark begins by noting: "The universities of the world have entered a time of disquieting turmoil that has no end in sight. As the difficulties of universities mounted across the globe during the last quarter of the twentieth century, higher education lost whatever steady state it may have once possessed. . . . Pushed and pulled by enlarging, interacting streams of demand, universities are pressured to change their curricula, alter their faculties, and modernize their increasingly expensive physical plant and equipment—and to do so more rapidly than ever" (Clark, 1998, pp. xiii–xiv).[6]

From his study of these cases, Clark (1998) extracted five common elements of their success:

1. A "strengthened steering core": "a greater systematic capacity to steer themselves than they had possessed 15 years earlier. . . . [an] administrative backbone [that] fused new managerial values with traditional academic ones" (pp. 5, 137)
2. An "enhanced development periphery": "outreach administrative units that promote contract research, contract education, and consultancy" (pp. 6, 138)
3. A "diversified funding base": "additional lines of income from pursued patrons" and "active cost containment" (pp. 6, 140)
4. A "stimulated academic heartland": "heartland departments" such as social sciences and humanities also "[buy] into entrepreneurial change" (pp. 7, 142)
5. An "entrepreneurial belief": "a work culture that embraces change" (pp. 7, 143–144)

There is a risk in such entrepreneurism. The search for added revenue has often become the end rather than the means, causing institutions to drift into activities marginal to, or incompatible with, institutional mission and values.

Diversified Funding

One goal of an entrepreneurial effort should be development of diversified funding sources as a means of creating greater stability and facilitating response to new opportunities in a time of volatility. Diversity in funding sources also helps institutions find resources for support of activities, such as outreach efforts required in service to the community, that may be difficult to fund as the escalating level of competition forces institutions to concentrate existing resources on key academic programs, limiting the institution's ability to cross-subsidize. It is, however, critical that the nature of any new funding stream be compatible with the institution's mission and values.

Reputation

The strategy should include building a positive reputation. Most institutions assume that reputation simply follows quality—with *quality* defined narrowly. In a world of intense competition, depending on this assumption is dangerous. The reputation that an institution has is a critical asset or liability. We know and respect the reputation of CalTech, Williams, Truman State, or Portland State, but such institutions are few and far between.[7] They have been willing to focus and not try to be all things to all people. We may agree or disagree with their chosen focus, but we, and they, know what it is. Too often, institutions are unclear about what exactly their special role is.

Beyond having a focus, concrete actions are needed to create a widespread and positive reputation. The academic community has frequently turned up its nose at the idea of public relations or the concept of brand, assuming that such activities sully the academic purity of the institution. Instead, institutions depend on constantly repeated rhetoric about the institution's quality. The advice from Socrates that "the best way to gain a good reputation is to endeavor to be what you desire to be" is necessary but not sufficient.

Institutions must do the hard work of building a positive and specific reputation. There is more at stake than attracting students and funding. Improving the confidence of stakeholders is essential to gaining and preserving autonomy. Reputation is the key for recruiting faculty and staff. In addition to defining and building its own special role and capacity, the institution must ensure that its role and skills are recognized by key constituencies: existing students, prospective students, parents, funders, alumni, faculty, potential faculty candidates, and the surrounding communities. Have polls and focus groups been done to determine the reputation that currently exists? Have all the constituencies been kept abreast of the changes and improvements of the institution and of the revised goals and strategy? Does the Website give a clear picture of the institution's special role and quality? Building a reputation, like every other aspect of building an effective university or college, needs careful analysis, a plan, skilled implementation, and constant assessment of progress.

Collaboration

The plan should describe the institution's objectives and intended collaboration with other organizations, spelling out the purposes, gains to be made, and limitations. As competition increases, so

higher education plays. Higher education serves society through teaching that is nonideological, research that is open and trustworthy, and service that helps address the difficult issues that society faces. Its objectivity and integrity can be trusted because its interests are beyond those of the marketplace. In return, society has extended unusual privileges to these institutions—academic freedom, the right to debate controversial issues facing society, financial support, tax exemption, and respect and trust.

Some of the benefits of the compact are immediate and tangible, such as tax exemption and subsidy. Some are more important but less tangible, such as academic freedom. The benefits hardest to quantify are at the core of the relationship between the academy and society: trust and respect. If higher education allows these profound benefits to erode, if higher education becomes just one more participant in the marketplace, the loss to higher education and to society will be fundamental and probably irreversible.

This compact now suffers from a slow but deeply concerning erosion—a slow weakening that is causing, in turn, erosion of the special nature of higher education. In part, this flows from an overstated sense that the benefits of higher education are private rather than public. In part, it flows from the increasing tendency for universities and colleges to act like businesses, focused more on revenue streams than public purposes (even to the point of presidents calling themselves CEOs). In part, it flows from an unwillingness to acknowledge and address the flaws that mar higher education's performance.

Serving the public purposes of higher education has never been more important. American society must address the revitalization of its economy, growing income disparity, the dogged problems of enhancing the lives of the least advantaged and ensuring their social mobility, the need for a workable system of health care, the frayed relationship with the rest of the world, the need for security in a newly insecure world, and rebuilding the civic engagement of its citizens. In short, for the United States to be a successful democracy and a model to the world, higher education must stand as a central source of hope, vision, and assistance.

For civic renewal to be effective, there must be a shared belief that society has the capacity to rise above narrow self-interest. This, in turn, requires institutions in the society with the capacity and will to lead the effort. Traditional candidates for that leadership are the university, the media, the church, and the government. Just listing these candidates makes plain how much we need a committed and effective system of higher education. For higher education to become simply another self-focused, revenue-oriented sector of society would be a tragedy of massive proportions. The task, then, is to rebuild the compact, renew the understanding between higher education and the public, and renew and strengthen the commitment to the public purposes of higher education.

The Long, Historical Growth of Public Expectations

For the three-plus centuries of American higher education, universities and colleges—both state-owned and private—have held a privileged position. With this special position have come responsibilities and expectations. As the country has grown and developed, the expectations that society holds for higher education have grown. When the first college was founded in 1636, two purposes were spelled out in its charter: to graduate enough "men of the cloth" to lead the colony's churches and to graduate "lettered gentlemen" able to lead the affairs of the colony. The act of the Connecticut legislature in 1701 that led to the founding of Yale University called for education for "employment both in Church and Civil State" (Frederick, 1971, p. 27). These two purposes—education for the workforce and for civic life—have remained the bedrock of public expectations to this day.

During the first half of the 1800s, another responsibility was acquired: moral development of young men from so-called better families. Typically, the institution's president taught the capstone course on moral philosophy. This responsibility remains today in a broader form as a responsibility to develop in students (now men and women) a sense of civic responsibility. Unfortunately, presidents are no longer expected to teach moral philosophy.

In 1862, the Land Grant College Act, sponsored by Congressman Justin S. Morrill of Vermont, opened a new dimension of expectations. The federal government put up blocks of the land it owned in the West so that states could sell the land and finance new institutions (or add to existing ones) focused on two important expansions of public expectation. The first was to expand the study of practical subjects and establish the means of bringing the knowledge and skills resident in the college to bear on problems of the community. Particular attention was to be paid to "agricultural science" and the "mechanic arts," the two prominent economic development issues of the day—the transformation of agriculture and the Industrial Revolution.

The second and equally significant challenge was to create the opportunity for education of the industrial classes. The latter function was echoed in the founding of a number of institutions created for the express purpose of providing opportunity for the less advantaged, as with City College of New York and the Illinois Institute of Technology.

During the same period, two new universities, Johns Hopkins and Cornell, were founded that furthered the push toward practical subjects as well as more formalized research, deepening two important expectations: that universities should engage in research and that the fruits of research would be put at the service of society by outreach activities and by graduating skilled experts able to help serve the community. In the early 1900s, these concepts were pushed further in the Wisconsin experiment with progressive government. The state and the University of Wisconsin undertook a multifaceted collaboration designed to improve the quality of state government (the "university in the service of the people"). The basic concept, in the words of Governor Robert La Follette, was: "In no state of the Union are the relationships between the university and the people of the state so intimate and so mutually helpful as in Wisconsin. We believe that the purpose of the university is to serve the people, and every effort is made through correspondence courses, special courses, housekeepers' conferences, farmers' institutes, experimental stations and the like to bring every resident of the state under the broadening and inspiring influence of a faculty of trained men" (La Follette, 1913, p. 31).

In 1944, another powerful change in expectations developed, almost unexpectedly, with passage of the GI Bill (formally the Servicemen's Readjustment Act), intended to help millions in transitioning from wartime service to peacetime jobs. The federal government committed itself to tuition benefits for every person who spent more than a minimum time in the service; the benefits

allowed attendance at any college or university that would admit
the veteran (or at union apprentice or vocational programs). The
result was a huge jump in college and university access, from 10
percent of each age group in 1940 to 20 percent in 1950, coupled
with the realization that many more young people could succeed
at and gain from college attendance than had been the accepted
wisdom. One result was a new surge in enrollment. Another was
an increase in federal and state government support of broader
access.

Several factors aided this enrollment surge. Public universities
and colleges began to expand in response to public pressure. Community colleges, which had been growing in number, exploded,
targeting several groups of students—those seeking more advanced
vocational skills, those who hadn't done well in high school but had
developed the motivation to go on, and those who were place-bound.

Access expanded in the 1950s and 1960s in another way. Nontraditional students, often older and working full-time or part-time,
began to gain access not only at community colleges but at universities as well. There were antecedents for this willingness to
admit the nontraditional student (a willingness still largely absent
or limited in much of the rest of the world), among them a small
number of law schools or other institutions devoted to the nontraditional student. Later, in the 1980s, when the demographics of
the eighteen to twenty-two age group forecast falling enrollments,
a broader range of institutions began active recruiting of nontraditional students to keep enrollments rising.

The 1950s saw another profound change in expectations. Recognizing the powerful impact that research had on the outcome
of World War II, and painfully aware of how dependent the United
States had been on British research and on scientists driven from
Europe by Nazi Germany, the federal government began an extensive program of research support in a new format: peer-reviewed,
competitive grants from multiple federal agencies (see Chapter
Ten for details). Soon American research led the world, and the
public added to its expectations of higher education the importance of world-leading research in every field.

In the 1960s, expectations about access expanded again. The
national debate over civil rights led to desegregation of essentially

public opposes use of quotas to furnish access to selective programs for minorities, they also indicate strong support for other modes of outreach to help the less advantaged gain opportunity through higher education.[4] There are clearly multiple modes by which higher education can meet the public's criteria and create effective opportunity for those still poorly served. A new debate, focused on successful modes of making opportunity available for the less advantaged, can set higher education on a positive course that has broad, informed public support.

Rebuilding the Compact Between Higher Education and the Public

Perhaps the most important point of all in creating a public debate is the realization that the structure of higher education must be built on the foundation of each institution's determination to discharge its responsibilities to society. The success of American higher education has depended on the broad social compact noted above—a widely shared understanding of what it is that higher education does for society and the support, privilege, and respect that society provides in return. Over time, this compact has become visibly frayed. Institutions often seem more self-focused than public-focused. As society continues to change, higher education has not always kept up with the new demands placed on it. As market forces play a greater role, the risk that higher education will fail to meet its side of the compact grows.

As each institution builds a special place in the overall scheme of higher education, it needs to ask what its responsibilities are to the public. Has the institution recognized the centrality of teaching and learning (even at research universities)? Has it recognized that education includes more than simply job skills, that it entails development and practice of civic skills? Has it considered how use of resources, such as student aid, shapes the basic nature of the institution? What expertise does it have that can be shared with society in ways that improve the community? Has the institution served the public as a center of open discussion of controversial issues in a way that values evidence and analysis or has it reneged on this responsibility in order to avoid offending funders or the community?

At the same time, state governments must take on the responsibility for clearly identifying and communicating their priorities and expectations. Accountability needs to be a clearly stated expectation and a workable plan, not simply a phrase to be bandied about as a signal of discontent. Research has shown that states with clear expectations receive better results from their institutions.[5]

As those of us in the higher education community look ahead, the future seems hard to predict and full of change and surprise. We will have to learn to live with a high level of risk and uncertainty. What is clear is that higher education will be even more important to meeting society's goals than it has already become today. Technology will open new possibilities for extending the university's reach and improving the capacity to teach and research. But technology is no respecter of tradition as to how organizations are organized. New forms of pedagogy are emerging. We will no doubt have to face the possibility of fundamental changes in what a university or college looks like. We must be certain to take seriously this great responsibility.

Governments today are struggling with the task of creating policies that encourage greater responsiveness and accountability on the part of universities and colleges. Every institution needs to join in that effort and help create a renewed understanding of what higher education will do for the public and what support—political and financial—the public will offer in return. Taking all these profound issues into account, there was never a period in which the opportunity for contributing to society has been as great as it is now.

Notes

Chapter One

1. Much has been written about the growing market and competition in higher education by other researchers. See, for example, MacTaggart and Associates, 1998; Kirp, 2003; Ruben, 2004; Berdahl, 2001; Brewer, Gates, and Goldman, 2002; Bok, 2003; Armstrong, 2001.

    Mario Martinez and Richard Richardson of the Alliance for International Higher Education Policy Studies analyzed governance models in New Jersey and New Mexico and concluded that "monopoly and regulated markets may produce strong performance in singular areas, but balanced markets produce consistent performance across a range of outcomes." See Martinez and Richardson, 2003. See also National Center for Public Policy and Higher Education, 2003.

Chapter Two

1. 11,309,399 students are in public institutions, out of a total of 14,791,224 (76.5 percent). See "Almanac 2002–3," 2002.
2. Princeton is not alone. For examples of the use of merit aid at the University of Massachusetts and Union College, please see Rimer, 2003, p. 16; Marcus, 2001.
3. Lowering tuition certainly is not the norm. In an opposite move, Miami University of Ohio is seeking to raise in-state tuition to match out-of-state tuition, a strategy it claims will give the school the money and flexibility needed to compete for the state's top students. Critics of the plan believe that this is mainly a ploy to improve the institution's *U.S. News & World Report* rankings by attracting "better" students and that the increased tuition will limit access for low-income students. "Miami Approves One-Tuition Plan," *Dayton Daily News,* Apr. 24, 2003 [http://www.daytondailynews.com/localnews/content/localnews/daily/0424miamituition.html].

4. For an example of enrollment management at work, see Kirp and Holman, 2002.

5. The University of Pennsylvania, for example, looked to early decision as one method to improve its enrollment and allure as a competitive university. In this instance, the strategy worked. In 2002, it tied for sixth place with Stanford in the *U.S. News & World Report* college rankings. When these rankings were first published in 1983, UPenn was not even ranked among the national universities (Fallows, 2003, p. 37–38). See also Arenson, 2002.

6. For more examples and details on how colleges and universities are competing for students as covered in the popular press, see Russell, 2002; Symonds, 2003; Guernsey, 1999; Levinson, 2002; O'Neill, 2001 (O'Neill wrote a six-part series on the subject); Arenson, 2002 (see also ad for CUNY's honors program in Jan. 12, 2003, edition of *New York Times,* p. 10); "Clemson University Wants to Be Ranked Top 20 Universities in Nation," *Associated Press Newswires,* Jul. 22, 2001; "S.D. Colleges Using Technology to Recruit Students," *Associated Press Newswires,* Apr. 7, 2002; Winston, 2001; Marcus, 2001; "Colleges Finding Fitness Centers Are Way to Draw, Keep Students," *Providence Journal,* July 28, 2002; "State Colleges Work Hard to Recruit Students," *Associated Press Newswires,* July 26, 2002; Crenshaw, 2002; Winter, 2003c.

7. As of October 2002, the cost of a full centerspread in "Education Life" was $89,078, and the cost of a full-page ad was $41,888 ("Education Life—Quarterly Tabloid Magazine: Sunday Nationwide Distribution," Feb. 2003, http://nytadvertising.nytimes.com/adonis/html/open/ed_1a.shtml).

8. According to Ross (2003), the author of *Public Relations and the Presidency: Strategies and Tactics for Effective Communications,* "After 30 years laboring in higher education's media-relations vineyard, I've seen little, if any, reliable data that directly relate the occasional mention of a college in major newspapers and magazines to continuing success in fund raising or to sustained increases in enrollment and retention."

9. For a discussion of prestige, see Brewer, Gates, and Goldman, 2002.

10. Currently, about 77 percent of colleges and universities offer online applications. More than one hundred thousand applications were processed within a two-month time span in 1999 through Xap.com, a company that creates online applications. That same year the University of California system alone received nineteen thousand online applicants; Guernsey, 1999.

11. For a discussion of the aid package wars in Pennsylvania, see O'Neill, 2001.

factsheets/Information%20about%20The%20Open%20University/
The%20Open%20University%20worldwide.pdf]. The Singapore-
MIT Alliance, an alliance between MIT, Nanyang Technological
University (NTU), and National University of Singapore (NUS), was
founded in 1998 to promote global engineering research. "The
Singapore-MIT Alliance: A New Model in Global Education," May
2003 [http://web.mit.edu/sma/].

27. For reading on GATS, see Knight, Mar. 2002a; Altbach, 2002a;
     Knight, Summer 2002b; Altbach, 2003.

28. "Does Erasmus Meet Its Objectives?" 2001; "What Is Socrates/Erasmus?"
     May 2003 [http://europa.eu.int/comm/education/erasmus/what.
     html]; European Union Online. "ECTS-European Credit Transfer
     System, Erasmus," Dec. 2001 [http://europa.eu.int/comm/education/
     socrates/ects.html]; "ECTS-European Credit Transfer System," May
     2003 [http://europa.eu.int/comm/education/socrates/ects.html].

Chapter Three

1. Sen. Joseph Lieberman gave a speech about holding colleges
    accountable. See Burd, 2002c, p. A25. The steady and unabating
    rise in tuition has also raised cries for new accountability. See Win-
    ter, 2003a.

2. Interview with Ray Kieft, senior policy advisor and academic officer
    of the Colorado Commission on Higher Education, conducted by
    Lara Couturier on July 17, 2002. See also "Performance Agreement:
    Colorado School of Mines and CCHE for FY 2002–2007," Feb. 11,
    2002, supplied by John Trefny, president, Colorado School of Mines;
    interview with Sheila Kaplan, president of Metropolitan State College
    of Denver, conducted by Lara Couturier, July 25, 2002. See also Met-
    ropolitan State College of Denver, 2003; Burdman, 2003; Prah, 2002.

3. In what is termed a gentlemen's agreement, Darden has agreed to
    ensure that 30 percent of its entering class are Virginia residents.
    These students pay $5,000 less tuition than students from out of state,
    and Virginia makes up half the difference. Virginia will also continue
    to give more than $500,000 a year in matching grants for "eminent
    scholars" as well as continue to own the land Darden sits on. See Kirp
    and Roberts, 2002; phase-out date updated via e-mail by David Kirp
    [kirp@uclink4.berkeley.edu]. "The Academic Marketplace." E-mail
    message to Frank Newman, (frank_newman@brown.edu), Aug. 20,
    2003. See also Kronholz, 2003.

4. Colorado State Rep. Keith King, in focus group facilitated by John
    Immerwahr, Nov. 8, 2001.

5. For an overview of market-based reforms in K–12, see Ladd, 2002.

6. Observatory on Borderless Higher Education, 2002. The Singapore government report is at [www.mti.gov/sg/public/ERC/frm_ERC_Default. asp?sid=124].

7. See, for example, the argument about the trend to privatize the state universities in Michigan. See Waldsmith, 2003; Breneman, 2002.

8. For interesting examples of this trend, see Allen, 2002.

9. NASSGAP reported that, "In the 2000–2001 academic year, the states awarded $4.681 billion in need and non-need–based student grant aid to more than three million students, an increase of 14.5% in expenditures over the $4.089 billion awarded in 1999–2000" (National Association of State Student Grant and Aid Programs, 2002).

10. For information on tuition increases, see American Council on Education, 2002b; College Board, 1999; Trombley, 2002. Between 1990 and 1999, federal research expenditures grew 25.3 percent (in constant 1998 dollars), with public universities outperforming private ones in this area. See Craig, 2002. For further information on increases in research funding, see Press and Washburn, 2000; Brainard, 2003.

11. See Jones, 2003; Trombley, 2003; American Association of State Colleges and Universities, 2002.

12. Another example of market forces gone wrong was passage of the Mental Retardation and Community Mental Health Centers Construction Act of 1963. The act sought to create community mental health centers that would help to relieve the burden on state hospitals. The community centers had to rely to a great extent on local and private sources of funding, however, which forced them to seek out paying customers. As a result, the centers began to focus on clients who needed services such as marriage counseling instead of the truly ill who were unable to pay for their services. The sought-out clients were referred to by one expert with the acronym YAVIS ("young, attractive, verbal, intelligent, and successful"). The president of the American Psychiatric Association said that the centers had "drifted away from their original purpose." See Gillon, 2000.

13. For a brief and entertaining description of the risk of expecting more from markets than they can produce, see Varian, 2003.

14. For thorough discussions of the market and the need for public policies, see Berdahl, 2001; see Martinez and Richardson, 2003.

Chapter Four

1. Institutions also seek prestige in other ways that lead to mission creep, including creation of honors colleges. See Selingo, 2002.

2. For evidence that technology is fundamentally reorganizing higher education, see Duderstadt, Atkins, and Van Houweling, 2002.

3. "October Certification Test Results Released," Massachusetts Department of Education, Dec. 8, 2000 [http://www.doe.mass.edu/news/news.asp?id=600]. The Florida Comprehensive Assessment Test, a high school graduation requirement, is another example. In 2002, half of the sophomores in Miami-Dade County and 40 percent of the sophomores in Broward County failed the exam; Grech, 2002. See also Morgan, 2002b.

4. In 1998, the National Commission on the Cost of Higher Education called upon colleges and universities to go public with information about their financial information and college costs. In response, the National Association of College and University Business Officers created a study to develop a uniform methodology for explaining costs. Despite these efforts, individual institutions devote very little attention to reducing costs. See National Commission on the Cost of Higher Education, Jan. 1998; see also National Association of College and University Business Officers. "Explaining College Costs: NACUBO's Methodology for Identifying the Costs of Delivering Undergraduate Education," Feb. 2002 [http://www.nacubo.org/public_policy/cost_of_college/]; Heterick, 2002; Stringer and others, 1999.

5. American Association of University Professors. "Background Facts: Part-Time Faculty," Mar. 2003 [http://www.aaup.org/Issues/part-time/Ptfacts.htm]. See also Coalition on the Academic Workforce. "Who Is Teaching in U.S. College Classrooms? A Collaborative Study of Undergraduate Faculty, Fall 1999," Mar. 2003 [http://www.theaha.org/caw/pressrelease.htm]; Smallwood, 2003.

6. There are a few exceptions, such as a "program contribution analysis" conducted by the University of Rhode Island, which shows that some liberal arts programs are more profitable than others, such as the hard sciences that were assumed to be generating revenue because of their grants and prestige. See University of Rhode Island Program Contribution Analysis, FY01: 2000–01, Apr. 2002.

7. Higher education observers have long commented on this phenomenon. The editorial page editor of the *Providence Journal,* for example, has commented on higher education's "insatiable thirst for more and more money," applying C. Northcote Parkinson's quip that "Expenditures rise to meet income." See Whitcomb, 2003.

8. For ideas on how to improve quality without increasing costs, see Massy, 2003. The Mellon Foundation is running a program called Cost Effective Uses of Technology in Teaching (CEUTT), which funded twenty-five projects at universities in the United States (and

one in South Africa) to gauge the effectiveness of instructional technologies (www.ceutt.org). See also Duderstadt, Atkins, and Van Houweling, 2002.

9. The University of Phoenix has developed a cost-efficient and effective way of developing course materials. Farrell, 2003a.

10. The Project on the Future of Higher Education believes that rising costs must, and can, be addressed. See Guskin and Marcy, 2003.

11. From 2000–2001 to 2001–2002, tuition rose 5.5 percent at private colleges and 7.7 percent at the publics. College Board, 1999. For information on recent tuition increases, see Trombley, 2002. The steady and unabated rise in tuition has raised an outcry, most recently sparking a proposal from Rep. Howard P. McKeon of California to penalize colleges and universities that raise their tuitions too quickly. Brownstein, 2001. In that same time period, state appropriations increased by more than 80 percent in California, Florida, Georgia, Louisiana, Mississippi, and Texas. Despite this, the state's share of the whole higher education pie has been decreasing because institutional budgets have increased through private grants and revenues. Winter, 2003a.

12. Grapevine Project. A National Database for Tax Support for Higher Education, Illinois State University. "50 State Summary Table," May 2003 [http://www.coe.ilstu.edu/grapevine/].

13. Pat Callan, president of the National Center for Public Policy and Higher Education, has said, "Costs keep going up astronomically. . . . You're playing with political dynamite if you push this too far." Quoted in Allen, 2002, p. 1.

14. For a commentary on how career enhancement (instead of just income) distorts the research process, see Kennedy, 2003.

15. For another example of a university seeking revenues from research, see "Schools Profit from Publicly Funded Research," Apr. 29, 2003 [www.cnn.com/2003/EDUCATION/04/29/patent. universities.ap/index.html].

16. For background information on Olivieri and the Apotex controversy, see Blumenstyk, 1999; Spurgeon, 2001, p. 1085; "Report Vindicates Dr. Nancy Olivieri," 2001; Aoki, 2001; Baird, Downie, and Thompson, 2002.

17. See, for example, Hoyle, 2002. See also Corrigan, 2002; Atwell and Wellman, 2002. As you might expect, the *Chronicle of Higher Education* has covered this topic in some detail; see Keohane, 2003; Basinger and Perry, 2002.

18. Higher education must work harder to find ways to encourage the civic education of today's students to ensure the efficacy of tomorrow's democracy. See Colby, Ehrlich, Beaumont, and Stephens,

2003; Institute of Politics, 2002; Harkavy, 2002. Elisa C. Diller, a National Service Fellow, compiled a list of seven facts that exemplify today's level of civic disengagement. As an example, one of the facts cited by Diller is that "Since the 1972 Presidential Election, when the voting age was reduced to 18, there has been nearly a 20% point decrease in voting among 18–24 year olds, with only 32% going to the polls in 1996." For the rest of Diller's work, see Diller, E. C. "Citizens in Service: The Challenge of Delivering Civic Engagement Training to National Service Programs," June 2002 [http://www.etr.org/nsrc/pdfs/fellows/diller.pdf]. According to the Committee for the Study of the American Electorate, in the 1996 election, 49 percent of eighteen- to twenty-four-year olds with four years of college voted; 39 percent of that age group with one to three years of college voted; and 22 percent of high school graduates aged eighteen to twenty-four voted. See Clymer, 2000.

19. For arguments about higher education's performance in a number of areas ranging from access to teacher education, see "Promoting Educational Excellence in the New Economy," 2001; "The Challenge for Education Reform," 2003.

20. For another opinion on higher education's flaws, see Lovett, 2002a. Mel Elfin, the editor emeritus of *U.S. News & World Report College Guide,* recently wrote a scathing evaluation of higher education's current status. Elfin concluded: "At a time when the public's patience with higher education's rising costs and falling standards is wearing thin, conducting academic business as usual risks a destructive crisis of confidence in an enterprise that, for all its deep-seated troubles, remains integral both to the well-being of our society and to the future of our democracy." See Elfin, 2003. A recent "Policy Perspective" from the National Center for Public Policy and Higher Education also criticized the focus on institutional growth and improvement rather than on meeting state needs. See "Of Precept, Policy and Practice," Fall 2002.

Chapter Five

1. For articles covering the views of governors, see Conklin, 2002; Klor de Alva, 2000. In one example of a gubernatorial initiative, South Dakota's Gov. Michael Rounds established the Rounds Grants Program in Course Redesign, providing incentive funding to encourage institutions to collaborate in redesigning their courses with the goals of reducing costs and improving quality. See South Dakota Board of Regents, 2003.

Chapter Six

1. For a further example of an industry that is best served by some regulation, see Philip Hilts's (2003) story of the Food and Drug Administration.

2. For recommendations for colleges and universities, see "The Civic Mission of Schools," 2003. For an example of a university-based program focused on civic engagement, see the work of Brian O'Connell at the Tufts University College of Citizenship and Public Service.

3. For a further discussion of community outreach, please see CEOs for Cities and Initiative for a Competitive Inner City, 2002; Lewin, 2003a.

4. See also Kirp and Holman, 2002; Bok, 2003; for K–12, see Ladd, 2002.

5. A number of excellent books have been written on this subject. See, for example, Duderstadt, 2000; Bowen and Shulman, 2001. There has also been a great deal of discussion in periodicals. See, for example, Reed, 2002; Gerdy, 2002; Eskin, 2001.

6. For a sampling of sportswriters' reactions, see "Foul Shots," 2003.

7. See Newman, 2000, for a fuller statement of the risks to research. As an example of a public statement against private sector dominance of research, see Atkinson and others, 2003.

8. For background, see Healy and Russell, 2003; Russell, 2003.

9. For an overview of reforms in New Zealand, see McLaughlin, 2003; see also note 21 of Chapter Seven.

10. For an analysis of the impact of competition at the K–12 level, see Fiske and Ladd, 2000c; see also Fiske and Ladd, 2000a.

11. LaRocque, N. (nlarocque@nzbr.org.nz), policy advisor to the New Zealand Business Roundtable. "Closed Institutions." E-mail message to Lara Couturier (lara_couturier@brown.edu), Aug. 18, 2002; Webster, J. (civil@clear.net.nz). "Re: Sent on Behalf of Frank Newman." Private e-mail message to Frank Newman (frank_newman@brown. edu), Aug. 4, 2002. LaRocque gave this list of public institutions in New Zealand that have been closed or merged (that is, ceased to be legal entities on their own) over the last decade: Wairarapa Community Polytechnic (essentially bankrupt, merged with Universal College of Learning); Wanganui Regional Community Polytechnic (essentially bankrupt, merged with Universal College of Learning); Central Institute of Technology (essentially bankrupt, merged with Hutt Valley Polytechnic to create Wellington Institute of Technology); Wellington Polytechnic (merged with Massey University—not due to bankruptcy); Palmerston North College of Education

(merged with Massey University—not due to bankruptcy). This data can be confirmed through the New Zealand Ministry of Education's Website. See "Number of Tertiary Providers," 2003.

Chapter Seven

1. V. Lynn Meek asserts, for example, that "nearly everywhere, higher education is being asked to be more accountable and responsive, efficient and effective and, at the same time, more entrepreneurial and self-managing" (Meek, 2003, p. 149).
2. See also Callan, 2002.
3. See Jones, 2003; Trombley, 2003.
4. The OECD has made similar pronouncements: "Accountability, transparency, efficiency and effectiveness, responsiveness and forward vision are now considered as the principal components of good public governance, which universities are and will increasingly be asked to implement." See Center for Educational Research and Innovation, 2002. See also Quddus and Rashid, 2000.
5. "Within the Organisation for Economic Co-operation and Development (OECD), comprised of the world's richest countries, the private share of total payments for post-secondary education ranges from 3% (Scandinavia) to 83% (South Korea)"; see "The Quiet Educational Revolution," 2002.
6. It should be noted that performance funding and budgeting declined slightly in 2002 as states tightened their budgets for the economic downturn. See Burke and Minassians, 2002.
7. Aims McGuinness tracks the restructuring of state systems: "Among the 50 states, Aims McGuinness identifies at least 19 different models for higher education governance and coordination, and 17 states altered these arrangements or experimented with different structures between 1992 and 2002." McGuinness, 2003, quoted from Volkwein and Zhou, 2003.
8. Terrence MacTaggart clarifies the distinction between decentralization and deregulation by stating that in decentralization "the rules do not change, but the level at which they are enforced does" (MacTaggart and Associates, 1998, p. 11). See also Annie E. Casey Foundation, 2000.
9. There are more questions than answers about the success of K–12 charter schools at this point. For a variety of perspectives, please see "Study: Charter Students Test Poorly," 2002; Bulkley and Fisler, 2002; Gewertz, 2002; Ladd, 2002; Miron and Horn, 2002.
10. Data from "Race of First-Time Full-Time First-Year Students," a table supplied by Fran Lanzer, research assistant, St. Mary's Office of Institutional Research.

11. Interview with Ray Kieft, senior policy advisor and academic officer of the Colorado Commission on Higher Education, conducted by Lara Couturier, July 17, 2002. See also "Performance Agreement," 2002.

12. A number of interviewees commented on quality of the institutions, presence of quality audits, and so forth. Examples are interview with Agneta Bladh, state secretary for education of Sweden, conducted by Lara Couturier, Aug. 14, 2002; Jan-Eric Sundgren, rektor, Chalmers University, conducted by Lara Couturier, Aug. 1, 2002; Roger Svensson, managing director of STINT Foundation, conducted by Lara Couturier, July 22, 2002; Clas Wahlbin, rektor, Jönköping University, conducted by Lara Couturier, July 25, 2002; Per Unckel, member of the Swedish Parliament and former minister of education and science, conducted by Lara Couturier, Nov. 7, 2002.

Additionally, see the National Agency for Higher Education quality audit reports, such as: "Report 2002: 16R—Renewed Quality Audit at Chalmers University of Technology, Gothenburg University and the Royal Institute of Technology," National Agency for Higher Education, 2002 [http://wwweng.hsv.se/en/iwt/startpage/startpage_en. jsp?home=location/].

There have been as well some evaluations of Chalmers at the department level; see Chalmers Environmental Initiative. "Environmental Research, Education and Outreach at the Chalmers University of Technology, Goteborg, Sweden." *International Evaluation,* Sept. 1998 [www.miljo.chalmers.se/cei/profile/inteval_1.htm]; Swedish Research Council. "Three Major Academic Laboratories: An Evaluation." Stockholm, 2002, p. 8 [www.vr.se/fileserver/index.asp?fil= ZY0MIMY9K0ZY].

13. Interview with Niels Grolin, kontorchef (head of secretariat) of Danmarks Tekniske Universitet (Technical University of Denmark), conducted by Lara Couturier, Nov. 26, 2002.

14. Interview with Keith King, conducted by Lara Couturier, July 24, 2002.

15. For an overview of the plan detailed by the institution, see "New Tuition and Scholarship Plan." Miami University of Ohio, Oct. 2003 [http://www.miami.muohio.edu/tuitionplan/qa.cfm]. For Joni Finney's statement as paraphrased by the *New York Times,* see Dillon, 2003. For a good explanation of the downside to this plan, see Breneman, 2003.

16. For information on the decline of public funding, see New Zealand's Vice-Chancellor's Commission, 2000a. For an overview of the reforms, see McLaughlin, 2003; New Zealand Ministry of Education, Nov. 1998; New Zealand's Vice-Chancellor's Commission, 2000b;

"Tertiary Education Reforms," 2002; interview with J. Webster, president/CEO of UNITEC of Auckland, New Zealand, conducted by Frank Newman, Paris, Sept. 11, 2000; LaRocque, 2001; see also Tertiary Education Advisory Commission, 2001.

17. The New Zealand's Vice-Chancellor's Commission reported that the country experienced a 20 percent decrease in higher education enrollments from the country's poorer districts, but that figure has been disputed. See New Zealand's Vice-Chancellor's Commission, 2000b. For pro-market arguments and a review of the debate about equity and student debt, see the Website of the Education Forum [www.educationforum.org.nz].

18. See note 11 in Chapter Six.

19. There were thirty-eight public institutions of higher education in New Zealand before the three closed or merged. "Number of Tertiary Providers," 2003. There are 1,713 public institutions in the United States ("Almanac Issue 2003–4," 2003).

20. Chance, B. (bcnored@aol.com). "Compact Bill." E-mail message to Lara Couturier (lara_couturier@brown.edu), Mar. 31, 2003.

21. Hebel illustrates the confusion surrounding the terminology in use at this point by saying, "Officials in Colorado, Massachusetts, and Virginia also are debating proposals to develop charter colleges, or governance structures akin to that model." See Hebel, 2000.

22. For further ideas on this subject, see CEOs for Cities, 2002; Lewin, 2003a.

23. As the researchers at the Alliance for International Higher Education Policy Studies (AIHEPS) concluded after conducting research on New Jersey and New Mexico, "On the basis of this AIHEPS research, as well as our own experience in many other settings, we assert that (1) the more explicitly a given state defines the purposes it seeks to achieve in supporting its higher education system, (2) the more clearly it conveys those expectations to institutions through the rules of the game, and (3) the more care and discernment it gives to the work of assessing how well its purposes are achieved, the more likely that state is to achieve optimal performance on the measures of preparation, affordability, participation, completion, and benefits, as defined by the *Measuring Up* report card series" (National Center for Public Policy and Higher Education, 2003, p. 6).

Chapter Eight

1. The Futures Project is indebted to Russell Edgerton for his thoughtful definitions of these needs and of the changes in society that make these skills essential.

2. According to research done by John Immerwahr for the National Center for Public Policy and Higher Education, most school leaders feel that too many students arrive at college unprepared. They also feel that institutions of higher education are offering too many remedial courses. Eighty-eight percent feel that too many new students need remedial education. Even though these same leaders feel the need for college graduates in society is growing, they think that admissions standards are too low to necessarily make a college diploma worth anything; Immerwahr, 1999b.

3. Of the students in the National Education Longitudinal Study from the lowest socioeconomic quintile, 49.8 percent had received no credential, 18 percent earned a certificate, 17 percent earned an associate, and 18 percent earned a bachelor degree or higher.
Special data analysis by Clifford Adelman, senior research analyst, U.S. Department of Education, Oct. 24, 2003.

4. For an interesting discussion of prestige and how it affects students in the college admissions process, see "Our First Annual College-Admissions Survey," 2003.

5. In 1986, the National Governors Association sponsored Time for Results, a report that encouraged institutions of higher learning to shift from an inputs-based assessment of quality to one that focuses on outputs, on actual learning achieved. This report focused what had been a wide-ranging discussion of quality into the specific requirement to assess student outputs. However, magazines, beginning with *U.S. News & World Report* in 1983, began to publish college rankings based on measurements other than quality as defined by learner outcomes and value added. They still ranked by input-based assessments of quality.

6. A similar situation has arisen in the K–12 public education world. Therefore, it can be helpful to examine the K–12 systemic response to these new pressures.

Chapter Nine

1. Educational requirements for a tool and die maker have increased. Requirements now include: "four or five years of apprenticeship and/or postsecondary education training; algebra, geometry, trigonometry, and statistics" (The Education Trust, 2003).

2. Further underscoring the importance of a college education are the results of a 2002 Rand study: "The highest paid workers will hold their own to 2015. Those in the 50th percentile—workers right in the middle of the distribution—have lost about 14 percent in real wages over the last 20 years; by 2015, they will be earning about 25 percent less than they earned in 1976. But the most striking consequence of current trends shows up in the figures for workers in the

bottom 10 percent. If current trends continue, these workers will be earning little more than half of what they earned in 1976. "Breaking the Social Contract: The Fiscal Crisis in Higher Education" (Council for Aid to Education, 1997).

3.   In 1940, only 1 percent of the black population held a college degree. See Herbold, 1994–1995.

4.   Among freshmen, 74.2 percent volunteered during their last year in high school, and 20.6 percent volunteer at least three hours per week (Sax and others, 1998; Clymer, 2000).

5.   Among the students enrolled in CCD's Division of Education and Academic Services, 84.5 percent maintained a GPA of 2.0 or higher, as did 92 percent of students using the reading lab at least three hours a week and 97 percent of students using the writing lab at least three hours a week (McClenney and Flores, 1998).

6.   Tinto and Riemer describe learning communities as "a kind of co-registration or block scheduling that enables students to take courses together. The same students register for two or more courses, forming a sort of study team." Sometimes a group of students will co-enroll in linked courses—for example, a course in writing and a course in history, or a course in math and a course in science. Students in a learning community may also participate in discussion sections to supplement large lecture courses. Effective learning communities are often centered around a core theme linking the courses together, a technique that Tinto and Riemer suggest "provides students with a coherent interdisciplinary experience that promotes a deeper type of learning than is possible in stand alone courses" (Tinto and Riemer, 2001).

Chapter Ten

1.   The 2000 economic impact survey found that "the average return on every $1 of state money invested in a NASULGC institution is $5." Other positive indicators included: the mean of sponsored research funding was $105 million, the mean number of jobs created at the universities was 6,562 (not including part-time students), and two-thirds of the graduates remained in the state for a "significant period of time" (National Association of State Universities and Land-Grant Colleges, Aug. 2001; see also Committee on the Future of the Colleges of Agriculture in the Land Grant University System, 1995).

Chapter Eleven

1.   For insights from current academic leaders on the challenges facing higher education and some solutions, see Ruben, 2004.

2.   Burton Clark outlined effective governance mechanisms (a strength-
      ened steering core) in the five universities he studied. See Clark, 1998.
3.   An example is the concern over the loss of civic involvement on the
      part of students, spurring the formation of the Campus Compact
      for Community Service in 1985. The original hope was to ultimately
      engage one hundred presidents and their institutions in the push
      to encourage students to participate in community service. Today,
      more than 850 colleges and universities are members. This effort
      did not, however, require faculty to acknowledge any flaws.
4.   In Japan, private universities are suffering from shrinking enroll-
      ment, and many have been forced to close. This is a case where the
      need for planning became clear. As the *Chronicle of Higher Education*
      suggested, "Many of the private universities that have remained suc-
      cessful started planning more than 10 years ago to find ways to
      attract students from the shrinking prospective-student pool as well
      as to bring in nontraditional students." See Brender, 2003a, p. A41.
5.   David Kirp warns against outsourcing core teaching and learning
      activities but reminds us that there are many areas in need of
      improvement: "The locally run bookstore was, more often than not,
      creakily inefficient. The venerable campus dining hall that featured
      'mystery meat' and potatoes on its menu was indifferent to students'
      wishes" (Kirp, 2002, p. B13).
6.   For a good summary of the longer book, see Clark, 2000.
7.   For a description of how Pres. John Sexton has encouraged focus
      and reputation at New York University, see Levine, 2003.
8.   The New England Resource Center for Higher Education wrote a
      research brief about the need for collaboration that was based on
      its experiences with a multi-institutional project. See New England
      Resource Center for Higher Education, 2001.
9.   As an example of collaboration, there is a new proposal for two state
      institutions in Rhode Island to create a joint campus in the city of Prov-
      idence. The Community College of Rhode Island would supply the first
      two years of courses, graduating students with an associate's degree.
      Then, right on the same campus, students could go on to four-year
      degrees through courses supplied by the University of Rhode Island.
      The hope is that by creating a campus focused on their needs, more
      low-income students, concentrated in the city of Providence, would
      make the transition to the baccalaureate degree (M. Davis, 2003).

Chapter Twelve
1.   The critical question is whether both the academic and the politi-
      cal leaders can work together to create an effective balance of

autonomy and accountability that preserves the public nature of higher education.

2. Discussion with the CEOs of higher education corporations, at the Conference on the "Impact of For-Profit Education on Both Public & Non-Profit," Institute on Education and Government, Teachers College, Columbia University, Jan. 4, 1999.

3. A recent "policy perspective" from the National Center for Public Policy and Higher Education argued for discussions that would clarify the roles and priorities of higher education. See "Of Precept, Policy and Practice," 2002.

4. The public sees a significant difference between using "quotas" and making extra efforts on behalf of people of color. As Public Agenda describes it, "Majorities of Americans say they support programs that offer 'assistance' for minorities in college admissions or jobs, but support drops dramatically if the question is reworded to ask about 'preferences.' Most Americans say it is important for colleges to have a racially diverse student body, and more than half say 'affirmative action' in college admissions should continue." According to a poll conducted by CBS News and the *New York Times*, 78 percent of whites and 37 percent of African Americans oppose quotas, and 70 percent of whites and 36 percent of African Americans oppose preferential treatment in hiring. However, 50 percent of whites are in favor of "special efforts to help minorities get ahead," and only 13 percent of whites are in favor of ending affirmative action immediately. See Public Agenda Online, 2003.

5. See note 23 of Chapter Seven.

References

"About ASARECA," May 2003 [http://www.asareca.org/about/about.htm].

"About the Commission," Feb. 2003 [http://www.cpec.ca.gov/Second-Pages/CommissionHistory.asp].

Adame, J. "Athletic Sponsorship Increasing at Stanford." *Stanford Daily,* May 4, 1998.

Adelman, C. *A Parallel Postsecondary Universe: The Certification System in Information Technology.* Washington, DC: U.S. Department of Education, Office of Educational Research and Improvement, U.S. Government Printing Office, 2000.

Advisory Committee on Student Financial Assistance. *Access Denied: Restoring the Nation's Commitment to Equal Educational Opportunity.* Washington, DC: Advisory Committee on Student Financial Assistance, 2001.

Allen, J. L. "Public Colleges Scramble for Funds." *Chicago Tribune,* Jan. 21, 2002, p. 1.

"Almanac 2002–3." *Chronicle of Higher Education,* Aug. 30, 2002, *49*(1), 23, 64.

"Almanac Issue 2003–4." *Chronicle of Higher Education,* Aug. 29, 2003, *50*(1).

Altbach, P. G. "The Private Sector in Asian Higher Education." *International Higher Education: The Boston College Center for International Higher Education,* Fall 2002a, pp. 10–11.

Altbach, P. G. "Knowledge and Education as International Commodities: The Collapse of the Common Good." *International Higher Education,* Summer 2002b, no. 28, 2–5.

Altbach, P. G. "Globalization and the University: Myths and Realities in an Unequal World." *Current Issues in Catholic Higher Education,* Winter 2003, *23,* 5–25.

Altschuler, G. C. "College Prep: Tricks of the Trade." *New York Times,* Jan. 13, 2002, p. 17.

Amacher, R. C., and Meiners, R. E. "Empowering Students by Increasing Competition Among Universities." *Veritas,* Winter 2001, p. 26.

American Association of State Colleges and Universities. "Financing State Colleges and Universities: What Is Happening to the Public in Public Higher Education?" *Perspectives,* May 2001, p. 2.

American Association of State Colleges and Universities. *State Fiscal Conditions.* Washington, DC: American Association of State Colleges and Universities, Sept. 2002.

American Council on Education. "Attitudes Toward Public Higher Education: National Survey Results." *KRC Consulting and Research,* 2002a, pp. 13–16.

American Council on Education. "Tuition Funds Account for Larger Share of Institutional Revenue, NCES Data Shows." *Higher Education and National Affairs,* Mar. 4, 2002b, *51*(4), 4.

"Among Offered Budget Ideas: Privatize UW-Madison," Mar. 31, 2003 [Madison.com].

Ancheta, A. "Revisiting Bakke and Diversity-Based Admissions: Constitutional Law, Social Science Research, and the University of Michigan Affirmative Action Case." Cambridge, MA: The Civil Rights Project, Harvard University. Revised May 2003, p. 14.

Andrews, E. L. "Fight Is Looming over Who Bears the Biggest Tax Burden." *New York Times,* Jan. 14, 2003, p. C1.

Annie E. Casey Foundation. "Success in School: Education Ideas That Count," Nov. 2000 [www.aecf.org/publications/success/decent.htm].

Aoki, N. "Journals Pool Clout to Ensure Integrity Pledge to Be Asked of Medical Authors." *Boston Globe,* Sept. 10, 2001, p. A1.

Araton, H. "When Skipping College Is a More Savory Option." *New York Times,* Mar. 7, 2003, p. D1.

Arenson, K. W. "To Raise Its Image, CUNY Pays for Top Students." *New York Times,* May 11, 2002, p. A16.

Armajani, B., Heydinger, R., and Hutchinson, P. "A Model for the Reinvented Higher Education System." The Public Strategies Group, June 6, 2001 [http://www.psgrp.com/index.html].

Armstrong, L. "A New Game in Town: Competitive Higher Education." *Information, Communication & Society,* 2001, *4*(4), 479–506.

Arnone, M. "The Wannabes: More Public Universities Are Striving to Squeeze into the Top Tier. Can States Afford These Dreams?" *Chronicle of Higher Education,* Jan. 3, 2003a, p. A18.

Arnone, M. "IRS Ruling on Naming Rights Could Remove Tax-Exempt Status of Some Construction Bonds." *Chronicle of Higher Education,* Apr. 8, 2003b.

Association of American Colleges and Universities. *Greater Expectations: A New Vision for Learning as a Nation Goes to College.* National Panel Report. Washington, DC: Association of American Colleges and Universities, 2002.

Association of Commonwealth Universities. "Executive Summary." *The Bulletin,* July 2001, *148,* 12–13.

Astin, A. W., and Astin, H. S. *Leadership Reconsidered: Engaging Higher Education in Social Change.* Battle Creek, MI: W. K. Kellogg Foundation, 2000, p. 2.

Atkins, D. E. "Information Technology and the Transformation of Scientific and Engineering Research." Paper presented at the First International Conference on the Economic and Social Implications of Information Technology, U.S. Department of Commerce, Washington, DC, Jan. 27–28, 2003.

Atkinson, R. C., Beachy, R. N., Conway, G., Cordova, F. A., Fox, M. A., and others. "Public Sector Collaboration for Agricultural IP Management." *Science,* July 11, 2003, *301,* 174–175.

Atwell, R. H., and Wellman, J. V. "College Presidents and Higher Education Policy." In *Measuring Up 2002,* San Jose, CA: National Center for Public Policy and Higher Education, 2002, pp. 66–67.

Bain, O. "University Autonomy from the Top Down: Lessons from Russia." *International Higher Education,* Spring 2002, *27,* 22–24.

Baird, P., Downie, J., and Thompson, J. "Clinical Trials and Industry." *Science,* Sept. 27, 2002, *297,* 2211.

Banks, M., and McBurnie, G. "Embarking on an Educational Journey— The Establishment of the First Foreign Full University Campus in Malaysia under the 1996 Education Acts: A Malaysian-Australian Case Study." *Higher Education in Europe,* 1999, *24,* 265–272.

Barlow, D. "The Prevailing Money Madness of NCAA Sports." *Education Digest,* Oct. 2001, p. 36.

Basinger, J. "New Chancellor at U. of Texas Carries a Price Tag of Nearly $800,000." *Chronicle of Higher Education,* July 9, 2002.

Basinger, J., and Perry, S. "Private Funds Drive Up Pay of Public University Presidents." *Chronicle of Higher Education,* Almanac 2002–3, Aug. 30, 2002, pp. 6–8.

Beerkens, E. "Moving Toward Autonomy in Indonesian Higher Education." *International Higher Education,* Fall 2002, *29,* 24–25.

Bell, J. "The Biology Labs On-Line Project: Producing Educational Simulations That Promote Active Learning." *Interactive Multimedia Electronic Journal of Computer-Enhanced Learning,* Wake Forest University. Oct. 1999 [http://imej.wfu.edu/articles/1999/2/01/printver.asp].

Bennell, P., and Terry, P. *The Internationalisation of Higher Education: Exporting Education to Developing and Transitional Economies.* London: Intermediate Technology Publications, 1998, p. 14.

Bennett, M. J. *When Dreams Came True: The GI Bill and the Making of Modern America.* Washington, DC: Brassey's, 1996.

Benson, L., and Harkavy, I. "Saving the Soul of the University: What Is to Be Done?" In K. Robins and F. Webster (eds.), *The Virtual University?*

Knowledge, Markets, and Management. London: Oxford University Press, 2003.

Berdahl, R. O. "Balancing Self-Interest and Accountability: St. Mary's College of Maryland." In T. J. MacTaggart and Associates (eds.), *Seeking Excellence Through Independence.* San Francisco: Jossey-Bass, 1998, pp. 70–77.

Berdahl, R. O. "Institutional Diversity, Markets and State Steering: Public Ends, Private Means." Paper presented at the 23rd Annual EAIR Forum, Porto, Portugal, Sept. 9–12, 2001.

Berdahl, R. O., and MacTaggart, T. J. "Charter Colleges: Balancing Freedom and Accountability." *White Paper,* No. 10. Boston: Pioneer Institute for Public Policy Research, 2000, pp. 3, 14.

Berglund, D., and Clarke, M. *Using Research and Development to Grow Economies.* Washington, DC: National Governors Association, 2000, p. 15.

Berinato, S. "Coming After You: Hungryminds.com—It's Not Just an Internet Portal, It's a New Way to Think." *University Business,* Mar. 2000 [www.universitybusiness.com].

Bernasconi, A. "Private Higher Education with an Academic Focus: Chile's New Exceptionalism." *International Higher Education,* Summer 2003, pp. 18–19.

"Billboard Quarterback." *New York Times,* Aug. 8, 2001, p. A16.

Blair, J. "Attendance Requirement Leaves College Sweating." *New York Times,* Nov. 23, 2002, p. D1.

Blumenstyk, G. "Universities Urged to Protect Scholars Whose Findings Anger Companies." *Chronicle of Higher Education,* Apr. 9, 1999, p. A44.

Blumenstyk, G. "Gains by For-Profit Institutions Fuel Growth Predictions for Higher-Education Companies." *Chronicle of Higher Education,* June 5, 2002.

Blumenstyk, G. " Sylvan Will Shed Its Tutoring Business to Focus on Higher Education." *Chronicle of Higher Education,* Mar. 21, 2003, p. A31.

Boehner, J. "Higher Education Policy." Presented at the Business-Higher Education Forum Summer 2003 Meeting, Washington, DC, June 19, 2003.

Boehner, J. A., and McKeon, H. P. "The College Cost Crisis." U.S. House Committee on Education and the Workforce and U.S. House Subcommittee on 21st Century Competitiveness, 2003 [http://edworkforce.house.gov/issues/108th/education/highereducation/CollegeCostCrisisReport.pdf].

Bok, D. "Are Huge Presidential Salaries Bad for Colleges?" *Chronicle of Higher Education,* Nov. 22, 2002, p. B20.

Bok, D. *Universities in the Marketplace: The Commercialization of Higher Education.* Princeton, NJ: Princeton University Press, 2003.

Bollag, B. "At Italian Universities, Advertising Has Arrived." *Chronicle of Higher Education,* Dec. 13, 2002, p. A42.

The Book of Knowledge. New York: Merrill Lynch, Apr. 9, 1999, p. 121.

Borja, R. R. "Virtual High Schools Gain Following." timesdispatch.com, Aug. 7, 2001.

Bowen, W. G., and Shulman, J. L. *The Game of Life.* Princeton, NJ: Princeton University Press, 2001.

Brainard, J. "Plan Released to Streamline Federal Grant-Application Process." *Chronicle of Higher Education,* June 1, 2001.

Brainard, J. "'Have-Nots' Seek More Funds from the NIH." *Chronicle of Higher Education,* Mar. 29, 2002, p. A23.

Brainard, J. "Congress Completes Budget with Increases for Pell Grants and the NIH." *Chronicle of Higher Education,* Feb. 21, 2003, p. A22.

Brender, A. "Japan's Private Universities Awash in Red Ink." *Chronicle of Higher Education,* Feb. 14, 2003a, p. A41.

Brender, A. "The Big Shrink: As Enrollments Dwindle in Japan, Universities Begin to Merge." *Chronicle of Higher Education,* Feb. 21, 2003b, p. A34.

Breneman, D. W. "For Colleges, This Is Not Just Another Recession." *Chronicle of Higher Education,* June 14, 2002, p. B7.

Breneman, D. W. "Why a Public College Wants to Send In-State Tuition Soaring." *Chronicle of Higher Education,* Apr. 25, 2003, p. B20.

Brent, D, "Knowledge Received/Knowledge Constructed: Principals of Active Learning in the Disciplines," Keynote, Faculty Development Workshop, Laurentian University, May 1, 1996 [http://www.ucalgary.ca/~dabrent/art/active.html].

Brewer, D. J., Gates, S. M., and Goldman, C. A. *In Pursuit of Prestige: Strategy and Competition in U.S. Higher Education.* New Brunswick, NJ: Transaction, 2002.

Brimah, T. "Roster of For-Profit Educational Institutions." *Education Commission of the States,* Dec. 1999, Aug. 10, 2000 [http://www.ecs.org].

Brown, K. "Online, on Campus: Proceed with Caution." *Science,* Aug. 31, 2001, *293*(5535), 1617–1619.

Brownstein, A. "Tuitions Rise Sharply, and This Time Public Colleges Lead the Way." *Chronicle of Higher Education,* Nov. 2, 2001, p. A52.

Bulkley, K., and Fisler, J. "A Decade of Charter Schools: From Theory to Practice." *Consortium for Policy Research in Education Policy Briefs,* RB-35, Apr. 2002, pp. 1, 9.

Burd, S. "Rift Grows over What Keeps Low-Income Students Out of College." *Chronicle of Higher Education,* Jan. 15, 2002a.

Burd, S. "Senator Calls for Improving Graduation Rates, Holding Colleges Accountable." *Chronicle of Higher Education,* Apr. 16, 2002b.

Burd, S. "Lieberman Calls for More Accountability from Colleges." *Chronicle of Higher Education,* Apr. 26, 2002c, p. A25.

Burd, S. "Education Department Hears Appeals to Make Colleges More Accountable for Student Performance." *Chronicle of Higher Education,* Mar. 10, 2003.

Burdman, P. "Colorado's 'Grand Experiment': Voucher Program Could Give the State's Colleges a New Lease on Life." *National CrossTalk,* Spring 2003 [http://www.highereducation.org/crosstalk/ct0203/news0203- colorado.shtml].

Burke, J. C., and Minassians, H. *Performance Reporting: The Preferred "No Cost" Accountability Program—the Sixth Annual Report.* Albany, NY: Nelson A. Rockefeller Institute of Government, 2002.

Business-Higher Education Forum. *Sharing Responsibility: How Leaders in Business and Higher Education Can Improve America's Schools.* Washington, DC: American Council on Education and National Alliance of Business, Winter 2001.

Butterfield, F. "Romney's Campus Plan Would Cut Deficit, and a Political Foe." *New York Times,* Feb. 27, 2003, p. A24.

Callan, P. M. *Coping with Recession: Public Policy, Economic Downturns and Higher Education.* San Jose, CA: National Center for Public Policy and Higher Education, 2002.

Cantor, N., and Schomberg, S. "Poised Between Two Worlds: The University as Monastery and Marketplace." *Educause Review,* Mar./Apr. 2003, pp. 13–21.

Carlson, S. "Survey Finds That Adding Technology to Teaching Is a Top Issue." *Chronicle of Higher Education,* Oct. 27, 2000, p. A46.

Carnevale, A. P., and Fry, R. A. "Crossing the Great Divide: Can We Achieve Equity When Generation Y Goes to College?" Prepared for the Educational Testing Service Leadership 2000 Series, Princeton, NJ, 2000.

Carnevale, A. P., and Fry, R. A. "Economics, Demography and the Future of Higher Education Policy." Commissioned Essay for Higher Expectations I. Washington, DC: National Governors Association, 2003 [http://www.nga.org/center/divisions/1,1188,C_ISSUE_BRIEF%5ED_1509,00.html].

Carnevale, D. "As Online Education Surges, Some Colleges Remain Untouched." *Chronicle of Higher Education,* Feb. 23, 2001, p. A41.

Cavalcanti, H. "Private Universities Gain Market Share." *Gazeta Mercantil,* Nov. 21, 2000.

Cavanagh, S. "Arizona 'Changing Directions' for State University System." *Education Week,* Jan. 15, 2003, p. 6.

Center for Educational Research and Innovation. "What Future for the University? A Position Note on CERI's Future University Project." Paris: Organisation for Economic Co-operation and Development, Nov. 2002.

Center on Budget and Policy Priorities. "Poverty Rates Fell in 2000 as Unemployment Reached 31-Year Low." Washington, DC: Center on Budget and Policy Priorities, Sept. 26, 2001a [http://www.cbpp.org/9-25-01pov.htm].

Centre for Higher Education Research and Information. "Research." *Higher Education Digest: The Guide to Current Higher Education Policy, Development and Research: Digest Supplement.* London: Centre for Higher Education Research and Information, Open University, Spring 2003, p. 2.

CEOs for Cities and Initiative for a Competitive Inner City. *Leveraging Colleges and Universities for Urban Economic Revitalization: An Action Agenda.* Boston: CEOs for Cities and Initiative for a Competitive Inner City, Spring 2002.

"The Challenge for Education Reform: Standards, Accountability, Resources and Policy." Washington, DC: Aspen Institute Congressional Program. Proceedings of the Tenth Conference, Feb. 14–19, 2003, *18*(2) [http://www.aspeninstitute.org/Programt1.asp?bid=825#pubEducatio].

Chance, W. "Comments to the House Higher Education Committee." Olympia, WA: Northwest Educational Research Center, Jan. 2003.

Charles, L. "Consultants: Free Institutions from Some State Regulations." *Inside Iowa State,* Oct. 25, 2002 [http://www.iastate.edu/Inside/2002/1025/regents.shtml].

Chellgren, M. R. "Report Lauds Higher Education Reform, Warns of Dangers Ahead." Associated Press, Oct. 21, 2002.

Choy, S. *Access and Persistence: Findings from 10 Years of Longitudinal Research on Students.* Washington, DC: American Council on Education Center for Policy Analysis, 2002, p. 15.

"The Chronicle Index of For-Profit Higher Education." *Chronicle of Higher Education,* developed by the Center for Research in Security Prices at the University of Chicago's Graduate School of Business, Feb. 14, 2003, *49*(23), A31.

"The Civic Mission of Schools." New York: Carnegie Corporation of New York and the Center for Information and Research on Civic Learning and Engagement, 2003, p. 34 [www.civicmissionofschools.org].

Clark, B. R. *Creating Entrepreneurial Universities: Organizational Pathways of Transformation.* Oxford: Pergamon for IAU Press, 1998, pp. xiii–xiv, 5–7, 137–142.

Clark, B. R. "Collegial Entrepreneurialism in Proactive Universities: Lessons from Europe." *Change,* Jan./Feb. 2000, pp. 10–19.

Clayton, M. "Don't Worry—It's on Us!" *Christian Science Monitor,* Feb. 13, 2001a.

Clayton, M. "Corporate Cash and Campus Labs." *Christian Science Monitor,* June 19, 2001b, p. 11.

Clotfelter, C. *Buying the Best: Cost Escalation in Higher Education.* Princeton, NJ: Princeton University Press, 1996.

Clymer, A. "College Students Not Drawn to Voting or Politics, Poll Shows." *New York Times,* Jan. 12, 2000, p. A14.

Cobb, E. B. "How to Get a FIPSE Grant." *FIPSE,* May 2003 [http://www.ed.gov/about/offices/list/ope/fipse/howtoget.html].

Colby, A., Ehrlich, T., Beaumont, E., and Stephens, J. *Educating Citizens: Preparing America's Undergraduates for lives of Moral and Civic Responsibility.* San Francisco: Jossey-Bass, 2003.

College Board. *Trends in College Pricing.* Washington, DC: College Board, 1999, p. 3.

College Board and National Association of Student Financial Aid Administrators. "Financial Aid Professionals at Work in 1999–2000." Washington, DC: College Board and National Association of Student Financial Aid Administrators, 2002, Tables 13, 19 [http://www.collegeboard.com/repository/2001sufapppfinalrepor_19093.pdf].

"College FCAT? Failure Could Hurt Alma Mater." *St. Petersburg Times Online,* May 1, 2003 [www.sptimes.com/2003/05/01/news_pf/State/College_FCAT_Failure_.shtml].

"College Presidents in U. System of Maryland Seek Autonomy." *Chronicle of Higher Education,* Oct. 30, 1998, p. A32.

"Colleges Lure Students with Lower Tuition." *The Cincinnati Post,* Jan. 16, 2002, p. 9A.

"Colleges Want to Sever Ties with State." *Columbian,* July 15, 2002, p. C2.

Collis, D. *When Industries Change Revisited: New Scenarios for Higher Education.* New Haven, CT: Yale University Press, Sept. 1999.

Collis, D. "Comments for 'Higher Education Goes to Market.'" Paper presented at the Higher Education Goes to Market Conference, Tampa, FL, Jan. 11–13, 2002.

Colorado Department of Higher Education. "Executive Summary Chapter 7—Remedial Education: Too Much, Not Enough?" June 20, 2001 [http://www.state.co.us/cche_dir/1289-7.html].

Committee for the Study of the American Electorate. "Final Post-Election Report." Washington, DC: Committee for the Study of the American Electorate, Oct. 1999, p. 1 [www.gspm.org/csae].

Committee on an Evaluation of the U.S. Department of Agriculture National Research Initiative Competitive Grants Program, National Research Council. *National Research Initiative: A Vital Competitive Grants Program in Food, Fiber, and Natural-Resources Research.* Washington, DC: National Academy of Sciences, 2000, p. 29.

Committee on the Future of the Colleges of Agriculture in the Land Grant University System, National Research Council. *Colleges of Agriculture at the Land Grant Universities: A Profile*. Washington, DC: National Academy Press, 1995.

Community College Survey of Student Engagement (CCSSE). "Engaging Community Colleges, National Benchmarks of Quality, 2003 Findings," 2003, p. 19.

Community College Survey of Student Engagement. "MetLife Foundation in Student Retention." Highlights. Mar. 2003, *2*(4).

Conklin, K. D. "After the Tipping Point." *Change*, Mar./Apr. 2002, pp. 24–29.

Corrigan, R. A. "Presidential Leadership: Moral Leadership in the New Millennium." *Liberal Education*, Fall 2002, pp. 6–13.

Council for Aid to Education. "Breaking the Social Contract: The Fiscal Crisis in Higher Education," 1997 [http://www.rand.org/publications/CAE/CAE100/index.html].

Council for Higher Education Accreditation. *A Statement to the Community: Transfer and the Public Interest*. Washington, DC: Council for Higher Education Accreditation, Nov. 2000, pp. 1, 3.

Couturier, L. K. "Balancing State Control with Society's Needs." *Chronicle of Higher Education*, June 27, 2003, p. B20.

Craig, D. D. *Top American Research Universities: An Overview*. Center for Studies in the Humanities and Social Sciences, University of Florida, Gainesville, FL, Jan. 2002.

Crane, M. "Thinking About a Merger? Join the Club." *The Bulletin*, Feb. 2003, pp. 6–8.

Crenshaw, A. B. "Price Wars on Campus." *Washington Post*, Oct. 15, 2002.

Darling-Hammond, L. "Unequal Opportunity: Race and Education." *Brookings Review*, 1998, *16*(2), 28–32 [http://www.brook.edu/dybdocroot/press/review/spring98/darling.htm].

Davis, J. S. *Unintended Consequences of Tuition Discounting*. Indianapolis, IN: Lumina Foundation for Education, *5*(1), May 2003.

Davis, M. "Expanding Opportunities." *Providence Journal*, Jan. 28, 2003, p. A1.

Delbanco, A. "Books Outline the Fierce Competition Among Elite Colleges." *New York Times*, Sept. 29, 2002, p. 13.

Dickeson, R. C. *Prioritizing Academic Programs and Services: Reallocating Resources to Achieve Strategic Balance*. San Francisco: Jossey-Bass, 1999.

Dickeson, R. C. "Containing College Costs: The Case for Reallocation." *Higher Expectations: Second in a Series of Essays on the Future of Postsecondary Education*. Washington, DC: National Governors Association, 2002.

Dillon, S. "Public University in Ohio to End Instate Tuition Break." *New York Times*, Apr. 5, 2003.

"Does Erasmus Meet Its Objectives?" Workshop Session Report, ACU Conference, *Bulletin,* July 2001, p. 36.

"Don't Dismiss UW Privatization." Madison.com, Apr. 5, 2003.

Doyle, D. P. "China Inc." *Education Week,* Jan. 19, 2000, p. 39.

Drape, J. "College Basketball: Football Powers Push onto Hardcourt." *New York Times,* Mar. 10, 2003, p. D1.

Drape, J., and Glier, R. "Georgia Withdraws from Postseason and Suspends Harrick." *New York Times,* Mar. 11, 2003, p. C19.

Drosjack, M. "UT President Lauds House Bill as 'Wise': Boards Would Have Power to Set Tuition." *Houston Chronicle,* Apr. 24, 2003 [http://www.chron.com/cs/CDA/story.hts/metropolitan/1882968].

Duderstadt, J. L. *Intercollegiate Athletics and the American University: A University President's Perspective.* Ann Arbor: University of Michigan Press, 2000.

Duderstadt, J., Atkins, D., and Van Houweling, D. *Higher Education in the Digital Age.* Westport, CT: American Council on Education and Praeger, 2002.

Earls, A. R. "The Public's Business." *Connection: Journal of the New England Board of Higher Education,* Winter 2003, *17*(4), 19, 21.

Edds, M. "Budget Cuts Spur Talk of a 'New Equation' at State's Public Colleges." *Virginia-Pilot,* Jan. 12, 2003, p. J5.

Eddy, E. D. *Colleges for Our Land and Time: The Land-Grant Idea in American Education.* New York: Harper & Brothers, 1957.

Eddy, E. D. *The Land-Grant Movement: A Capsule History of the Educational Revolution Which Established Colleges for All the People.* Washington, DC: American Association of Land-Grant Colleges and State Universities, Centennial Office, 1962.

Edgerton, R. "A 21st Century Education." Chapter IV in the *Pew Forum Report,* unpublished, 2003a.

Edgerton, R. "A Land of Lost Opportunity." Chapter I in the *Pew Forum Report,* unpublished, 2003b.

The Education Resources Institute and the Institute for Higher Education Policy. "Missed Opportunities: A Look at Disadvantaged College Aspirants." Washington, DC: The Education Resources Institute and the Institute for Higher Education Policy, 1997.

The Education Trust. "High Schools in America 2003." Prepared for the United States Department of Education, Washington, DC, 2003.

Educational Testing Service. "Quality, Affordability, and Access: Americans Speak on Higher Education," June 2003 [www.ets.org/aboutets/americaspeaks/2003find.html].

Ehrenberg, R. *Tuition Rising: Why College Costs So Much.* Cambridge, MA: Harvard University Press, 2000.

Elfin, M. "Longtime Observer Gives Low Grade to Trends in U.S. Higher Education." *Key Reporter,* Winter 2003, pp. 9–15.

Engle, C., and Truax, H. "The Carrot or the Stick?" *Environmental Action,* May-June 1990, *21*(6), 12.

Eskin, B. "Contract Sport." *Lingua Franca,* Apr. 2001, pp. 6–8.

Etzkowitz, H. "Networked Research: An EC Model for U.S.?" *Science's Compass,* Apr. 13, 2001, p. 219.

"Expert Report of Walter Allen and Daniel Solorzano." Choices Project, Access, Equity and Diversity in Higher Education, Aug. 2002 [http:// www.sscnet.ucla.edu/issr/choices/reports/allen_solorzano.pdf].

FairTest: The National Center for Fair and Open Testing. "The SAT: Questions and Answers," July 2001 [www.fairtest.org/facts/satfact].

Farag, I. "Higher Education in Egypt: The Realpolitik of Privatization." *International Higher Education,* Winter 2000, *18,* 16.

Farrell, E. F. "Phoenix's Unusual Way of Crafting Courses." *Chronicle of Higher Education,* Feb. 14, 2003a, p. A10.

Farrell, E. F. "Career Education Corp. to Acquire Whitman Education Group in $230-Million Deal." *Chronicle of Higher Education,* Mar. 27, 2003b.

Feemster, R. "An Interview: Howard 'Buck' McKeon." *National CrossTalk,* Spring 2003, p. 2.

"Financial Aid Professionals at Work in 1999-2000: Results from the 2001 Survey of Undergraduate Financial Aid Policies, Practices, and Procedures." The College Board and the National Association of Student Financial Aid Administrators. [http://www.collegeboard.com/ repository/2001sufappfinalrepor_19093.pdf].

Fiske, E. B., and Ladd, H. F. "A Distant Laboratory: Learning Cautionary Lessons from New Zealand's Schools." *Education Week,* May 17, 2000a, p. 38.

Fiske, E. B., and Ladd, H. F. "A Level Playing Field? What We Can Learn from the New Zealand School Reform." *American Educator,* Fall 2000b, p. 28.

Fiske, E. B., and Ladd, H. F. *When Schools Compete.* Washington, DC: Brookings Institution, 2000c.

Fitzsimmons, W. R. "Entering the Elite." *Harvard Magazine,* May-June 2003, pp. 15–20.

Florida Department of Education. Florida Community College System, 2002 SREB, IPEDS Graduation Rate Survey and SREB Two Year Retention Study, 2002 [http://www.fldoe.org/news/pr_12_30_02/ SREB_GRS_2002_Adhoc.pdf].

"France: Structures of the Education and Initial Training Systems in the European Union." England: Eurydice/Cedefop, 1995, July 15, 2000 [http://www.felixent.force9.co.uk/europe/fr/06html].

"Foul Shots: Sportswriters on the Basketball Scandals." *Chronicle of Higher Education,* Mar. 28, 2003, p. B14.

Frank, R. H. "Higher Education: The Ultimate Winner-Take-All Market?" In M. Devlin and J. Meyerson (eds.), *Forum Futures: Exploring the Future of Higher Education, 2000 Papers.* San Francisco: Jossey-Bass, 2001.

Frank, R. H. "Higher Education: The Ultimate Winner-Take-All Market?" Paper presented at the "Higher Education Goes to Market" Conference, Tampa, FL, Jan. 11–13, 2002.

Frederick, R. *Curriculum: A History of the American Undergraduate Courses of Study.* San Francisco: Jossey-Bass, 1971, p. 27.

"The French Education System." Education in the European Union. Land Salzburg, June 2003 [http://www.land.salzburg.at/htblha/cyber/FRANAN.HTM].

Friedman, B. M. "Globalization: Stiglitz's Case." Review of *Joseph E. Stiglitz, Globalization and Its Discontents,* in *New York Review,* Aug. 15, 2002, p. 50.

Fund for the Improvement of Postsecondary Education—Comprehensive Program. "Funding," 2004 [http://www.ed.gov/programs/fipsecomp/funding.html].

"Funding: Texas State Library and Archives Commission," May 2003 [http://www.tsl.state.tx.us/ld/funding/lsta/].

Galbraith, K. "British Universities Attract an Increasing Number of Foreign Students, Agency Says." *Chronicle of Higher Education,* Feb. 5, 2003.

Gallagher, M. "The Emergence of Entrepreneurial Public Universities in Australia." Paper presented at the IMHE General Conference 2000, Paris, Sept. 2000, pp. 3, 8.

Gardiner, L. F. "Why We Must Change: The Research Evidence." *NEA Higher Education Journal,* Spring 1998, pp. 71–88 [http://www.nea.org/he/heta98/s98pg71.pdf].

"GATS—Fact and Fiction." World Trade Organization, Aug. 2002 [http://www.wto.org/english/tratop_e/serv_e/gatsfacts1004_e.pdf].

Gerdy, J. R. "Athletic Victories, Educational Defeats." *Academe,* 2002, *88*(1).

Gewertz, C. "Miami-Dade Will Launch Choice Plan." *Education Week,* Nov. 6, 2002, p. 1.

Gibbons, M. "Science's New Social Contract with Society." *Nature,* Dec. 1999, *402*(supp.), C81–C84.

Gibbons, M. "Message from the Secretary General." In *Review of 2002.* London: Association of Commonwealth Universities, 2003, p. 5.

Gibson, R. "Initiative for Excellence." Committee to Limit Political Interference with Universities, Apr. 2001. Paper presented at the Education Commission of the States 2001 National Forum on Education Policy, Philadelphia, July 18–21, 2001.

Giesecke, H. C. "Expansion and Development of Private Higher Education in East Central Europe." *International Higher Education,* Summer 1999, p. 2.

Gilbert, A. D. "The Idea of a University Beyond 2000." *Policy,* Autumn 2000, *16*(1), 31ff.

Gillon, S. M. *That's Not What We Meant to Do: Reform and Its Unintended Consequences in Twentieth-Century America.* New York: W.W. Norton, 2000.

"Global Development: Monash Around the World." Monash University, Mar. 2003, Apr. 28, 2003 [http://www.monash.edu.au/intoff/globaldevelopment/index2.html].

Golden, M. "Dirty Dealings." *Wall Street Journal,* Sept. 13, 1999, p. R13.

Gornitzka, A., Smeby, J., Stensaker, B., and de Boer, H. "Contract Arrangements in the Nordic Countries—Balancing Accountability and Trust?" Paper presented at the European Association for Institutional Research (EAIR) Forum, Prague, Sept. 8–11, 2002, pp. 7–11.

Gose, B. "Meeting Community Needs." *Chronicle of Higher Education,* Aug. 1, 2003, p. A23.

Gould, P. "EU Funding Bonanza Begins." *Materials Today,* Feb. 2003, pp. 44, 49.

Gouras, M. "Higher Ed Bill Called Landmark Legislation." *Bismarck Tribune,* Apr. 29, 2001, p. 5B.

"Governor, Leaders Support Greater College Autonomy." *Baltimore Sun,* Feb. 16, 1999, Local, p. 2B.

Graham, P. A., and Stacey, N. G. (eds.). *The Knowledge Economy and Postsecondary Education.* Washington, DC: National Academy Press, 2002.

Grapevine Project. A National Database for Tax Support for Higher Education, Illinois State University. "50 State Summary Table," May 2003 [http://www.coe.ilstu.edu/grapevine/].

Grech, D. A. "FCAT Failure Rate Is 'Scary.'" *Miami Herald,* May 23, 2002.

Green, K. "The New Computing—Revisited." *EducauseReview,* Jan.–Feb. 2003, pp. 32–39.

Green, M., Eckel, P., and Barblan, A. *The Brave New (and Smaller) World of Higher Education: A Transatlantic View.* Washington, DC: American Council on Education, 2002.

Guedegbe, C. M. "Higher Education Reform in Benin in a Context of Growing Privatization." *International Higher Education,* Summer 1999, *16,* 12.

Guernsey, L. "Spam Your Way to a Good Education." *New York Times,* Dec. 23, 1999, p. G1.

Gumport, P. J. "Academic Restructuring: Organizational and Institutional Imperatives." *Higher Education: The International Journal of Higher Education and Educational Planning,* 2000, *39,* 67–91.

Guskin, A., and Marcy, M. "Creating a Vital Campus in a Climate of Restricted Resources: 10 Organizing Principles." Paper presented at the Annual Meeting of the Association of American Colleges and Universities, Seattle, Jan. 24, 2003.

Hafner, K. "Lessons Learned at Dot-Com U." *New York Times,* May 2, 2002.

Hagan, M. "Northwestern U. Athletic Teams Might Lose Sponsor as Adidas Cuts Back on Deals." *Daily Northwestern,* Nov. 14, 2001.

Hammond, B. "Savvy Graduates Shop for College." *Portland Oregonian,* June 6, 2002, p. A01.

Hanson, M. "University System Getting More Control over Budget." *Bismarck Tribune,* Oct. 4, 2000, p. 1B.

Harkavy, I. "Honoring Community, Honoring Place." Keynote delivered at the Eighth National Gathering of Educators for Civic Engagement, Pablo, MT, June 2002.

Hart, C. Public Information Officer for University System of Maryland. E-mail to Milena Ivanova, Mar. 15, 2001 [milena_ivanova@brown.edu].

Harvey, W. B. *Minorities in Higher Education 2001–2002: Nineteenth Annual Status Report.* Washington, DC: American Council on Education, 2002, p. 12.

Hashim, H. "Looking Up to Malaysia." *New Straits Times* (Malaysia), Jan. 5, 2000, p. 10.

Hawpe, D. "In the Rankings That Count, Kentucky Wouldn't Make the Tournament." *Courier-Journal,* Feb. 12, 2003, p. A8.

Healy, P. "Consultants Told Romney of Waste in Public Colleges." *Boston Globe,* Mar. 25, 2003, p. B1.

Healy, P., and Russell, J. "Higher Tuitions, Merger of Six Colleges Proposed." *Boston Globe,* Feb. 27, 2003, p. A1.

Hearn Jr., T. K. "Where the Culture Clash Is Leading College Sports." *Trusteeship,* Nov.-Dec. 2002, p. 21.

Hebel, S. "Community College of Denver Wins Fans." *Chronicle of Higher Education,* May 7, 1999, p. A37.

Hebel, S. "Movement to Create Charter Colleges Gathers Supporters— and Critics." *Chronicle of Higher Education,* Nov. 3, 2000, pp. A31, A34.

Hebel, S. "Colorado Institutions Seek to Escape Limits on Spending." *Chronicle of Higher Education,* June 7, 2002, p. A29.

Hebel, S., and Schmidt, P. "Voters Approve Florida Governance Shift, Major Bond Measures in California and Virginia." *Chronicle of Higher Education,* Nov. 15, 2002, p. A26.

Heller, D. E. "Aid Matters: Merit Aid Is the Wrong Tool to Attract the Best and the Brightest." *Connection,* Summer 2003, *18*(1), 24–25.

Heller, D., and Marin, P. (eds.). *Who Should We Help? The Negative Social Consequences of Merit Scholarships.* Cambridge, MA: Civil Rights Project, Harvard University, Aug. 23, 2002, p. 17.

Henkel, M., and Little, B. *Changing Relationships Between Higher Education and the State.* London: Jessica Kingsley Publishers, 1999, pp. 52–68.

Herbold, H. "Never a Level Playing Field: Blacks and the GI Bill." *Journal of Blacks in Higher Education,* Winter 1994–1995, p. 106.

Heterick, B. "Explaining College Costs." *Learning Marketspace,* Mar. 1, 2002 [LFORUM-L@lists.rpi.edu].

Hibbard, H. "The Public Corporation: A Better Way to Deliver Public Services in a Resource-Constrained Environment?" *Oregon Tax Research,* Feb. 1997, p. 3.

Hill, M. "More Power Urged for College Heads." *Baltimore Sun,* Dec. 23, 1998, Local, p. 1B.

Hill, M. "College Controls Would Shift; Some Schools Would Not Need Commission Approval." *Baltimore Sun,* Mar. 2, 1999a, Local, p. 1B.

Hill, M. "Higher Education Bill Welcomed by State University Officials: School Presidents Get Expanded Authority to Create Programs." *Baltimore Sun,* Apr. 15, 1999b.

Hilts, P. *Protecting America's Health.* New York: Knopf, 2003.

"Hispanic Students Bring New Challenges." CNN.com/education, June 3, 2003 [http://cnn.com/2003/EDUCATION/06/03/Hispanic.students.ap/index.html].

Hoffman, E. "Bill to Give CU Enterprise Status Makes Fiscal Sense." *Denver Post,* Apr. 15, 2003.

Hoover, E. "The Changing Environment for College Admissions." *Chronicle of Higher Education,* Nov. 29, 2002, pp. A30–A31.

Hoyle, M. J. "Have College Presidents Lost Their Voice?" *Trusteeship,* Sept./Oct. 2002, p. 13.

Immerwahr, J. "The Price of Admission: The Growing Importance of Higher Education." A Report by Public Agenda for the National Center for Public Policy and Higher Education, San Jose, CA: National Center for Public Policy and Higher Education, 1998 [http://www.highereducation.org/reports/price/price.shtml].

Immerwahr, J. "Doing Comparatively Well: Why the Public Loves Higher Education and Criticizes K–12." A Report by Public Agenda for the National Center for Public Policy and Higher Education and the Institute for Educational Leadership. Washington, DC: Institute for Educational Leadership, Oct. 1999a.

Immerwahr, J. "Taking Responsibility: Leaders' Expectations of Higher Education." A Report by Public Agenda for the National Center for Public Policy and Higher Education, San Jose, CA: National Center for Public Policy and Higher Education, 1999b, p. 8 [http://www.highereducation.org/reports/responsibility/responsibility.pdf].

Immerwahr, J. "Meeting the Competition: College and University Presidents, Faculty, and State Legislators View the New Competitive Academic

Arena." A Report by Public Agenda for the Futures Project: Policy for Higher Education in a Changing World. Providence, RI: The Futures Project: Policy for Higher Education in a Changing World, Oct. 2002 [http://www.futuresproject.org/publications/MeetingtheCompfinal.pdf].

Immerwahr, J., and Foleno, T. "Great Expectations: How the Public and Parents—White, African American, and Hispanic—View Higher Education." A Report by Public Agenda for the National Center for Public Policy and Higher Education. San Jose, CA: National Center for Public Policy and Higher Education, 2000 [http://www.highereducation.org/reports/expectations/expectations.shtml].

Institute of Politics. *The Institute of Politics Survey of Student Attitudes: A National Survey of College Undergraduates.* Cambridge, MA: Kennedy School of Government, Harvard University, 2002.

"International Roundup." *Monash Magazine,* Monash University, 6, Spring-Summer 2000 [http://www.monash.edu.au/pubs/monmag/issue6-2000/pg23.html].

"Investment Strategy: Who's Eligible." *EPSCOR,* May 2003 [http://www.ehr.nsf.gov/epscor/investment/eligible.cfm].

Johnston, D. B. "Financing Higher Education: Who Should Pay and Other Issues." In P. G. Altbach, R. O. Berdahl, and P. J. Gumport, (eds.), *The American University in the 21st Century: Higher Education and Society.* (3rd ed.). Baltimore, MD: Johns Hopkins University Press, 1997.

Jones, D. "State Shortfalls Projected Throughout the Decade." *Policy Alert,* Feb. 2003.

Jonsson, P. "High School Athletics Under a Microscope." *Christian Science Monitor,* Apr. 1, 2003, p. 17.

Jordan, S. M. "Vouchers in Public Higher Education: A Bad Idea Whose Time Has Come?" *National CrossTalk,* Fall 2002, *10*(4), 12–13.

Josephsen, K. "GOP Lawmakers Vow to Support Universities." *Pantagraph,* Apr. 16, 2003, p. A6.

Judy, R., and D'Amico, C. "Workforce 2020 Work and Workers in the 21st Century." Hudson Institute, Indianapolis, IN, May 1998.

June, A. W. "Tapping the Land to Bring Life Back to Campus." *Chronicle of Higher Education,* Aug. 1, 2003a, p. A26.

June, A. W. "Remaining the Province of Women." *Chronicle of Higher Education,* Aug. 1, 2003b, p. A28.

Kanter, R. M. *The Change Masters.* New York: Free Press, 1985.

Katz, S. N. "Excellence Is by No Means Enough." *Common Knowledge,* 2002, *8*(3), 427–438.

Kay, M. "Senate Eases Up on Tuition Control." *American Statesman,* May 27, 2003a.

Kay, M. "Bill to Deregulate Tuition Advances." *American Statesman,* Apr. 30, 2003b.

Kay, M., and Jayson, S. "State Leaders Embracing Uncapped Tuitions." *American Statesman,* Feb. 13, 2003.

Kellogg Commission on the Future of State and Land Grant Universities. *Renewing the Covenant: Learning, Discovery, and Engagement in a New Age and Different World.* Prepared for the National Association of State Universities and Land-Grant Colleges, Mar. 2000, pp. 4, 9 [http://www.nasulgc.org/publications/Kellogg/Kellogg2000_covenant.pdf].

Kelly, K. F. *Meeting Needs and Making Profits: The Rise of For-Profit Degree-Granting Institutions.* Denver: Education Commission of the States, July 2001, Nov. 26, 2001 [http://www.ecs.org/clearinghouse/27/33/2733.htm].

Kennedy, D. "Research Fraud and Public Policy." *Science,* Apr. 18, 2003, pp. 300, 393.

Keohane, N. O. "When Should a College President Use the Bully Pulpit?" *Chronicle of Higher Education,* Feb. 7, 2003, p. B20.

Kertesz, L. "Oregon Academic Medical Center Breaks State Tie." *Modern Healthcare,* Jan. 30, 1995, p. 20.

Kettl, D. F. "Creating High-Performance Postsecondary Education." Commissioned Essay for Higher Expectations I. Washington, DC: National Governors Association, 2001 [http://www.nga.org/cda/files/HIGHEREDREINVENTINGHIED.pdf].

King Jr., A. S., Governor of Maine. State of the State Address, Jan. 22, 2002.

Kirp, D. L. "Pop Quiz: What Do the University of Chicago, University of Illinois-Chicago, DeVry Institute, unext.com and Hamburger University Have in Common?" Paper presented at the Center for Studies in Higher Education, University of California-Berkeley, Oct. 2000.

Kirp, D. L. "Higher Ed Inc.: Avoiding the Perils of Outsourcing." *Chronicle of Higher Education,* Mar. 15, 2002, p. B13.

Kirp, D. L. *Shakespeare, Einstein, and the Bottom Line: The Marketing of Higher Education.* Cambridge, MA: Harvard University Press, 2003.

Kirp, D. L., and Holman, J. T. "This Little Student Went to Market." *The American Prospect,* Oct. 7, 2002, *13*(18) [http://www.prospect.org/print-friendly/print/V13/18/kirp-d.html].

Kirp, D. L., and Roberts, P. S. *Mr. Jefferson's 'Private' College: Darden Business School Secedes from the University of Virginia.* New York: Teacher's College, Columbia University, 2002 [http://www.ncspe.org/publications_files/126_OP55.pdf].

Klor de Alva, J. "Re-making the Academy." *Educause Review,* Mar.-Apr. 2000, pp. 32–40.

Knight, J. "Trade in Higher Education Services: The Implications of GATS." *Observatory on Borderless Higher Education,* Mar. 2002a.

Knight, J. "Trade Creep: Implications of GATS for Higher Education Policy." *International Higher Education,* Summer 2002b, no. 28, 5–7.

Knox, R. A. "Biomedical Results Often Are Withheld: Study Examines Researcher's Financial Links to Corporations." *Boston Globe,* Apr. 16, 1997, p. A1.

Kohler, P. O. *The First Year: A Report to the Employees of the Public Corporation.* Portland: Oregon Health and Science University, Aug. 1996, p. 3.

Konrad, R. "E-learning Companies Look Smart Even in a Down Market." CNET News.com, Mar. 6, 2001 [http://news.cnet.com/news/0–1007–202–5043194.html].

Kronholz, J. "Schools Trim State Ties—As Share of Funding Declines, Colleges Want More Tuition, More Students from Elsewhere." *Wall Street Journal,* Apr. 18, 2003, p. B1.

Kuh, G. "Assessing What Really Matters to Student Learning: Inside the National Survey of Student Engagement." *National Survey of Student Engagement,* May 2003 [http://www.iub.edu/~nsse/html/change.shtml].

Kumar, A. "Debate Begins on New Board." *St. Petersburg Times,* Nov. 11, 2002, p. 1B.

Kumar, A. "A College FCAT? The Debate Begins." *St. Petersburg Times,* May 1, 2003, p. 18.

Kuttner, R. *Everything for Sale.* Chicago: University of Chicago Press, 1996, p. 4.

La Follette, R. M. *La Follette's Autobiography.* Madison: University of Wisconsin Press, 1960. (Originally published 1913.)

Ladd, H. F. *Market-Based Reforms in Urban Education.* Washington, DC: Economic Policy Institute, 2002.

Lapovsky, L., and Hubbell, L. L. "Positioning for Competition." In *Proceedings from the NACUBO Forum on Tuition Discounting,* Apr. 27, 2000 [www.nacubo.org/website/members/issues/bulletins/Discounting.pdf].

LaRocque, N. *Shaping the Tertiary Education System: An Assessment of the Second Report of the Tertiary Education Advisory Commission Entitled "Shaping the System."* Auckland: Education Forum, 2001.

Lee, M.N.N. *Private Higher Education in Malaysia.* Monograph Ser. 2/1999. Penang, Malaysia: School of Educational Studies, Universiti Sains Malaysia, 1999, pp. 2, 4.

Levine, M. "Ivy Envy." *New York Times,* June 8, 2003.

Levinson, A. "Colleges Hamper Credit Transfers." *MSNBC,* July 14, 2002. [http://www.msnbc.com/news/775704.asp?0na=x2314290-.

Lewin, T. "Universities Learn Value of Neighborliness." *New York Times,* Mar. 12, 2003a.

Lewin, T. "New Online Guides Rate Professors." *New York Times,* Mar. 24, 2003b, p. 11.

Lewis, D. R., Hendel, D. D., and Dundar, H. "Wither Private Higher Education in Transition." Paper presented at the Annual Meeting of the European Association for Institutional Research, Prague, Czech Republic, Sept. 9, 2002, pp. 15–17.

Lewis, L., and others *Distance Education at Postsecondary Education Institutions: 1997–98.* Washington, DC: National Center for Education Statistics, NCES #2000–013, Dec. 1999 [http://nces.ed.gov/pubs2000/2000013.pdf].

Lindsay, J. M. "The New Apathy: How an Uninterested Public Is Reshaping Foreign Policy." *Foreign Affairs,* Sept.-Oct. 2000, *79*(5), 2–8.

Litsky, F. "Villanova Is Latest to Face Scandal." *New York Times,* Mar. 9, 2003a, p. 1.

Litsky, F. "Study Finds Winning Teams Losers in the Classroom." *New York Times,* Mar. 25, 2003b, p. S4.

Lively, K. "Autonomy Comes at a Price for Oregon's Public Colleges." *Chronicle of Higher Education,* July 14, 1995.

Lohmann, S. "Can't the University Be More Like Business?" Paper presented at the "Higher Education Goes to Market" Conference, Tampa, FL, Jan. 11–13, 2002.

Lohmann, S. "Darwinian Medicine for the University." In R. Ehrenberg, (ed.), *Governing Academia.* Ithaca, NY: Cornell University Press, 2004.

Longman, J., and Fountain, J. "Phenom's School Tries to Avoid Getting Caught Up in the Game." *New York Times,* Feb. 8, 2003, p. D1.

Lorenzo, G. "eArmyU and the Future of Distance Education." Technology Source, May/June 2002 [http://ts.mivu.org./default.asp?show=article&id=998].

Lovett, C. "A Clash of Cultures Between Public Universities, Public Officials." *NASULGC NewsLine,* Mar. 2000, *9*(3), 8.

Lovett, C. M. "Cracks in the Bedrock." *Change,* Mar.-Apr. 2002a, pp. 11–15.

Lovett, C. M. "The Dumbing Down of College Presidents." *Chronicle of Higher Education,* Apr. 5, 2002b, p. B20.

Lowery, C. "Kelsey-Jenney College Shuts Its Doors." *Chronicle of Higher Education,* July 5, 2002, p. A27.

MacGregor, K. "South Africa: The Race for Portable Qualifications." *The Courier* [UNESCO], Nov. 2000 [http://www.unesco.org/courier/2000_11/uk/doss23.htm].

Mackey, E. "Legislatures for the 21st Century." *Chronicle of Higher Education,* June 7, 2002, p. B20.

MacTaggart, T. J., and Associates. *Seeking Excellence Through Independence: Liberating Colleges and Universities from Excessive Regulation.* San Francisco: Jossey-Bass, 1998, pp. 11, 189.

Macy, B. "From Rusty Wire Fences to Wrought-Iron Gates, How the Poor Succeed in Getting to—and Through—College." *College Board,* Jan. 2000.

Mahtesian, C. "Higher Ed: The No-Longer Sacred Cow." *Governing,* July 1995, pp. 20–26.

"Managing for Results in Maryland State Government," Dec. 2002 [http://www.dbm.state.md.us/html/manage4results.html].

Mandel, M. J. "The Right to Pollute Shouldn't Be for Sale." *Business Week,* May 22, 1989.

Mangan, K. S. "Perfecting the Sales Pitch." *Chronicle of Higher Education,* Feb. 21, 2003, pp. A30–A31.

Marcus, A. "Welcome to the Bazaar." *Business 2.0 Magazine,* Oct. 2001.

Martin, J., and Samels, J. E. "We Were Wrong: Try Partnerships, Not Mergers." *Chronicle of Higher Education,* May 17, 2002, p. B10.

Martinez, J. C. "CU Backs Bill to Secure 'Enterprise Status.'" *Denver Post,* Apr. 24, 2003.

Martinez, M. C., and Richardson, R. C. "A View of the Market Through Studies of Policy and Governance." *American Behavioral Scientist,* Mar. 2003, *46*(7), 883–901.

Massachusetts College of Art. "A New Partnership with the Commonwealth." Sept. 2003 [http://www.massart.edu/about/news/pdf/mca_economic_broch.pdf].

Massy, W. *Honoring the Trust: Quality and Cost Containment in Higher Education.* Bolton, MA: Anker, 2003.

Mathews, J. "Colleges Upgrade Their Image." *Washington Post,* May 6, 2003, p. A10.

Mazuzan, G. T. *The National Science Foundation: A Brief History.* Washington, DC: Office of Legislative and Public Affairs, National Science Foundation, 1994, p. 1.

McBurnie, G. "The Business of International Branch Campuses: Four Australian Case Studies." *International Higher Education,* Fall 2002, *29,* pp. 4–5.

McClenney, B. N., and Flores, R. M. "Community College of Denver Developmental Education." In *Developmental Education: A Twenty-First Century Social and Economic Imperative.* Mission Viejo, CA: League for Innovation in the Community College, 1998, p. 45.

McClenney, K. "The Learning-Focused Institution: Characteristics, Evidence, Consequences." *Pew Forum Working Paper*, No. 6, Draft. San Diego, CA: The Pew Forum on Undergraduate Learning, Jan. 2003.

McCormick, A. C. (ed.). *The Carnegie Classification of Institutions of Higher Education.* 2000 Edition. Menlo Park, CA: The Carnegie Foundation for the Advancement of Teaching, 2001.

McGuinness, A. C. "Models of Postsecondary Education Coordination and Governance in the States." *Education Commission of the States,* 2003 [www.ecs.org].

McKinley, J. C. "At Indiana, Players Dig in Over Firing of Knight." *New York Times,* Sept. 12, 2000, p. D9.

McLarin, K. J. "Deregulating Higher Education: Colleges Hail an Agency's Demise." *New York Times,* Apr. 12, 1994, p. B1.

McLaughlin, M. "Tertiary Education Policy in New Zealand." *Ian Axford (New Zealand) Fellowships in Public Policy,* Feb. 2003, *6*, 20–25.

McLendon, M. K. "Setting the Governmental Agenda for State Decentralization of Higher Education." Dissertation, University of Michigan, Ann Arbor, 2000, p. 17.

McMahon, E. M. "Institutional Independence and Public Oversight: The New Jersey and Maine Experiments." *Connection,* Spring 1997, *12*(1), 43.

McMillin, L. A., and Berberet, W. G. (eds.). *A New Academic Compact: Revisioning the Relationship Between Faculty and Their Institutions.* Bolton, MA: Anker, 2002, p. xi.

Mederly, P. "New Slovak Higher Education Law: The Corner-Stone of Fully Autonomous and Accountable Universities." Paper presented at the IMHE General Conference, Paris, Sept. 16–18, 2002.

Meek, V. L. "On the Road to Mediocrity? Governance and Management of Australian Higher Education in the Market Place." In A. Amaral, G. A. Jones, and B. Karseth (eds.), *Governing Higher Education: National Perspectives on Institutional Governance.* Dordrecht, The Netherlands: Kluwer, 2002, pp. 254–255, 262.

Meek, V. L. "Governance and Management of Australian Higher Education: Enemies Within and Without." In A. Amaral, V. L. Meek, and I. M. Larsen (eds.), *The Higher Education Managerial Revolution?* Dordrecht, The Netherlands: Kluwer, 2003, p. 149.

Meek, V. L., and Wood, F. Q. "The Market as a New Steering Strategy for Australian Higher Education." *Higher Education Policy,* 1997, *10*(3/4), 266, 267, 270.

Metropolitan State College of Denver. "Board of Trustees," Feb. 2003 [http://www.mscd.edu/welcomectr/trustees/index.htm].

Miron, G., and Horn, J. *Evaluation of Connecticut Charter Schools and the Charter School Initiative.* Kalamazoo, MI: The Evaluation Center, Western Michigan University, Sept. 2002.

Morgan, A. W. "Adaptation and Change in Russian Universities." *International Higher Education,* Winter 2002a, *26,* 11–12.

Morgan, R. "Some Teacher-Education Colleges Circumvent Reporting Requirements, GAO Says." *Chronicle of Higher Education,* Oct. 10, 2002b.

Morphew, C. "Program Duplication in Higher Education: A Longitudinal Study of Seven State Systems." Unpublished doctoral dissertation. Stanford University, Stanford, CA, 1996.

Mortenson, T. "Educational Attainment by Family Income 1970–1994." *Postsecondary OPPORTUNITY,* Nov. 1995, *14,* 1.

Mortenson, T. "Shutting the College Doors: Are We Cutting Off the Middle Class?" Paper presented at the Education Commission of the States, 2002 National Forum on Education Policy. Hollywood, CA, July 2002.

Mortenson, T. G. "The Education Pipeline in Ohio: International, State and Time-Series Comparisons." Paper presented at the Governor's Commission on Higher Education and the Economy, Columbus, OH, Aug. 27, 2003, pp. 12, 16, 17 [http://www.postsecondary.org/archives/Reports/EducOH82703.pdf].

Mullen, J. "Graduates Deficient in 'Soft' Skills." *People Management,* 1997, *3*(22), 18.

Mumper, M. "The Future of College Access: The Declining Role of Public Higher Education in Promoting Equal Opportunity." *Annals of the American Academy of Political and Social Science,* Jan. 2003, *585,* 101.

Myers, M. T. "A Student Is Not an Input." *New York Times,* Mar. 26, 2001.

National Association of Manufacturers, Andersen, and Center for Workforce Success. *The Skills Gap 2001: Manufacturers Confront Persistent Skills Shortages in an Uncertain Economy.* Washington, DC: National Association of Manufacturers, DC2001.

National Association of Manufacturers, Center for Workforce Success, and Thornton, G., LLP. *The Skills Gap—The Shortage of Qualified Workers: A Growing Challenge to the American Economy.* Washington, DC: Manufacturing Institute, DC1998, pp. 2, 8.

National Association of State Student Grant and Aid Programs (NASSGAP). *32nd Annual Survey Report, 2000–2001 Academic Year.* Albany: New York State Higher Education Services Corporation, Apr. 2002.

National Association of State Universities and Land-Grant Colleges. "Shaping the Future: The Economic Impact of Public Universities."

Washington, DC: National Association of State Universities and Land-Grant Colleges, Aug. 2001, pp. 3–4 [http://www.nasulgc.org/publications/EconImpact.pdf].

National Center for Postsecondary Improvement. "Beyond Dead Reckoning: Research Priorities for Redirecting American Higher Education." Stanford, CA: School of Education, Stanford University, 2002, pp. 3, 15, 21–22 [http://www.stanford.edu/group/ncpi/documents/pdfs/beyond_dead_reckoning.pdf].

National Center for Public Policy and Higher Education. *Measuring Up 2000: The State-by-State Report Card for Higher Education.* San Jose, CA: National Center for Public Policy and Higher Education, 2000.

National Center for Public Policy and Higher Education. "Fund for the Improvement of Postsecondary Education: The Early Years." June 2002, pp. 3, 31–32, 40 [http://www.highereducation.org/reports/fipse/fipse.shtml].

National Center for Public Policy and Higher Education. *Purposes, Policies, Performance: Higher Education and the Fulfillment of a State's Public Agenda.* San Jose, CA: National Center for Public Policy and Higher Education, Feb. 2003.

National Commission on the Cost of Higher Education. "Straight Talk About College Costs and Prices." Washington, DC: American Council on Education, Jan. 1998, p. 11 [http://www.acenet.edu/washington/college_costs/1998/07july/straight_talk.html].

National Governors Association. "Postsecondary Education Reform in Kentucky," Nov. 2001a [http://www.nga.org/center/divisions/1,1188,C_ISSUE_BRIEF^D_2566,00.html].

National Governors Association. *Influencing the Future of Higher Education: The NGA Center for Best Practices 2001–2004 Postsecondary Education Agenda.* Washington, DC: National Governors Association, 2001b [http://www.nga.org/cda/files/FUTUREHIGHERED.pdf].

National Governors Association. *Higher Expectations: Second in a Series of Essays on the Future of Postsecondary Education. Influencing the Future of Higher Education.* Washington, DC: National Governors Association, 2002.

National Research Council. *Investing in the National Research Initiative: An Update of the Competitive Grants Program of the U.S. Department of Agriculture.* Washington, DC: National Academy Press, 1994, p. 2.

National Research Council. *How People Learn.* Washington DC: National Academy Press, 2000.

National Research Council of the National Academies. *Preparing for the Revolution.* Washington, DC: National Academies Press, 2002.

National Survey of Student Engagement. "The College Student Report, 2003 Overview." National Survey of Student Engagement 2003, p. 1.

Naughton, J. "St. Mary's Grows Up." *Washington Post Magazine*, July 22, 2001.

"NCSL Education Expert Projects Key State Issues for Higher Education." *NASULGC Newsline*, Jan. 1999, p. 12.

"Need Grows for More Federal Financing of Research Facilities." *NASULGC Newsline*, 2003, *12*(1), 7.

Nelson, B. *Higher Education at the Crossroads: An Overview Paper.* Canberra, Australia: Commonwealth Department of Education, Science and Training, Apr. 2002, pp. 5–7 [http://www.backingaustraliasfuture.gov.au/publications/crossroads/default.htm].

Nelson, B. *Our Universities: Backing Australia's Future.* Canberra, Australia: Commonwealth Department of Education, Science and Training, May 2003 [http://www.backingaustraliasfuture.gov.au/].

"New Century Scholarship Program." State of Utah, Aug. 15, 2002 [http://www.utahsbr.edu/html/new_century.html].

New England Resource Center for Higher Education. "Lessons on Supporting Change Through Multi-Institutional Projects." *NERCHE Brief*, Nov. 2001.

"New Tuition and Scholarship Plan." Miami University of Ohio, Oct. 2003 [http://www.miami.muohio.edu/tuitionplan/qa.cfm].

New Zealand Ministry of Education. "Tertiary Education in New Zealand: Policy Directions for the 21st Century." White Paper, Nov. 1998 [http://www.minedu.govt.nz/Tertiary/Review/wp/chap].

New Zealand's Vice-Chancellor's Commission (NZVCC). "Another Year Slips By." *NZVCC Newsletter*, Aug. 2000a [www.nzvcc.ac.nz].

New Zealand's Vice-Chancellor's Commission (NZVCC). "The Priorities: Funding, Student Financial Support, Differentiation and Research." *NZVCC Newsletter*, Feb. 2000b, *55* [http://www.nzvcc.ac.nz/pubs/newsletter55/text/priorities.html].

Newman, F. "The Era of Expertise: The Growth, the Spread and Ultimately the Decline of the National Commitment to the Highly Trained Expert, 1945 to 1970." Unpublished doctoral dissertation, Department of History, Stanford University, Stanford, CA, 1981.

Newman, F. "Saving Higher Education's Soul." *Change*, Sept./Oct. 2000, pp. 17–23 [http://www.futuresproject.org/publications/soul.pdf].

Newman, F., and Scurry, J. E. "Higher Education in the Digital Rapids," June 2001 [www.futuresproject.org].

Nickel, M. "Task Force Redesigns Faculty Governance." *George Street Journal*, Sept. 13, 2002.

North Dakota University System. "Creating a University System for the 21st Century." *1st Annual Accountability Measures Report*, Bismarck, ND, Dec. 2001.

Novak, R. "A Legislature's Tool for Making Higher Education More Responsive." *AGB Trusteeship,* Sept.-Oct. 2001, p. 36.

Novak, R., and Johnson, N. "The Oregon Experience." In D. F. Kettl, "Creating High-Performance Postsecondary Education." National Governors Association's Influencing the Future of Higher Education Initiative, May 2001, pp. 33–34 [http://www.nga.org/center/divisions/1,1188,C_ISSUE_BRIEF^D_1509,00.html].

"Number of Tertiary Providers," Sept. 2003 [www.minedu.govt.nz/index.cfm?layout=document&documentid=7107&indexid=7211&indexparentid=6142].

Oblinger, D. G., and Verville, A. *What Business Wants from Higher Education.* Phoenix, AZ: Oryx Press, 1998, pp. 19–27, 71–73.

Observatory on Borderless Higher Education. "Singapore—A Regional Hub for Higher Education?" *VC-NET,* Oct. 31, 2002.

O'Connell, B. "Citizen Participation and Influence in America.: Impressive Performance and Alarming Shortfalls." *Public Integrity,* Spring 2003, 5(2), 163.

"October Certification Test Results Released," Massachusetts Department of Education, Dec. 8, 2000 [http://www.doe.MAedu/news/dec00/1208pr.html].

"Of Precept, Policy and Practice." A Special Supplement to *National CrossTalk,* Fall 2002 [http://www.highereducation.org/crosstalk/pdf/0402-policy_perspectives.pdf].

"OHSU: An Historical Chronology," June 2003 [http://www.ohsu.edu/about/history.html].

OHSU Foundation. "About the Foundation," July 5, 2001 [www.ohsu.edu/ohsufoundation/about_foundation.html].

Olson, L. "Panel Suggests State Compact for Research." *Education Week,* Apr. 9, 2003, p. 1.

O'Neill, J. M. "An Exacting Education in Economic Realities." *Philadelphia Inquirer,* Jan. 28, 2001 through Feb. 2, 2001 (six-part series).

"Online High School Program." Distance Learning Programs (DANTES), Jan. 8, 2002 [http://voled.doded.mil/dantes/dl/hs.htm].

Oregon Revised Statutes, ORS 353.010, Title 30. *Education and Cultural Facilities,* Chapter 353. Portland: Oregon Health Sciences University.

Orfield, G. *Schools More Separate: Consequence of a Decade of Resegregation.* Cambridge, MA: The Civil Rights Project, July 2001.

"Our First Annual College-Admissions Survey." *Atlantic Monthly,* Nov. 2003, pp. 104–140.

"Owens Ties CU's Purse Strings." *Denver Post,* May 28, 2003.

Palomba, C., and Banta, T. *Assessment Essentials: Planning, Implementing, and Improving Assessment in Higher Education.* San Francisco: Jossey-Bass, 1999, p. 16.

Pascarella, E. T., and Terenzini, P. T. *How College Affects Students: Findings and Insights from Twenty Years of Research.* San Francisco: Jossey-Bass, 1998, p. 592.

Pearlstein, S. "On California Stage, a Cautionary Tale." *Washington Post,* Aug. 21, 2001, p. A01.

Peirce, N., and Johnson, C. "Bright Futures? Human Capital Dilemmas Cloud New England Outlook." *Connection,* Summer 2003, *18*(1), 15.

Perez, C. "The Truth Behind the Hype: A Closer Look at the SAT." Paper presented at 2002 New England Association for College Admission Counseling Conference, Fairfield University, May 2002.

"Performance Agreement: Colorado School of Mines and CCHE for FY 2002–2007," Feb. 11, 2002, supplied by John Trefny, president, Colorado School of Mines.

Performance Indicator Advisory Committee. *Establishing Performance Indicators to Assess Progress Toward Meeting the Goals of the Illinois Commitment.* Springfield: Illinois Board of Higher Education, Aug. 2002.

The Pew Research Center for the People and the Press. "Conflicted Views on Affirmative Action," May 14, 2003.

Phillips, K. *Wealth and Democracy.* New York: Broadway Books, 2002, pp. 136, 137.

Phipps, R. A. *Access to Postsecondary Education: What Is the Role of Technology?* Attachment 2, Washington, DC: National Postsecondary Education Cooperative (NPEC), *20,* March 2002, p. 2.

"Plan to Test Student Learning, Enact Performance Measures Top IBHE Agenda." News from the Illinois Board of Higher Education, January 28, 2003 [http://www.ibhe.state.il.us/Media%20Center/2003/HTM/0128_Agenda.htm].

Pollack, A. "Three Universities Join Researcher to Develop Drugs." *New York Times,* July 31, 2003, early ed., p. C1.

"Postsecondary Education," July 2002 [http://www.sreb.org/main/HigherEd/higheredindex.asp].

Potter, W. "Texas Legislature Gives Public Colleges the Power to Set Tuition." *Chronicle of Higher Education,* June 13, 2003a, p. A25.

Potter, W. "North Carolina and Texas Try to Buck Trend of Tuition Increases." *Chronicle of Higher Education,* Feb. 21, 2003b, p. A23.

Prah, P. M. "Colorado Considers Vouchers for Higher Ed," Dec. 23, 2002 [http://www.stateline.org/stateline/?pa=story&sa=showStoryInfo&id=278678].

"President's Fiscal 2001 Budget Would Increase Support for Basic Research by 7 Percent." *NASULGC Newsline,* 2000, *9*(3), 11.

Press, E., and Washburn, J. "The Kept University." *Atlantic Monthly,* Mar. 2000 [http://www.theatlantic.com/issues/2000/03/press.htm].

"Promoting Educational Excellence in the New Economy: The Challenges for National Policy." Washington, DC: Aspen Institute Congressional Program, Proceedings of the Eighth Conference, 16.2, Feb. 16–19, 2001.

Public Agenda Online. "Red Flags: Affirmative Action: What a Difference a Word Makes," May 2003 [http://www.publicagenda.org/issues/red_flags.cfm?issue_type=higher_education].

Pulley, L. J. "Relying on Admissions, Not Fund Raising." *Chronicle of Higher Education*, Aug. 1, 2003, p. A27.

Pusser, B. "Higher Education, the Emerging Market, and the Public Good." In P. A. Graham and N. G. Stacey (eds.), *The Knowledge Economy and Postsecondary Education*. Washington, DC: National Academy Press, 2002, p. 114.

Pusser, B., and Doane, D. J. "Public Purpose and Private Enterprise." *Change*, Sept.-Oct. 2001, pp. 19–22.

Quddus, M., and Rashid, S. "The Worldwide Movement in Private Universities." *American Journal of Economics and Sociology*, July 2000, *59*(3), 487–516.

"The Quiet Educational Revolution." *Economist*, Sept. 23, 2002.

Rai, S. "Rift in India Leads MIT to Abandon a Media Lab." *New York Times*, May 8, 2003.

Randall, L. "Way Cool Rec Centers." *New York Times*, Nov. 10, 2002, p. 7.

Reed, C. B. "It's Time to Stress Academics, Then Athletics—in That Order." *Trusteeship*, Nov./Dec. 2002, p. 5.

Reindl, T., and Brower, D. "Financing State Colleges and Universities: What Is Happening to the 'Public' in Public Higher Education?" *Perspectives*, American Association of State Colleges and Universities, May 2001.

"Report Vindicates Dr. Nancy Olivieri." *Bulletin Online*, Nov. 2001, *48*(9) [http://www.caut.ca/english/bulletin/2001_nov/default.asp].

Riding, A. "The New E.U." *New York Times*, Jan. 12, 2003.

Rimer, S. "For a Price, Colleges Offer Students Privacy." *New York Times*, Jan. 27, 2003a, p. A1.

Rimer, S. "High School Is Virtual, but the Caps and Gowns Are Real." *New York Times*, June 19, 2003b.

Rios, R. "Brief of the Authors of the Texas Ten Percent Plan as Amicus Curiae in Support of the Respondents." *Jennifer Gratz and Patrick Hamacher v. Lee Bollinger et al., Respondents*, 2003, p. 1.

Robbins, L. "At Texas Tech, Some Professors Balk at Knight." *New York Times*, Mar. 15, 2001, p. D1.

Roberts, S. "Therapeutic Treatments for Title IX." *New York Times*, Feb. 2, 2003a, p. 11.

Roberts, S. "When University President Turns into Team Cheerleader, It's Trouble." *New York Times,* Mar. 9, 2003b, p. 3.

Rocca, F. X. "Study Notes an Uptick in Programs Taught in English at European Colleges." *Chronicle of Higher Education,* Jan. 3, 2003.

Rooney, M. "Virginia Tech Bans Speakers with Extreme Views and Relaxes Antidiscrimination Clause." *Chronicle of Higher Education,* Mar. 13, 2003.

Ross, J. "Colleges Should Stop Counting Their National News Clips." *Chronicle of Higher Education,* Feb. 21, 2003, p. B16.

Roy, C. "Romney Cancels Chat with UMass Chiefs." *Boston Globe,* Apr. 1, 2003, p. B2.

Ruben, B. D. (ed.). *Pursuing Excellence in Higher Education: Eight Fundamental Challenges.* San Francisco: Jossey-Bass, 2004.

Ruppert, S. S. *Where We Go from Here: State Legislative Views on Higher Education in the New Millennium. Results of the 2001 Higher Education Issues Survey.* Colorado: Educational Systems Research, National Education Association of the United States, 2001, pp. i, iv–iv, 35.

Russell, J. "Colleges Turn to 'Instant' Admissions." *Boston Globe,* May 30, 2002, p. A1.

Russell, J. "Romney Draft Plan for Colleges Offers Few Concessions." *Boston Globe,* Apr. 10, 2003, p. B6.

St. John, E. P., Musoba, G. D., Simmons, A. B., and Chung, C. "Meeting the Access Challenge: Indiana's Twenty-First Century Scholars Program." Indianapolis, IN: Lumina New Agenda Series, 2002, *4*(4).

Samuels, S. H. "With Honors." *New York Times,* Aug. 5, 2001.

Sax, L. J., Astin, A. W., Korn, W. S, and Mahoney, K. M. *The American Freshman: National Norms for Fall 1998.* Los Angeles: Higher Education Research Institute, UCLA Graduate School of Education, 1998.

Schmidt, P. "Some Campuses Want to Leave U. of Maryland System." *Chronicle of Higher Education,* Nov. 20, 1998.

Schmidt, P. "Maryland Urged to Keep University System Intact." *Chronicle of Higher Education,* Feb. 5, 1999, p. A38.

Schmidt, P. "States Push Public Universities to Commercialize Research: Conflict-of-Interest Fears Take Back Seat to Economic Development." *Chronicle of Higher Education,* Mar. 29, 2002, p. A26.

Schmidt, P. "Happily Stuck in a Power Vacuum." *Chronicle of Higher Education,* May 16, 2003, p. A23.

"Schools Profit from Publicly Funded Research," Apr. 29, 2003 [www.cnn.com/2003/EDUCATION/04/29/patent.universities.ap/index.html].

Schultze, C. L. *The Public Use of Private Interest.* Washington, DC: The Brookings Institution, 1977, p. 30.

Scott, S. V. "The Academic as Service Provider: Is the Customer 'Always Right'?" *Journal of Higher Education Policy and Management,* Nov. 1999, *21*(2), 193ff.

Selingo, J. "Mission Creep? More Regional State Colleges Start Honors Programs to Raise Their Profiles and Draw Better Students." *Chronicle of Higher Education,* May 31, 2002, p. A19.

Shapera, T. "The Best College in the Country." *Trust,* Winter 2002, *5*(1), 14–19.

Simmons, M. "The Sad State of NCAA Football," Apr. 2002 [http://www.askmen.com/sports/business_60/75b_sports_business.html].

Sivin-Kachala, J., and Bialo, E. R. "The 2000 Research Report on the Effectiveness of Technology in Schools, 7th Edition." Washington, DC: Published for the Software Information Industry Association, 2000, p. 25.

Sizemore, B. "Universities Look to Cut Some Ties with State." *Virginia-Pilot,* Jan. 4, 2003, p. A1.

Smallwood, S. "United We Stand? Part-Time Professors Are Forming Unions, but Many Wonder If Teaming Up with Full-Timers Would Be Better." *Chronicle of Higher Education,* Feb. 21, 2003, p. A10.

Smith, L. H. "Norman Borlaug Announces Lifelong Learning Company." About NBU: Press Room, Norman Bourlaug University, Sept. 2000 [http://www.nbulearn.com/netscape/index.htm].

Sosin, J. "National Leadership Dialogue Series: Higher Education's Role in Serving the Public Good." Paper presented at the Kellogg Forum on Higher Education for the Public Good, Ann Arbor, MI, Oct. 2002 [http://www.kelloggforum.org/activities/national_summit.html#summit].

South Dakota Board of Regents. "Governor Rounds' Grants for Course Redesign Summer 2003," June 2003 [http://www.ris.sdbor.edu/RoundsGrant.htm].

Southwick, R. "Fewer Foreign Students, More Women Earn Science and Engineering Doctorates in U.S., Report Finds." *Chronicle of Higher Education,* May 1, 2002.

Special data analysis by Clifford Adelman, senior research analyst, U.S. Department of Education, Oct. 24, 2003.

Sporn, B. "World Class Reform of Universities in Austria." *International Higher Education,* Fall 2002, *29,* 19.

Spurgeon, D. "Report Clears Researcher Who Broke Drug Company Agreement." *British Medical Journal,* Nov. 10, 2001, p. 1085.

The Star, 1997. Cited in Lee, M.N.N. *Private Higher Education in Malaysia.* Monograph Ser. 2, 1999. Penang, Malaysia: School of Educational Studies, Universiti Sains Malaysia, 1999, p. 3.

"State Investment Effort in Higher Education, FY1962 to FY2003." *Postsecondary Education Opportunity,* Dec. 2002, *126.*

State of North Dakota Office of the Governor. "Governor Signs Landmark Higher Education Legislation." News Releases for May 2001, May 2,

2001 [http://www.governor.state.nd.us/media/news-releases/2001/05/010502.html].

Stensland, J. "Bill Would Give Research Colleges Leeway." TheState.com, Mar. 29, 2003a, p. B1.

Stensland, J. "Plan Debated to Eliminate College Oversight Board." TheState.Com, Apr. 27, 2003b, p. B1.

Stephens, S. "Conference Sees Roadblocks in College Path." *The Plain Dealer,* Sept. 26, 2002.

Stiglitz, J. "The Roaring Nineties." *Atlantic Monthly,* Oct. 2002 [www.theatlantic.com/issues/2002/10/stiglitz.htm].

Stolberg, S. G. "Report Says Profit-Making Health Plans Damage Care." *New York Times,* July 14, 1999, p. A18.

Stringer, W. L., Cunningham, A. F., Merisotis, J. P., Wellman, J. V., and O'Brien, C. T. "Cost, Price and Public Policy: Peering into the Higher Education Black Box." Institute for Higher Education Policy. Indianapolis, IN: *USAGroup Foundation New Agenda Series,* Aug. 1999, *1*(3), 9.

"Structures of the Education and Initial Training Systems: France." Eurydice, CEDEFOP, European Commission, 1995. [http://www.eurydice.org/Documents/struct/en/struct.htm].

"Study: Charter Students Test Poorly." *Providence Journal,* Sept. 3, 2002, p. A4.

Suggs, W. "How Gears Turn at a Sports Factory." *Chronicle of Higher Education,* Nov. 29, 2002, p. 32.

Suggs, W. "Denied Varsity Status, BYU Men's Soccer Team Gets a Professional Franchise Instead." *Chronicle of Higher Education,* Mar. 10, 2003.

Sullivan, J. "Board Approves Tuition Flexibility for State Schools." *Bismarck Tribune,* Feb. 22, 2002, p. 9A.

Suroor, H. "India Invites Investment from Its Expats." *Times Higher Education Supplement,* Dec. 2000, *1,* 12.

"The swissUp Ranking," Nov. 14, 2001 [http://www.swissup.com/ran_methodology.cfm?upid=EN].

Symonds, W. C. "Colleges in Crisis." *BusinessWeekOnline,* Apr. 28, 2003.

The Task Force on Higher Education and Society. *Higher Education in Developing Countries: Peril and Promise.* Washington, DC: World Bank, 2000, pp. 107, 111.

Tertiary Education Advisory Commission. *Shaping the Strategy.* Wellington, New Zealand, July 2001.

"Tertiary Education Reforms 'Not Backed by Evidence.'" *Education Forum,* July 2002, *10.*

Thompson, N. "The Best, the Top, the Most." *New York Times,* Aug. 3, 2003.

Tinto, V., and Riemer, S. "Remedial Education in Higher Education: Learning Communities." June 22, 2001 [http://soeweb.syr.edu/Faculty/Vtinto/index.html].

"Top Financial Aid Tips," Feb. 2003 [http://education.yahoo.com/college/essentials/articles/college/college-financial-toptips.html].

Totty, M., and Grimes, A. "The Old College Try." *Wall Street Journal*, Mar. 12, 2001 [http://interactive.wsj.com/public/current/articles/SB984068180221773257.htm].

Trombley, W. "Tuition Is Rising as States Face Budget Difficulties." In *Measuring Up 2002*. San Jose, CA: National Center for Public Policy and Higher Education, 2002, pp. 60–63.

Trombley, W. "The Rising Price of Higher Education." Special Supplement to *National CrossTalk*, Winter 2003.

"Turf Battles Still Endanger State's Higher Education." *Paducah Sun*, Oct. 21, 2002.

Twigg, C. A. Improving Learning and Reducing Costs: New Models for Online Learning. *Educause Review*, Sept./Oct. 2003a, pp. 28–38.

Twigg, C. A. *Improving Learning and Reducing Costs: Lessons Learned from Round I of the Pew Grant Program in Course Redesign*. New York: Center for Academic Transformation, Rensselaer Polytechnic Institute, 2003b.

"Universities Ask for Freedom to Set Own Tuition Policies." Eugene, OR: Associated Press Newswires, Jan. 27, 2003.

"Universities Can Play Important Role in Innovation, Economic Development." *NASULGC Newsline*, 2003, *12*(1), 8.

University Business. "Making Quality Work." July/August 2001 [http://www.university business.com/magazine/0207/cover.mhtml].

University of Rhode Island Program Contribution Analysis, FY01: 2000–2001. Kingston, RI: Budget Office, Office of Strategic Planning and Institutional Research, Apr. 2002.

"University of Wisconsin System: Plan 2008: Educational Quality Through Racial and Ethnic Diversity," UW System Board of Regents, May 1998 [http://www.uwsa.edu/multcult/plan/planfinl.htm].

"University of Wisconsin System Minority and Disadvantaged Student Annual Report." Apr. 2002 [http://www.uwsa.edu/oadd/2001-2002%20M-D.doc].

University System of Maryland. "The USM in 2010: Responding to the Challenges That Lie Ahead; the 10 Year Plan." July 7, 2000, p. 20.

University System of Maryland. "System Overview of USM," Mar. 16, 2001a [http://www.usmd.edu/Overview/charter.html]. (Public corporation bill SB-682.)

University System of Maryland. System Overview of USM. "The USM as a Public Corporation/Charter System," Mar. 20, 2001b [http://www.usmd.edu/Overview/charter.html].

University System of Maryland. "USM Timeline," Jan. 2002 [www.usmd.edu/Overview/Timeline.html].

U.S. Census Bureau. "Health Insurance Coverage: 1999." *Current Population Reports.* By Robert J. Mills. Sept. 2000 [http://www.census.gov/prod/2000pubs/p60–211.pdf].

U.S. Department of Education. *Distance Education at Postsecondary Education Institutions: 1997–98.* NCES 2000–013, Washington, DC: National Center for Education Statistics, Dec. 1999.

U.S. Department of Education. 2000 White House Education Press Release and Statements. Fact Sheet on Agenda for Higher Education. "A New Opportunity Agenda for Higher Education: Making Critical Investments in Education and Training," Jan. 20, 2000.

U.S. Department of Education. "What Is the U.S. Department of Education?" Jan. 2003 [http://www.ed.gov/pubs/overview/whatis.html].

U.S. Department of Education, National Center for Education Statistics. *Transfer Behavior Among Beginning Post Secondary Students: 1989–1994.* NCES 97–266. Washington, DC: U.S. Government Printing Office, 1997, p. 3 [www.nces.ed.gov].

U.S. Department of Education, National Center for Education Statistics. *The Condition of Education 2002.* Washington, DC.: U.S. Government Printing Office, 2002.

U.S. Department of Labor. "Executive Summary. Futurework: Trends and Challenges for Work in the 21st Century," 1999 [www.dol.gov/dol/asp/public/futurework/execsum.htm].

U.S. General Accounting Office. "Agricultural Research: USDA's Outreach to Minority-Serving Institutions Could Improve Grant Competition." GAO-03–541, May 2003 [http://www.gao.gov/new.items/d03541.pdf].

U.S. House Committee on Education and the Workforce and U.S. House Subcommittee on 21st Century Competitiveness. "The College Cost Crisis." Sept. 4, 2003. [http://www.edworkforce.house.gov/issues/108th/education/highereducation/CollegeCostCrisisReport.pdf].

Uvalic-Trumbic, S., and Varoglu, Z. *Survey of the 2002 Breaking News and the UNESCO Global Forum on Quality Assurance, Accreditation and the Recognition of Qualifications.* Observatory on Borderless Higher Education, Apr. 2003 [www.obhe.ac.uk].

Van Der Werf, M. "The Precarious Balancing Act at Small Liberal-Arts Colleges." *Chronicle of Higher Education,* July 30, 1999, p. A32.

Van Der Werf, M. "Acting Like a For-Profit College." *Chronicle of Higher Education,* Aug. 1, 2003a, p. A24.

Van Der Werf, M. "Slashing Prices Draws a Crowd." *Chronicle of Higher Education,* Aug. 1, 2003b, p. A25.

Varian, H. R. "Economic Scene." *New York Times,* May 8, 2003, p. C2.

Vernez, G., and Mizell, L. "Goal to Double the Rate of Hispanics Earning a Bachelors Degree." Santa Monica, CA: Rand Education, Center for Research on Immigration Policy, 2001, pp. vii–viii.

Volkwein, J. F., and Zhou, J. "Measuring Up: Examining the Connections Between State Governance Structures and Performance." Paper presented at the ASHE Forum on Public Policy in Higher Education, Portland, OR, Nov. 13, 2003.

Waldsmith, L. "A State Debates Higher Ed Cuts." *Detroit News,* Mar. 16, 2003, p. 11.

Walsh, J. "Community Colleges Gain New Respect: Two-Year Schools Are Offering More Challenging Courses—as Well as a Way to Save on Tuition." *Star Tribune,* Jan. 5, 2003, p. 1A.

Wan, C. "First Step in Supporting Private Tertiary Education: Private College Will Get Aid for Upgrade." *South China Morning Post,* Jan. 20, 2000, p. 7.

Ward, D., and Hawkins, B. L. "Presidential Leadership for Information Technology." Paper presented at Transforming Universities Through Information Technology, National Academies, Washington, DC, Apr. 15–16, 2003.

"Web-Based Surgical Simulators and Medical Education Tools," Apr. 15, 2002 [http://synaptic.mvc.mcc.ac.uk/simulators.html].

"Weekly Bulletin." *Journal of Blacks in Higher Education.* June 5, 2003.

Wellman, J. V. "Statewide Higher Education Accountability: Issues, Options and Strategies for Success." In National Governors Association, *Higher Expectations: Second in a Series of Essays on the Future of Postsecondary Education. Influencing the Future of Higher Education.* Washington, DC: National Governors Association, 2002.

Werbach, K. "Clicks and Mortar Meets Cap and Gown: Higher Education Goes Online." Release 1.0, Sept. 15, 2000, p. 6 [www.edventure.com].

West Virginia Higher Education Policy Commission. "It All Adds Up: Compact for the Future of West Virginia," May 2003 [http://www.hepc.wvnet.edu/news/extendedgoals.pdf].

Westheimer, J., and Kahne, J. "What Kind of Citizen? Political Choices and Educational Goals." *Campus Compact Reader,* Winter 2003, p. 2.

Whitcomb, R. "Higher Education's Binge." *Providence Journal,* Jan. 17, 2003, p. B6.

Wilgoren, J. "Spiraling Sports Budgets Draw Fire from Faculties." *New York Times,* July 29, 2001, p. 12.

Winston, G. "Why Can't a College Be More Like a Firm?" In J. Meyerson (ed.), *New Thinking on Higher Education: Creating a Context for Change.* Bolton, MA: Anker, 1997, p. 4.

Winston, G. "Is Princeton Acting Like a Church or a Car Dealer?" *Chronicle of Higher Education,* Feb. 23, 2001, p. B24.

Winter, G. "Junior Colleges Try Niche as Cheap Path to Top Universities." *New York Times,* Dec. 15, 2002, p. 1.

Winter, G. "Lawmaker Proposes a Measure to Restrain Tuition Increases." *New York Times,* Mar. 7, 2003a, p. A21.

Winter, G. "Squeezed Colleges See Credit Ratings Drop." *New York Times,* Apr. 15, 2003.

Winter, G. "Jacuzzi U.? Battle of Perks to Lure Students." *New York Times,* Oct. 5, 2003c, p. 1.

Winter, G., and Rimer, S. "Alumni Pressure Harvard to Put Reins on Spending." *New York Times,* Feb. 25, 2003, p. 18.

Woodbury, R. L. "How to Make Your College No. 1 in U.S. News & World Report . . . and Lose Your Integrity in the Process." *New England Board of Higher Education,* Spring 2003, pp. 18–20.

World Bank, Task Force on Higher Education and Society. *Higher Education in Developing Countries: Peril and Promise.* Washington, DC: World Bank, 2000, p. 29.

Yeager, M. "FSU, UF to Suggest Budget Deal." *Tallahassee Democrat,* Tallahassee.com, Mar. 27, 2003.

Yeager, M. "FSU, UF Seek to Ensure Funding." *Tallahassee Democrat,* Tallahassee.com, Mar. 1, 2004.

Young, J. "Early Applicants Have Strong Advantage at Elite Colleges, Book Argues." *Chronicle of Higher Education,* Mar. 7, 2003, p. A38.

Yudof, M. G. "Higher Tuitions: Harbinger of a Hybrid University." *Change,* Mar./Apr. 2002a, pp. 17–20.

Yudof, M. G. "Is the Public Research University Dead?" *Chronicle of Higher Education,* Jan. 11, 2002b, p. B24.

Zumeta, W., and Raveling, J. S. "Attracting the Best and the Brightest." *Issues in Science and Technology,* Winter 2002–2003, p. 37.

Name Index

Subject Index

Please remember that this is a library book,
and that it belongs only temporarily to each
person who uses it. Be considerate. Do
not write in this, or any, library book.